HAVING THE WORLD IN VIEW

John McDowell

Having the World in View

Essays on Kant, Hegel, and Sellars

HARVARD UNIVERSITY PRESS

Cambridge, Massachusetts, and London, England   2009

Library of Congress Cataloging-in-Publication Data

McDowell, John Henry.
  Having the world in view : essays on Kant, Hegel, and Sellars / John McDowell.
    p. cm.
  Includes bibliographical references (p.) and index.
  ISBN 978-0-674-03165-4 (alk. paper)
  1. Kant, Immanuel, 1724–1804.   2. Hegel, Georg Wilhelm Friedrich, 1770–1831.
3. Sellars, Wilfrid.   I. Title.
  B2798.M4235 2009
  190—dc22 2008013843

Contents

IV   Sellarsian Themes

Preface

The title of this collection is the title under which I presented versions of the essays in Part I as the Woodbridge Lectures at Columbia University in 1997.

Those essays appear here under what I used as the subtitle of those lectures. Their topic is Wilfrid Sellars's deeply Kantian account of perceptual experience. In the experience of rational subjects, things are given to them to be known, in knowledge of a kind only rational subjects can have, knowledge that is a standing in the space of reasons. Is this givenness a case of what Sellars rejects as the Myth of the Given? No, but that is only because the experience of rational subjects, experience in which things are given for rational knowledge, itself draws on capacities that belong to the rational intellect, the understanding.

Even as enjoyed by rational subjects, perceptual experience involves sensibility. And sensibility is not peculiar to rational subjects. As Sellars interprets what a Kantian account would require, sensibility constrains the involvement of the understanding in experience from outside. I contrast that with a conception according to which the role of sensibility in a Kantian account is that it is sensory consciousness that is informed by conceptual capacities in the experience of rational subjects. When I wrote the essays in Part I, I thought Sellars's picture included this informing of sensory consciousness by capacities that belong to the understanding, and that he added external constraint, by what he calls "sheer receptivity", as a distinct further role for sensibility. I retract that reading of Sellars in Essay 6. (Readers should be alert to what this is an instance of: I would not now affirm everything on every page of this collection.)

Sellars holds that it is not as possessors of significance that words bear relations to elements in extra-linguistic reality. In Essay 3 I discuss how this doctrine, which I think we should reject, conspires with other features of

Sellars's thinking to make the contrasting conception of the role of sensibility invisible to him.

If, as I recommend, we deny that the rational intellect needs a certain sort of external constraint, even in its empirical operations, we are sounding what can be easily heard as a Hegelian note. In Essays 2 and 3 I make some remarks about the Hegelian character of the denial, and that is the central topic of the first two essays in Part II.

Of the other essays in Part II, Essay 6 is a further discussion of the contrast that shapes the essays in Part I, between Sellars's view of the role of sensibility in a Kantian account of experience and the alternative I recommend. And in Essay 7 I try to motivate and defend the thought—which is common between Sellars's version of Kantianism and the alternative I recommend— that experience can make rational knowledge available only by itself involving the understanding.

The first two essays in Part III sketch readings of parts of Hegel's *Phenomenology of Spirit*. Essay 8 begins with a restatement of some material from Essay 4; I use that to introduce an interpretation of the Master/Slave dialectic, according to which the point of that section of the *Phenomenology* is closer to the main theme of this collection than it is on more standard readings. Essay 9 is further removed from the topic of having the world in view, but there is a counterpart here to a feature of my preferred treatment of that theme. If, as I recommend, we deny that sensibility constrains the understanding from outside, then, even though sensibility is characteristic of animals as such, not just rational animals, we are debarred from conceiving the sensibility of rational animals as simply separate from the rationality they manifest in their guise as experiencing the world. In Essay 9 I find in Hegel's treatment of action an analogous drive towards integrating the rationality of rational animals, now in their guise as agents, with their bodily nature, even though embodiment, like sensibility, is characteristic of animals as such, not just rational animals.

Essay 10 brings together some of the main points in the reading of Kant and Hegel that underlies the treatment I recommend for the theme of having the world in view.

Part IV contains miscellaneous essays on Sellarsian topics. Essay 11 largely repeats material from Part I, adding more comparison between Sellars and Donald Davidson. In Essay 12 I urge that Sellars's "Empiricism and the Philosophy of Mind" should be read, not as dismissing empiricism altogether, but as recommending a reformed empiricism, an empiricism structured so as to avoid the Myth of the Given. Essay 13 discusses Sellars's doctrine, which figures in Essay 3 and again in Essay 11, that significance is not a matter of relations between bearers of significance and elements in extra-linguistic reality. In Essay 14 I offer one more treatment of the question how we should conceive the kind of experience that makes rational knowledge available, in the face of the pitfall constituted by the Myth of the Given. This essay makes more of the Kantian notion of intuition than I manage in any of the others, including Essays 2 and 3 where that notion is central.

I have cited works by author's name and title, relegating other details to the bibliography at the end of the volume.

Many people have helped with this volume. I want to express special thanks to James Conant, who helped with the substance of many of the essays, and did indispensable editorial work on the collection.

HAVING THE WORLD IN VIEW

PART I

Sellars, Kant, and Intentionality

Sellars on Perceptual Experience

1. In his seminal set of lectures "Empiricism and the Philosophy of Mind", Wilfrid Sellars offers (among much else) the outlines of a deeply Kantian way of thinking about intentionality—about how thought and language are directed towards the world. Sellars describes *Science and Metaphysics: Variations on Kantian Themes*, his major work of the next decade after "Empiricism and the Philosophy of Mind", as a sequel to "Empiricism and the Philosophy of Mind" (p. vii). The later work makes explicit the Kantian orientation of the earlier; Sellars now shows a conviction that his own thinking about intentionality (and, indeed, about everything) can be well expounded through a reading of Kant. I do not think it is far-fetched to attribute to Sellars a belief on the following lines: no one has come closer to showing us how to find intentionality unproblematic than Kant, and there is no better way for us to find intentionality unproblematic than by seeing what Kant was driving at. That means rethinking his thought for ourselves, and, if necessary, correcting him at points where we think we see more clearly than he did what he should have been doing. Sellars does not hesitate to claim, on some points, to have a better understanding of the requirements of Kantian thinking than Kant himself achieved.

Now, I share this belief I have read into Sellars, that there is no better way for us to approach an understanding of intentionality than by working towards understanding Kant. I also believe that coming to terms with Sellars's sustained attempt to be a Kantian is a fine way into beginning to appreciate Kant, and thereby—given the first belief—into becoming philosophically comfortable with intentionality. I mean this as a partly backhanded compliment to Sellars. Sellars makes the way he thinks he has to correct Kant perfectly clear, and I want to suggest that the divergence is revealing. I think a fully Kantian vision of intentionality is inaccessible to Sellars, because of a deep structural feature of his philosophical outlook. I believe we can bring the way Kant actually thought about intentionality, and thereby—given that first belief—how we ourselves ought to think about intentionality, into clearer focus by reflecting on the difference between what Sellars knows Kant wrote and what Sellars thinks Kant should have written.[1]

The reading of Kant that I aim to give a glimpse of in this and the next two essays is under construction in a collaborative enterprise that I am privileged to be engaged in with my colleagues James Conant and John Haugeland. Here I want to make a standard prefatory remark, which I mean in a less ritualistic manner than is perhaps usual. Conant and Haugeland should receive full credit for anything in what follows that is helpful towards the understanding of Kant, and thereby towards the understanding of intentionality. The blame for anything unhelpful, or simply wrong, is mine alone. In particular, Conant and Haugeland should not be held responsible for the perhaps perverse idea that we can approach an understanding of Kant through seeing how close Sellars comes to Kant's picture; nor should they be held responsible for the details of my reading of Sellars.[2]

2. Sellars's master thought in "Empiricism and the Philosophy of Mind" is this. There is a special category of characterizations of states or episodes that occur in people's lives, for instance, characterizations of states or episodes as *knowings*; and, we might add, corresponding characterizations of the people in whose lives the states or episodes occur, for instance, characterizations of people as *knowers*. In giving these characterizations, we place whatever they

---

1. It is a measure of how difficult it is to come to terms with Kant that this sort of indirect approach can be helpful. In "Zwei Naturalismen auf Englisch", Dieter Henrich describes my references to Kant, in my earlier engagement (in *Mind and World*) with the issues I shall be considering in these three essays, as "platitüdinnahen". No doubt it is nearly platitudinous that sensibility must have a central role in any even approximately Kantian attempt at making intelligible the very idea of intentionality, the directedness of subjective states or episodes towards objects. But that is nearly platitudinous just because it is neutral between Sellars's reading of Kant and the quite different picture I was trying to give. Sellars thinks a properly Kantian position requires that conceptual episodes occur in perception in a way that is guided by "sheer receptivity". I do not believe that is a correct picture of the transcendental role of sensibility in a properly Kantian position. If this belief were platitudinous, Sellars could not have understood Kantian thinking as he does. I hope this will become clearer in these three essays.

2. I have also benefited from years of fruitful exchange with Robert Brandom, and from his very helpful comments on a draft of these essays.

characterize in "the logical space of reasons" (§36). Sellars's thesis is that the conceptual apparatus we employ when we place things in the logical space of reasons is irreducible to any conceptual apparatus that does not serve to place things in the logical space of reasons. So the master thought as it were draws a line; above the line are placings in the logical space of reasons, and below it are characterizations that do not do that.

That is a merely negative specification of what we must distinguish from placings in the logical space of reasons. But Sellars is concerned to warn against a particular philosophical pitfall, the temptation to suppose, of certain specific below-the-line characterizations, that they can fulfil tasks that can in fact be fulfilled only by above-the-line characterizations. This temptation is urgent in respect of some, in particular, of the characterizations that function below Sellars's line, and we need a positive specification of the characterizations that activate the temptation. Sellars sometimes suggests this helpful way of putting his thought: characterizations that affirm *epistemic* facts need to be distinguished from characterizations that affirm *natural* facts.[3] In these terms, his central thesis is that we must not suppose we can understand epistemic states or episodes in terms of the actualization of merely natural capacities—capacities that their subjects have at birth, or acquire in the course of merely animal maturation. I think "epistemic" here amounts to something like "concept-involving"; I shall justify this interpretation shortly.

Assuming this interpretation for the moment, we can bring Sellars's thought into direct contact with Kant. The logical space of reasons, on this reading, is the logical space in which we place episodes or states when we describe them in terms of the actualization of conceptual capacities. Now what corresponds in Kant to this image of the logical space of reasons is the image of the realm of freedom. The way to understand the correspondence is to focus on the Kantian idea that conceptual capacities are essentially exercisable in judging. It is true, and important, that judging is not the only mode of actualization of conceptual capacities; I shall be exploiting the point in these three essays. But even so, judging can be singled out as the paradigmatic mode of actualization of conceptual capacities, the one in terms of which we should understand the very idea of conceptual capacities

---

3. See §17, and note the echo of §5, where Sellars warns of a mistake in epistemology that is "of a piece with the so-called 'naturalistic fallacy' in ethics". At §36, he contrasts placing things in the space of reasons with "empirical description"; I think this formulation is less helpful.

in the relevant sense. And judging, making up our minds what to think, is something for which we are in principle responsible—something we freely do, as opposed to something that merely happens in our lives. Of course a belief is not always, or even typically, a result of our exercising this freedom to decide what to think. But even when a belief is not freely adopted, it is an actualization of capacities of a kind, the conceptual, whose paradigmatic mode of actualization is in the exercise of freedom that judging is. And this freedom, exemplified in responsible acts of judging, is essentially a matter of being answerable to criticism in the light of rationally relevant considerations. So the realm of freedom, at least the realm of the freedom of judging, can be identified with the space of reasons.

Sellars describes the logical space of reasons as the space "of justifying and being able to justify what one says".[4] We can see this as a distinctively twentieth-century elaboration of a Kantian conception, the conception of the capacity to exercise, paradigmatically in judgment, a freedom that is essentially a matter of responsiveness to reasons. The twentieth-century element is the idea that this capacity comes with being initiated into language.

3. At a pivotal point in "Empiricism and the Philosophy of Mind" (Part VIII), Sellars addresses the question whether empirical knowledge has foundations. His answer is nuanced.

In an empiricistic foundationalism of the usual kind, it is not just that the credentials of all knowledge are ultimately grounded in knowledge acquired in perception. Beyond that, the grounding perceptual knowledge is atomistically conceived. Traditional empiricists take it that each element of the grounding knowledge can in principle be acquired on its own, independently not only of other elements of the grounding perceptual knowledge, but also of anything in the world view that is grounded on this basic stratum of knowledge.

What Sellars objects to in traditional empiricism is just this supposed independence. He writes:

> There is clearly *some* point to the picture of human knowledge as resting on a level of propositions—observation reports—which do not rest on other propositions in the same way as other propositions rest on them. On the other hand, I do wish to insist that the metaphor of "foundation" is mis-

---

4. §36. This connects with the perhaps infelicitously labelled thesis of "psychological nominalism": see §29, §31, and, for an anticipation early in the lectures, §6.

leading in that it keeps us from seeing that if there is a logical dimension in which other empirical propositions rest on observation reports, there is another logical dimension in which the latter rest on the former.[5]

Sellars does not deny that there is a logical dimension in which observation reports are basic. His point is just to insist on the other logical dimension, in which observation reports depend on the world view that is grounded on them, that is, dependent on them in the logical dimension that a traditional empiricism restricts itself to. The result is a picture that is still in a way empiricist, by virtue of its acknowledgment of one of these logical dimensions, though it is separated from traditional empiricism by virtue of its insistence on the other.

Of course Sellars's point here is at least partly epistemological, in an intelligibly narrow sense; he is telling us how we should conceive the credentials in virtue of which a world view counts as knowledgeably held. But the divergence from traditional empiricism means that we cannot take Sellars to be doing epistemology in some sense that contrasts with reflecting about intentionality. It is indeed perceptual *knowledge* (knowledge expressed in observation reports) about which he is here urging that it depends, in respect of the concepts that figure in it, on a world view. But that is just a case of something more general; his thought is that the conceptual equipment that is operative in perceptual experience generally, whether the experience is such as to yield knowledge or not, is dependent on a world view, in the logical dimension that the metaphor of "foundation" risks leading us to forget. We can capture this part of the picture by saying that the intentionality, the objective purport, of perceptual experience in general—whether potentially knowledge-yielding or not—depends, in that logical dimension, on having the world in view, in a sense that goes beyond glimpses of the here and now. It would not be intelligible that the relevant episodes present themselves as glimpses of the here and now apart from their being related to a wider world view in the logical dimension Sellars adds. But the wider world view depends, in turn, in the logical dimension that figures in traditional empiricism, on perceptual experience that is capable of yielding knowledge, in the form of glimpses of the here and now. With this mutual dependence, the non-traditional empiricism that Sellars espouses constitutes a picture both of the credentials of empirical knowledge and of the intentionality of empirical thought in general.

---

5. §38. Compare §19.

This makes it unsurprising that we find Sellars speaking of "the epistemic character, the 'intentionality' ", of expressions such as "thinking of a celestial city".[6] When he introduces the image of the logical space of reasons, he singles out the episodes or states whose characterizations place them in the space of reasons as episodes or states of *knowing*.[7] And of course episodes or states of knowing would have an epistemic character in an etymologically obvious sense. But it would be wrong to conclude that Sellars's concern is narrowly epistemological. In the remark about "thinking of a celestial city", he makes this clear by showing that he is willing to equate epistemic character with intentionality, and to talk of epistemic character in a case in which there need be no question of knowing. In the remark about "thinking of a celestial city", "epistemic" can amount to no more than "concept-involving".[8] This is the interpretation I announced and promised to vindicate.

I have been urging that Sellars's non-traditional empiricism is not only a picture of the credentials of empirical knowledge, a topic for epistemology in a narrow sense, but also a picture of what is involved in having one's thought directed at the world at all, the topic of reflection about intentionality. This enables me to forestall a possible objection to the proposal that we read Kant, Sellars's model, as a philosopher of intentionality. I do not mean the feeble objection that "intentionality" is not a Kantian term. "Intentionality" is a scholastic term, which did not come back into mainstream philosophical currency until (I think) Brentano, but obviously that does not prevent us from supposing that the topic is a Kantian topic. What I have in mind is rather the potentially more challenging objection that Kant's concern is epistemological. As a putative reason for supposing that Kant is not concerned with intentionality, I can neutralize this by saying: certainly Kant's concern is epistemological—in just the way in which Sellars's is.

Against a "neo-Kantian" reading of Kant, Heidegger says: "The *Critique of Pure Reason* has nothing to do with a 'theory of knowledge'."[9] I think we can make the point Heidegger is trying to make more effectively—certainly we

---

6. §7. Compare §§24, 25. Consider also the implication, at §17, that looking red is an epistemic as opposed to a natural fact about objects. Looking red is not an epistemic fact in the etymologically obvious sense that I mention in the text below.

7. §36.

8. See *Science and Metaphysics*, p. 23: for purposes of the philosophy of mind, "the intentional is that which belongs to the conceptual order".

9. *Kant and the Problem of Metaphysics*, p. 11. Heidegger's word is "Erkenntnistheorie", which might have been translated "epistemology"; see Taft's note, p. 188.

can put it in a form in which it is easier to swallow—by saying, not that epistemology is *no* concern of the first *Critique*, but that it is no more *the* concern of the first *Critique* than it is of "Empiricism and the Philosophy of Mind" or of *Science and Metaphysics*.

4. Early in "Empiricism and the Philosophy of Mind" (§7), Sellars diagnoses "the classical concept of a sense datum" as "a mongrel resulting from a crossbreeding of two ideas": first, an idea of non-concept-involving sensory episodes, such as sensations of red; and, second, an idea of non-inferential knowings that such-and-such is the case. This is a mongrel, a conflation, because attributions of non-concept-involving episodes belong below the line drawn by Sellars's master thought, whereas attributions of knowings belong above it. When Sellars repeats the diagnosis a few pages later, he extracts from it a programme for the rest of the lectures: "to examine these two ideas and determine how that which survives criticism in each is properly to be combined with the other" (§10). The programme, then, is to arrive at an acceptable picture of how the sensory and the conceptual—sensibility and understanding—combine so as to provide for the intentionality of perceptual experience, and (the same function viewed from a different angle) to provide for how perceptual experience figures in the acquisition of a knowledgeable view of the world. We have looked ahead in Sellars's work, so we know that this case of intentionality, the intentionality of perceptual experience, is going to be in one way basic to intentionality in general, though not in a way that involves its being intelligible in advance of the idea of having a world view that goes beyond the immediate deliverances of perception.

The above-the-line element in the mongrel conflation is the idea of non-inferential knowings. Sellars mostly focuses on one sensory modality, and considers seeings.[10] But in pursuing his programme in connection with this particularization to one sensory modality of the above-the-line element in the mongrel, he expands the topic from seeings to a wider class of experiences, which he initially introduces as ostensible seeings. Seeings are a

10. For a self-conscious comment on this, see *Science and Metaphysics*, p. 9. There is a minor complication (nothing turns on it): seeings are not, as such, non-inferential knowings or acquirings of knowledge (that was how the above-the-line elements in the mongrel conflation were first introduced), but rather opportunities to know, which may not be taken. Consider how it might be intelligible to say this: "I thought it merely looked to me as if the tie was green, but I now realize that I was seeing it to be green."

singled-out subclass of ostensible seeings.[11] Evidently Sellars takes it that for purposes of separating and correctly combining what survives criticism in the ideas that are conflated into the mongrel, what matters is to understand the wider class. The goal is to understand the intentionality of visual experience in general, whether potentially knowledge-yielding or not.

Ostensible seeings are experiences in which it looks to their subject as if things are a certain way, and Sellars devotes some effort to elucidating that idea. Centrally important here is the image of an experience as, "so to speak, making an assertion or claim", or as "containing" a claim (§16). Sellars introduces this image in an explicitly promissory way, pointing forward to the culmination of "Empiricism and the Philosophy of Mind". There he vindicates a notion of non-overt conceptual episodes, on the ground that they can be understood by analogical extension from overt conceptual episodes, linguistic acts.[12] Visual experiences "make" or "contain" claims in that they are conceptual episodes, actualizations of conceptual capacities, and as such are to be understood on the model of linguistic performances in which claims are literally made.

This bears some elaboration. I have mentioned the Kantian view that conceptual capacities have their paradigmatic mode of actualization in judgings. We can approach the idea that visual experiences are conceptual episodes, and as such "make" or "contain" claims, through this identification of judging as the paradigmatic kind of conceptual episode. Consider, say, judging that there is a red cube in front of one. There is a conceptual capacity that would be exercised both in making that judgment and in judging that there is a red pyramid in front of one, and another conceptual capacity that would be exercised both in judging that there is a red cube in front of one and in judging that there is a blue cube in front of one. In judging that there is a red cube in front of one, one would be exercising (at least) these two capacities together. What does "together" mean here? Not just that one would be exercising the two capacities in a single act of judgment; that would not distinguish judging that there is a red cube in front of one from judging, say,

---

11. For seeings as veridical members of a class of ostensible seeings, see "Empiricism and the Philosophy of Mind", §7. This points towards the discussion of "looks" statements in Part III. I shall comment in Essay 3 below on the idea, which is implicit in at least the first version of "Empiricism and the Philosophy of Mind", that veridicality is all it takes for an ostensible seeing to be a seeing.

12. The first phase of the myth of Jones; for the application to perceptual experience, see §60.

that there is a red pyramid and a blue cube in front of one. In a judgment that there is a red cube in front of one, the two conceptual capacities I have singled out would have to be exercised with a specific mode of togetherness: a togetherness that is a counterpart to the "logical" or semantical togetherness of the words "red" and "cube" in the verbal expression of the judgment, "There is a red cube in front of me". Here we see the point of the idea that non-overt conceptual episodes are to be understood on analogy with linguistic acts; it affords a way to make a distinction that we need to make.[13]

The conceptual episodes Sellars is concerned with, when he speaks of visual experiences as "containing" claims, are not as such cases of judging. Even if one does judge that things are as they look, having them look that way to one is not the same as judging that they are that way. In some cases, perhaps, one does judge that things are a certain way when they look that way—acquiring the belief that they are that way by freely making up one's mind that they are that way. But more typically, perceptual belief-acquisition is not a matter of judging, of actively exercising control over one's cognitive life, at all. Unless there are grounds for suspicion, such as odd lighting conditions, having it look to one as if things are a certain way—ostensibly seeing things to be that way—becomes accepting that things are that way by a sort of default, involving no exercise of the freedom that figures in a Kantian conception of judgment.

So there is a disconnection between perceptual experience and judging. But even so, we can exploit the apparatus of the conception of judging I have sketched in order to vindicate Sellars's image of experiences as "containing" claims. A free, responsible exercise of certain conceptual capacities, including at least the two I mentioned, with a suitable mode of togetherness would be judging that there is a red cube in front of one. Now we can say that in an ostensible seeing that there is a red cube in front of one—an experience in which it looks to one as if there is a red cube in front of one—the *same* conceptual capacities would be actualized with the *same* mode of togetherness. This cashes out the idea that an experience so described "contains" a claim,

---

13. I mean this quick sketch of a conception of judging, as the joint exercise of different conceptual capacities, to recall Gareth Evans's discussion of "the Generality Constraint": *The Varieties of Reference*, pp. 100–5. Evans's discussion has its roots in P. T. Geach's account of judging on analogy with saying, in *Mental Acts*. Geach's analogical account of judging is roughly contemporary with Sellars's in "Empiricism and the Philosophy of Mind"; independent of it; and (I would argue) more satisfactory, in being free of the scientistic baggage with which Sellars encumbers his version. But I shall not be considering the scientistic details of Sellars's version in these essays (though Sellars's scientism will matter in other contexts).

whose content is just what one would be judging in the corresponding judgment. But this actualization of the relevant conceptual capacities, unlike the one that would be involved in the corresponding judgment, would be involuntary; that is why I say "actualization" rather than "exercise".

This idea of conceptual capacities being involuntarily actualized in perceptual experience partly captures the point of a striking remark Sellars makes about the way an experience "contains" a claim; he says that the claim "is, so to speak, evoked or wrung from the perceiver by the object perceived" (§16 bis). When Sellars says this, he is talking about experiences of seeing, but the point he is making surely applies also to members of the wider class, ostensible seeings, even the ones that are not seeings. Ostensible seeings are experiences that, as conceptual episodes, "contain" claims, but in a special way that differentiates them from conceptual episodes of other kinds. They "contain" their claims as ostensibly *necessitated* by an object ostensibly seen. In *Science and Metaphysics*, Sellars puts the same point by saying that if one says it looks to so-and-so as though there were a red and rectangular physical object in front of him, one is attributing to so-and-so (who may of course be oneself) a conceptual representation, of a particular kind, that there is a red and rectangular physical object in front of him; and the kind is "that kind of conceptual representation which is being under the visual *impression* that . . . there is (or of there being) a red and rectangular physical object in front of one" (p. 14; my emphasis). In the language of "Empiricism and the Philosophy of Mind", this is to say that ostensible seeings "contain" their claims in a distinctive way, one that distinguishes them from other conceptual episodes; they "contain" their claims as ostensibly visually *imposed* or *impressed* on their subject.[14]

14. I have, I think charitably, discounted "evoked or wrung *from the perceiver*" in the formulation Sellars uses in "Empiricism and the Philosophy of Mind". A claim evoked from a perceiver would surely be a claim that the perceiver makes. But it seems wrong to imply that a perceiver makes the claim his experience "contains"—wrong even before we widen the focus from seeings to ostensible seeings. Whether an ostensible seeing is a seeing turns on whether its "contained" claim is true, and that is a separate question from whether its subject makes (endorses) the claim. (See n. 10 above.) So even a seeing, let alone a merely ostensible seeing, does not necessarily "contain" a claim made by its subject. Where I have marked an omission in my citation of the parallel remark from *Science and Metaphysics*, Sellars glosses "being under the visual impression that" with "(visually taking it to be the case that)", and this seems wrong in the same way. We can correct Sellars on this without posing a threat to something he wants to insist on, that one gets to have conceptual episodes (representations) of the relevant kind occur in one's life at all only by acquiring the capacity to make the claims they "contain".

So it is not simply that conceptual episodes of the relevant kind consist in actualizations of conceptual capacities that are involuntary. (We have that also with other kinds of conceptual episodes; for instance, when one is, as we say, struck by a thought.) In visual experiences conceptual capacities are actualized with suitable modes of togetherness; this is how we cash out the idea that the episodes "contain" claims. But they are actualized with an involuntariness of a specific kind; in a visual experience an ostensibly seen object ostensibly impresses itself visually on the subject. And presumably parallel things are to be said about other sensory modalities.[15]

5. I have been considering what survives criticism, from the above-the-line element of the mongrel conflation, in a conception of visual experience that would be acceptable by Sellars's lights. Sellars's programme for "Empiricism and the Philosophy of Mind" presupposes in addition that something survives criticism from the below-the-line element in the mongrel conflation, and needs to be acceptably combined with conceptual episodes of the distinctive kind I have been discussing, in a total picture of visual experience. In the course of executing his programme, Sellars says it is "clear" that there is more to visual experience than conceptual episodes of that distinctive kind; and specifically, that a full picture must also include non-concept-involving episodes of the kind exemplified, in the original description of the mongrel conflation, by sensations of red.[16] But why is this supposed to be clear?

The question is especially pressing when we realize how much goes into what we already have above Sellars's line—how much goes into the idea of a conceptual episode of the relevant kind. Even after we have said not just that a visual experience "contains" a claim but also that the "contained" claim is, so to speak, "evoked" by an ostensibly seen object, Sellars still says it is clear that we need to add something about visual episodes of a non-conceptual

15. Compare the conception of experience I recommended in *Mind and World*, where I wrote of states or episodes in which conceptual capacities are operative in sensibility. I think such a formulation simply captures, in explicitly Kantian language, the way Sellars shows us how to conceive perceptual experience—at any rate what he sees as the above-the-line element in the total truth about perceptual experience. In *Mind and World* (e.g. pp. 140–1) I focused on the below-the-line role that he credits to sensibility, and missed the fact that he has an above-the-line conception of perceptual impressions that matches the conception I was recommending.

16. "Empiricism and the Philosophy of Mind", §16 bis. Compare the use of "of course" at §22; and again at §45.

kind. In his view, conceptual episodes of the relevant kind are already, as the conceptual episodes they are, cases of *being under the visual impression* that such-and-such is the case. It is not that as conceptual episodes they are phenomenologically colourless, so that they would need to be associated with visual sensations in order that some complex composed of these conceptual episodes and the associated visual sensations can be recognizably visual. These conceptual episodes are already, as the conceptual episodes they are, shapings of visual consciousness.[17] If we need a below-the-line element in our picture, it is not in order to ensure that the picture depicts states or episodes of visual consciousness.

So why does Sellars think our total account of visual experience needs to include visual sensations as well? About the presence of the corresponding element in the mongrel conflation, he says:

> [This] idea clearly arises in the attempt to explain the facts of sense perception in scientific style. How does it happen that people can have the experience which they describe by saying "It is as though I were seeing a red and triangular physical object" when either there is no physical object there at all, or, if there is, it is neither red nor triangular? The explanation, roughly, posits that in every case in which a person has an experience of this kind, whether veridical or not, he has what is called a 'sensation' or 'impression' 'of a red triangle.'[18]

And in the view that emerges as his own, in the course of "Empiricism and the Philosophy of Mind", it is not in this explanatory motivation for its below-the-line element that the mongrel conflation goes wrong, but just in the way it conflates the below-the-line element so motivated with the above-the-line element, episodes that would have to be actualizations of conceptual capacities. Sensations figure in the picture, at least initially, as posited on the ground that they are needed for an explanatory purpose.[19]

17. Contrast, for instance, Robert B. Brandom, *Making It Explicit: Reasoning, Representing, and Discursive Commitment*. In his chapter 4, Brandom undertakes to give an account of observational claims and observational knowledge while sedulously avoiding any mention of sensory consciousness. Brandom here diverges from something that is quite central to Sellars's thinking.

18. "Empiricism and the Philosophy of Mind", §7.

19. See §§21–22; a programmatic passage, and he returns to its programme, and executes it in the rest of the lectures. Much of the work needed is in qualifying the idea of sensations as posited, in order to make room for immediate self-attribution of sensations. This is why I say "at least initially".

What explanatory purpose? In "Empiricism and the Philosophy of Mind", the envisaged explanation is, as we have seen, "in scientific style". And the question that the explanation is to answer seems to be this, to put it in terms that become available during the execution of Sellars's programme: how is it that the *same* claim would be "contained" in, say, each member of a trio of possible experiences of which one is a case of seeing that there is a red and triangular physical object in front of one, one is a case in which something in front of one looks red and triangular although it is not, and one is a case in which it looks to one as if there is something red and triangular in front of one although there is nothing there at all?[20]

If what we still need to ask for is an explanation of the *sameness* of claims "contained" in such a trio of experiences, the request for an explanation apparently assumes that we are already entitled to think of experiences as "containing" some claims or other, independently of the explanation we are asking for. After all, we might say, the idea that experiences "contain" claims is already accounted for in the part of the story that belongs above the line; we have already entitled ourselves to it by talking about actualizations of conceptual capacities, before questions arise about a below-the-line element in the total story. But in that case it is not clear why we should suppose that our explanatory need can be met only by finding a sameness at the level of visual *sensations*—items in consciousness—between the members of such a trio, as opposed to a sameness at the level of, say, patterns of light impinging on retinas. When he elaborates "the attempt to explain the facts of sense perception in scientific style" by positing sensations, Sellars himself says: "The core idea is that the *proximate cause* of such a sensation is only for the most part brought about by the presence in the neighborhood of the perceiver of a red and triangular physical object."[21] In this remark, Sellars is suggesting that we should expect to find a sameness between seeings and ostensible seeings that "contain" the same claims, at a level that he here specifies as that of *proximate causes* of sensations; for instance, at the level of retinal images. But then why not suppose a sameness at this level will do the explanatory work for which Sellars thinks we need to appeal to

20. See §45 for a formulation on these lines. Sellars notes at §22 that it is not strictly accurate to say that the same claim is "contained" in each member of such a trio: the claim "contained" in each of the first two is referential, whereas the claim "contained" in the third is not. This will start to be significant in Essays 2 and 3 below, but it does not matter here, any more than it does at the point where Sellars acknowledges it.

21. §7; emphasis altered.

sensations? Conceptual episodes of the relevant kind are triggered by impacts from the environment on a perceiver's sensory equipment. If the impacts are suitably similar, there is nothing puzzling about a similarity between the conceptual episodes they trigger. And it is not clear why it should seem necessary to describe these suitably similar impacts in terms of non-conceptual impingements *on consciousness* (sensations), as opposed to saying that consciousness comes into play only with conceptual episodes, triggered by non-mentalistically described impacts on sensory equipment. It seems that what Sellars here introduces as proximate causes of sensations can themselves meet the explanatory need, conceived as he seems to conceive it in "Empiricism and the Philosophy of Mind". The sensations look like idle wheels.

In *Science and Metaphysics* (p. 18), Sellars explicitly confronts an objection on these lines. And he responds in a way that changes the picture rather radically from the one he seemed to be giving in "Empiricism and the Philosophy of Mind". First, he no longer formulates the explanation-seeking question in terms of the sameness of the claims "contained" in different possible experiences—as if we could anyway help ourselves to the idea that experiences "contain" claims at all. The explanation-seeking question now is: how is it that sensory relatedness to the environment takes the form of conceptual episodes, episodes that, in the terminology of "Empiricism and the Philosophy of Mind", "contain" claims, at all?[22] And second, the explanatory need that sensations are supposed to satisfy is not a need for scientific understanding, as it seemed to be in "Empiricism and the Philosophy of Mind"; rather, it is *transcendental*.[23] I think these are two ways of putting the same thought: the reason Sellars thinks our complete account of visual experience must include visual sensations—non-conceptual visual episodes—is that he thinks this is the only way we can find it intelligible that there should so much as be the conceptual shaping of sensory consciousness that constitutes the above-the-line element in his account of visual experience.

22. At p. 18, in the course of urging that the explanatory question is not specially about non-veridical experiences, Sellars writes: "even in normal [veridical] cases there is the genuine question, 'Why does the perceiver *conceptually represent* a red (blue, etc.) rectangular (circular, etc.) object in the presence of an object having these qualities?"

23. See p. 9. Sellars says that manifolds of sensation are "postulated on general epistemological or, as Kant would say, transcendental grounds". I think this equation, in the context of the understanding I am offering of "the 'sense impression inference' ", reinforces the impression given by his willingness to equate "intentionality" with "epistemic character" in "Empiricism and the Philosophy of Mind"; he does not conceive epistemology narrowly.

"Transcendental" figures here in a recognizably Kantian sense. The explanation Sellars envisages is transcendental because it is needed, he thinks, in order to vindicate the legitimacy of the apparatus—the talk of experiences as actualizations of conceptual capacities, which as such "contain" claims, but in a distinctively sensory way—in terms of which we enable ourselves to conceive experiences as ostensibly *of objects* at all.[24] Sellars thinks his picture, with sensations playing such a transcendental role, just is the picture Kant would have given if he had been fully clear about the drift of his own thinking.

On this reading of "the 'sense impression inference'" as it figures in *Science and Metaphysics*,[25] visual sensations or sense impressions are not simply an extra part of the truth about visual experiences, over and above the part that deals with the distinctive way in which visual experiences "contain" claims. That is how it might have seemed from "Empiricism and the Philosophy of Mind". But in the view Sellars urges in *Science and Metaphysics*, it is not that visual experiences "contain" claims in their distinctive way, and then there is a simply additional fact about them, that they involve visual sensations. The reason we have to acknowledge the "additional" fact, in Sellars's view, is that only so can we be entitled to have spoken as we did when we gave our above-the-line characterization of visual experiences—when we spoke of visual experiences as "containing" claims, and so having objective purport, in the distinctive way they do.

Sellars's "sense impression inference" is a piece of transcendental philosophy, in the following sense: it is directed towards showing our entitlement to conceive subjective occurrences as possessing objective purport. Notice that that description of transcendental philosophy implies nothing in particular about the nature of the activity. There is a temptation to suppose transcendental philosophy would have to be done at a standpoint external to that of the conceptual goings-on whose objective purport is to be vindicated—a standpoint at which one could contemplate the relation between those conceptual goings-on and their subject matter from sideways on. Sellars's move fits this conception; he undertakes to vindicate the objective purport of conceptual occurrences from outside the conceptual order. I shall be taking issue

---

24. See, e.g., *Critique of Pure Reason*, A11–12/B25: "I entitle *transcendental* all knowledge which is occupied not so much with objects as with the mode of our knowledge of objects in so far as this mode of knowledge is to be possible *a priori.*"

25. For the phrase, see p. 17.

with this conception of transcendental philosophy. It is important to see that this is not to take issue with the very idea of transcendental philosophy.[26]

6. When Sellars vindicates the idea of inner episodes, at the culmination of "Empiricism and the Philosophy of Mind", he does so in two phases: first for conceptual episodes and then for non-conceptual episodes. Each phase has two stages, and the structure is parallel in each phase. First, there is an account of how concepts of episodes of the relevant kind could have been introduced in the context of a theory; at this stage the episodes are envisaged as attributable, to others or oneself, only inferentially, in a way mediated by the theory. But then, second, there is an account of how a non-inferential, self-attributing ("reporting") employment of the relevant conceptual apparatus could have been introduced, by training people in such a way as to leave them immediately disposed to make self-attributions—"immediately" in the sense that they do not need to advert to the evidence that the theory provides for—on occasions when, according to the theory, those attributions are correct. By the end of "Empiricism and the Philosophy of Mind", conceptual episodes, including those that "contain" claims in the distinctive way in which visual experiences do, and non-conceptual sensory, and in particular visual, episodes—impressions or sensations—are on a level, in respect of being available for non-inferential self-attribution.[27]

In *Science and Metaphysics* Sellars modifies this picture in a way that belongs, I think, with the fact that he now explicitly sees "the 'sense impression inference'" as transcendentally driven. He suggests that the visual impressions or sensations that "the 'sense impression inference'" requires us to posit are states of consciousness, but not objects of consciousness; or—the same

26. The idea that transcendental philosophy would have to be done from a special standpoint is implicit at p. 293 of Richard Rorty, *Philosophy and the Mirror of Nature*, where Rorty writes of the "demand . . . for some transcendental standpoint outside our present set of representations from which we can inspect the relations between those representations and their object". Kant distinguishes "transcendental" and "transcendent" (see, e.g., A296/B352-3). In Rorty's phrase "transcendental" could be replaced by "transcendent". Not that that shows Rorty to be misusing "transcendental"; he is suggesting that transcendental philosophy requires a transcendent standpoint. That is what I think we should dispute. When I wrote disparagingly about Kant's "transcendental story" in *Mind and World* (pp. 41-3, 95-8), I was acquiescing, in a way I now regret, in a reading of parts of Kant's transcendental activity that fits Rorty's phrasing. (I would still disparage the philosophy such a reading finds in Kant.)

27. See §59 for conceptual episodes, and §62 for non-conceptual episodes.

thought differently expressed—that these impressions or sensations are states of consciousness that are not apperceived, where "apperception" can be explained as "non-inferential self-knowledge".[28] He is suggesting, then, that the transcendentally posited visual impressions or sensations figure in visual consciousness in a way that does not amount to their achieving the immediate or non-inferential attributability to oneself that he works to secure at the culmination of "Empiricism and the Philosophy of Mind".

Now it is hard to see how, on Sellarsian or indeed any principles, there could be a class of items in consciousness whose members were permanently and constitutionally incapable of being apperceived, incapable of being directly available for self-attribution. Sellars cannot mean to be suggesting that the visual impressions or sensations that, according to his transcendental "sense impression inference", must figure in episodes of "outer sense" are, simply as the visual impressions or sensations they are, incapable of being objects of consciousness. I think his thought must rather be on the following lines. The visual impressions or sensations in question are not apperceived *when they are playing their transcendental role.* That is not to say that they are not *apperceivable.* It is just to say that if they do get to be apperceived—if they do become objects for consciousness—they can no longer be playing their transcendental role, that of enabling episodes of "outer sense", episodes that "contain" claims about the environment. One can focus one's attention on the manifold of "sheer receptivity" that was, a moment before, enabling one's attention to be directed towards the ostensibly seen environment. But in doing so—in bringing it within the scope of one's apperception—one ensures that it ceases to perform that function.

I think this thought strengthens Sellars's position by immunizing it against a certain objection. If it were right to endorse Sellars's "sense impression inference", it would be a good idea to construe its conclusion in this way. Considering only "Empiricism and the Philosophy of Mind", I used to think one could complain that the below-the-line items that figure in Sellars's picture of visual experience would be opaque; not something through which the environment could intelligibly be revealed to us, but at best something on the basis of which, if we knew enough about how features of the environment cause these affections of our sensory capacities, we could infer conclusions about the environment.[29] In "Empiricism and the Philosophy of Mind", the

---

28. *Science and Metaphysics*, pp. 10, 11. For the gloss on "apperception", see p. 72.
29. See *Mind and World*, p. 145.

only way Sellars considers for something to be in consciousness is for it to be an object of consciousness. This leaves it seeming that the sensations that are part of Sellars's picture of perceptual experience would have to be objects of consciousness, on pain of not figuring in consciousness at all. If that were not what Sellars wants, why does he need to work at securing that they can be objects of consciousness, as he does at the culmination of "Empiricism and the Philosophy of Mind"? And if we try to make out that they are objects of consciousness, it does seem that they would engross the attention, and prevent it from fixing itself—except indirectly, through inference—on environmental objects, although it was perception of environmental objects that we were supposed to be trying to make intelligible.

But the picture Sellars gives in *Science and Metaphysics* is immune to any such objection. Now Sellars can concede that if a manifold of visual sensations is figuring as an object for its subject's consciousness, the subject's attention can no longer pass through it to features of the environment directly, but at best inferentially. But this leaves unthreatened the idea that such a manifold is transcendentally required for perceptual awareness of the environment. Sellars is now equipped to say that the transcendentally required manifold, when it is doing its transcendental job, figures in consciousness not as an object, in which case it would indeed prevent the free passage of the subject's attention to the environment, but precisely as that through which the subject's attention is directed without hindrance to features of the ostensibly seen environment. The idea is that attention, which involves apperception, can be directed either at the ostensibly seen environment or at the visual sensations that were enabling the environment to be ostensibly seen, but not both; if the attention is directed at the sensations, they can no longer be enabling the ostensible seeing of environmental objects.

This complication, however, does not undermine the fact that a Sellarsian account of the non-inferential self-attribution of visual sensations—when it does occur, as it surely can—will have the structure established in "Empiricism and the Philosophy of Mind". The concepts under which visual sensations are apperceived when they are—which is not when they are enabling episodes of "outer sense"—will be concepts whose original home is a transcendentally required theory concerning how manifolds of sensations enable episodes of "outer sense". When visual sensations become objects for consciousness, it will be under concepts whose original function is to connect these episodes, in a theory-mediated way, with the claim-"containing" character of visual experiences.

Some people think we can vindicate a role for sensations in the total picture of visual experience on the basis of a theoretically innocent introspection. The idea is that sensational properties are introspectively available in any case, whatever we say about what figures, in this conception, as the subsequent question how, if at all, the sensational properties of experiences relate to their claim-"containing" character. I have ignored this conception, because it makes no contact with Sellars's thinking.[30]

It is important not to be misled by the fact that Sellars uses the word "impression" both in the phrase "being under the visual impression that . . .", which characterizes a kind of conceptual episode, and for the below-the-line element in his picture of perceptual experience.[31] Conceptual episodes that belong to the kind, being under the visual impression that . . . , are, simply as conceptual episodes, available for apperception when they occur.[32]

30. See, e.g., chapter 1 of Christopher Peacocke, *Sense and Content*. Peacocke says the sensational properties of visual experience are arrayed in a two-dimensional visual field, and he does not suggest that "two-dimensional" here means anything different from what it might mean in describing, say, a surface in the environment. By Sellars's lights this is naive; for Sellars the spatiality of the arrangement of visual sensations is not the spatiality of "outer" configurations, but something that needs to be understood by analogical extension from it, in a sophisticated exercise of concept-formation.

Even on their own terms, I think Peacocke's phenomenological arguments are unconvincing, but I shall not argue this here. Perhaps the thinness of the supposedly independent phenomenological considerations reveals that Peacocke's conception of what a supposedly innocent introspection would yield is really controlled by an implicit acceptance of something like Sellars's transcendental thought.

There is another putative ground for supposing that visual experiences must have a sensational aspect, equally non-Sellarsian, which I shall also not discuss in these essays. This is the thought that there must be a two-dimensional sensational array to serve as a vehicle for the representational content of a visual experience, somewhat as an arrangement of pigment on a surface is a vehicle for the representational content of a picture.

31. See *Science and Metaphysics*, p. 19, where Sellars distinguishes "an impression of a red rectangle" from "an impression of a man lurking in the corner". The latter would, as he says, be "a conceptual state" (or episode); one of the kind identified at p. 14, the kind "being under the visual impression that . . .".

32. This is not to say that they are actually apperceived. The "I think" of apperception must be *able* to accompany all my representations (*Critique of Pure Reason*, B131), which is not to say that it actually accompanies them. But conceptual representations are available for apperception in a way that differs from that in which, in a plausibly Sellarsian picture, perceptual sensations are; apperceiving the latter would require equipping oneself with something new, a conceptual representation involving concepts whose primary home is the transcendental theory of how conceptual representations of outer reality are guided by manifolds of "sheer receptivity".

Impressions in the other sense, in contrast, can be apperceived only when they are not serving as the below-the-line element in the total truth about some perceptual experiences.

The fact that the same word naturally acquires these two uses is perhaps suggestive about the shape of Sellars's picture. When a conceptual episode is apperceived as belonging to the kind, being under the visual impression that . . . , what is apperceptively available, according to Sellars's picture, is *that* the flow of one's conceptual representations, of the sort involved in normal perceptual activity, is being guided into "containing" the relevant claim by the flow of one's impressions in the below-the-line sense, and perhaps this is why "being under the visual impression that . . ." is an appropriate specification of the kind to which the conceptual representation apperceivably belongs. But apperception does not embrace the specifics of *how* this guidance is effected; if the formerly guiding items get to be apperceived, they can no longer be performing their guiding function.[33]

7. Sellars thinks this picture is essentially the one Kant is aiming at, although he has to acknowledge that it is not to be found adequately set out on Kant's pages. For one thing, Kant "tends to restrict the term 'consciousness' to apperceiving and the apperceived as such", which makes it difficult to find in Kant the idea that impressions or sensations can figure in consciousness without being apperceived.[34] A more substantial problem is that Sellars has to find Kant seriously confused in his thesis that space is the form of outer sense.[35] One is bound to wonder whether Sellars has Kant wrong. And, since Sellars's reading of Kant is, perfectly properly, shaped by Sellars's own conviction about how we should conceive perceptual experience, that is inextricably bound up with wondering whether Sellars is mistaken in thinking that sound philosophy requires impressions or sensations to be credited with the role he attributes to them. These are my questions for the next of these three essays.

33. For the image of guiding, see *Science and Metaphysics*, p. 16.

34. See *Science and Metaphysics*, p. 11.

35. See *Science and Metaphysics*, p. 8: "the idea that Space is the form of outer sense is incoherent."

The Logical Form of an Intuition

1. In the first of these three essays, I elicited from Sellars a picture of the intentionality of perceptual experience—visual experience, to stay with the case Sellars mostly concentrates on.

Sellars's picture has elements both above and below a line that importantly shapes his thinking. The line separates characterizations of occurrences in people's lives that need to be understood in terms of the actualization of conceptual capacities from characterizations that do not need to be understood in those terms.

Above the line in a Sellarsian picture of a visual experience, there is a conceptual episode of a distinctive kind. Just by virtue of being a conceptual episode, such an episode "contains" a claim about the environment. But episodes of this kind are differentiated from conceptual episodes of other kinds in that they "contain" their claims in a distinctive way: as ostensibly required from or impressed on their subject by an ostensibly seen object.

Below the line in a Sellarsian picture of a visual experience, there is a complex or manifold of visual sensations, non-concept-involving visual episodes or states. Why does Sellars think the picture has to include this element as well as conceptual episodes of the relevant kind? Not to ensure that the picture respects phenomenological facts—as if there would be nothing sensory, let alone visual, about the episodes that are in view before we advert to this below-the-line element. On the contrary, the above-the-line episodes that figure in Sellars's picture of visual experience are, as conceptual episodes of their special kind, already conceived as conceptual shapings of sensory, and in particular visual, consciousness. Sellars's thought is rather this: it is for transcendental reasons that we need to acknowledge the below-the-line element in the picture. The idea is that we are entitled to talk of conceptual episodes in which claims are ostensibly visually impressed on subjects—the above-the-line element in the picture—only because we can see the flow of such conceptual representations as guided by manifolds of sensations; non-concept-involving episodes or states in sensory, and specifically visual, consciousness.

Sellars takes this picture to be fundamentally Kantian, although he complains that Kant failed to make the necessary distinction clear even to himself. As I suggested at the end of Essay 1, this invites us to consider a different exegetical possibility. Perhaps the idea that perception involves a flow of conceptual representations guided by manifolds of "sheer receptivity" is not Kantian at all. I am going to urge that that is indeed so; the idea is foisted on Kant by Sellars, even with his eyes open to the price, which is that he needs to accuse Kant of confusion. Sellars is willing to pay the price, because he is convinced that the idea is required for a satisfactory execution of Kant's project. In this essay and the next I am going to urge that Sellars is wrong about that, too. I want to suggest that, so far from helping to make us comfortable with the intentionality of perception, and thereby contributing towards making us comfortable with intentionality in general, the below-the-line element in Sellars's picture actually stands in the way of a useful conception of how perception and thought are directed towards objects—one we can find, at least in germ, in Kant, once we discard Sellars's interpretation of the transcendental role Kant credits to sensibility.

2. Sellars is firm in his conviction that what Kant usually calls "intuitions" are representations of individuals that already involve the understanding, the faculty associated with concepts. He suggests that an intuition on this interpretation of the term should be taken to represent an individual as a *this-such*.[1] I think this is very helpful, and I am going to exploit it. In an intuition on this interpretation of the term, sensibility and understanding are both involved. We might describe intuitions on this interpretation as shapings of sensory consciousness by the understanding—to echo the wording I used in connection with Sellars's conception of the conceptual episodes, as such "containing" claims, that figure above the line in the picture of perceptual experience he gives in "Empiricism and the Philosophy of Mind".

1. See *Science and Metaphysics*, p. 3: "On this model, which I take to be, on the whole, the correct interpretation, intuitions would be representations of *thises* and would be conceptual in that peculiar way in which to represent something as a *this* is conceptual." This is elaborated at pp. 4–7, where Sellars suggests that representing something as a *this* is representing it as a *this-such*.

But as I have said, Sellars is convinced that Kant also needs to speak about sensibility in a way that belongs below his line, as the talk of sensory consciousness with which we can gloss this first notion of intuition does not, because in intuitions, on this first interpretation, sensory consciousness is already shaped by the faculty of concepts. Sellars thinks the transcendental role that Kant needs sensibility to play consists in its supplying manifolds of sensory items that are not shaped by the understanding, to guide the flow of conceptual representations in perception. So Sellars thinks Kant needs the word "intuition"—his most general term for sensibility in operation—to apply also to occurrences in which the understanding, the faculty of concepts, is not involved: "We seem . . . to be led to a distinction between intuitions which do and intuitions which do not involve something over and above sheer receptivity."[2]

Sellars sees it as a failure on Kant's part that he does not distinguish these two interpretations of "intuition". And Sellars sees this failure as an implicit counterpart to the mongrel conflation that, in "Empiricism and the Philosophy of Mind", he finds in the classical concept of a sense datum:

> Kant's use of the term 'intuition', in connection with human knowledge, blurs the distinction between a special sub-class of *conceptual* representations of individuals which, though in some sense a function of receptivity, belong to a framework which is no sense prior to but essentially includes general concepts, and a radically different kind of representation of an individual which belongs to sheer receptivity and is in no sense conceptual.[3]

This is just like the mongrel conflation: a failure to separate items that belong above and below Sellars's line.

The fact that Sellars finds this implicit conflation in Kant helps to account for some features of the above-the-line notion of intuitions that he finds in Kant. In Sellars's reading, Kant's above-the-line notion of intuitions is distorted, in some of its applications, by the implicit conflation with a below-the-line notion.

An intuition on the above-the-line interpretation represents its object as a *this-such*. For instance, a visual intuition might represent its object as *this cube*. Now what does the word "cube" contribute to such a specification of the content of an intuition? According to Sellars, Kant thinks it can be

---

2. *Science and Metaphysics*, p. 4; see also p. 7 (§17).
3. *Science and Metaphysics*, p. 7; compare "Empiricism and the Philosophy of Mind", §7.

something prior to the concept of a cube, as that concept might figure in a judgment that something is a cube. In Sellars's reading, Kant thinks the concept of a cube—the concept that figures predicatively in such a judgment—is derived, by an analytic activity of the understanding, from something that is not yet that concept, figuring in intuitions that, even though they do not involve that concept, are nevertheless enabled to represent their object as *this cube* by a synthetic operation of the understanding functioning in the guise of the productive imagination.[4]

On this view, *cube* in a representation of an object as *this cube* can be prior to *cube* in a judgment that something *is a cube*. As Sellars remarks, this suggestion of a priority is "puzzling".[5] But it might seem to make sense in the context of the counterpart Sellars finds in Kant to the mongrel conflation of "Empiricism and the Philosophy of Mind". The idea Sellars finds in Kant is that some intuitions are only proto-conceptual. This can be seen as a response to the pressure—*ex hypothesi* not properly understood by Sellars's Kant, who is implicitly entangled in the mongrel conflation—to have the mongrel notion of an intuition provide for an idea that can in fact become clear only when the conflation is unmasked; only as the idea of an episode that is not conceptual at all.

Sellars says: "Kant's thesis . . . requires the existence of completely determinate 'basic' perceptual this-suches."[6] This fits the view that Kant thinks concepts proper, at least at a basic level, are derived by abstraction from representations of *this-suches* that are only proto-conceptual. Taking Kant's thinking to be distorted by an implicit commitment to the mongrel conflation fits with finding in Kant, as Sellars does, a conception of how the most basic empirical concepts are formed that is in a certain sense abstractionist.[7]

---

4. See *Science and Metaphysics*, pp. 4–7.

5. *Science and Metaphysics*, p. 5.

6. *Science and Metaphysics*, p. 7.

7. The abstractionism is of a peculiar kind. Elsewhere (e.g., "Phenomenalism", p. 90) Sellars credits Kant with seeing that concepts cannot be abstractively derived from *sensation*, in a process we would have to picture in terms of content being transferred into the intellect "as Jack Horner transferred the plum" (compare *Science and Metaphysics*, p. 20). In the position he attributes to Kant in *Science and Metaphysics*, it is not sensation from which concepts are abstractively derived, but intuitions conceived as already shaped by the understanding. But the position still violates a basic Sellarsian conviction, that the capacity to experience things as thus-and-so should be seen as coeval with the capacity to judge that they are thus-and-so.

3. On Sellars's view of the requirements for a properly Kantian position, the Transcendental Aesthetic should have dealt with forms exemplified in manifolds of intuition on the second interpretation of the term— manifolds of sensory impressions that are prior to any operations of the understanding, and that transcendentally subserve intuition on the first interpretation of the term, according to which intuitions involve the understanding as well as sensibility. Kant's topic in the Aesthetic, in so far as the Aesthetic bears on "outer sense", should have been a form exemplified in the manifolds of "sheer receptivity" that transcendentally enable outwardly directed episodes in which the understanding is also operative. Kant says the form of outer sense is space. If his topic had been what Sellars thinks it should have been, Kant would have had to mean that space informs the below-the-line element in the transcendental picture of outer awareness as a shaping of sensory consciousness by the understanding. But—as Sellars complains—space, as Kant considers it in the Aesthetic, is a form of outer intuitability on the first interpretation, a form of availability to intuition on the interpretation according to which intuition already involves the understanding. It is a form in accordance with which the *this-suches* that are objects of outer intuition on the first interpretation of the term, episodes of sensory consciousness shaped by the understanding, are given to the subjects of those episodes. That is: what space informs is above the line, and the Aesthetic fails to discuss what it should have discussed, a form that does its informing work below the line.[8]

In making this complaint, Sellars ignores a certain reading of how the Aesthetic fits in the overall scheme of the *Critique*. On this reading, we are supposed to account for the outwardness of outer sense by invoking space as an autonomous form of sensibility, intelligible independently of any involvement on the part of the understanding. When Kant then brings the understanding into play, in the Transcendental Analytic, the outwardness that, on this reading, the Aesthetic has already provided for takes on a new form, as directedness towards determinate *objects*. On this reading, space as the Aesthetic considers it would after all do its informing work below

---

Largely below the surface in *Science and Metaphysics* is a detailed picture of how the productive imagination generates intuitions out of (strictly) sensory material, which helps account for the view of concept-formation Sellars attributes to Kant. See Sellars's paper "The Role of the Imagination in Kant's Theory of Experience". I cannot go into this here.

8. See *Science and Metaphysics*, pp. 8, 28–30.

something corresponding to Sellars's line, with operations of the understanding above the line.

Sellars's complaint leaves no room for this reading. The complaint implies that as he reads Kant, the idea that space informs an outward directedness of subjectivity cannot be understood independently of the idea that objects are available to outer intuition on the first interpretation of the term, according to which intuitions are shapings of sensibility by the understanding. That is: space as the Aesthetic considers it, under the title of the form of outer sense, is not meant to be fully intelligible until we have the Analytic as well as the Aesthetic. For Sellars, space as an autonomous form of "sense as such"—what Kant, he thinks, should have concerned himself with—would have to be, not an already outer matrix or arena waiting, as it were, to be determinately populated with objects, but a form of inner states or episodes. Our comprehension of it would have to be constructed by analogical extension from our comprehension of space as the outer matrix in which intuitions on the first interpretation, shapings of sensibility by the understanding, locate objects.[9]

I think Sellars here shows a fine understanding of how Kant intends the thesis that space is the form of outer sense, and a fine understanding of the possibilities for making sense of spatiality as the matrix in which outer objects are given to us. The reading Sellars ignores does not fit Kant, and it does not make philosophical sense.[10] What I dissent from in Sellars is his conviction that Kant's failure to discuss a formedness of "sense as such",

---

9. See *Science and Metaphysics*, p. 29. The Appendix on inner sense (pp. 230–8) offers a parallel move with respect to time as the form of inner sense.

10. I have to be dogmatic here. On the philosophical question, I simply follow Sellars. On the question of fit with Kant (on which I am also following Sellars, though disagreeing with him over whether what he finds in Kant is a ground for complaint), see the footnote at B160. Kant there says that in the Aesthetic he represented the formal intuition, space, "as belonging merely to sensibility", but that was misleading; it does indeed "precede any concept", but it presupposes an operation of the understanding. I suppose a defender of the reading I am following Sellars in setting aside might claim that the form of outer intuition, which Kant here distinguishes from the formal intuition, could still, for all that the footnote says, be a topic for an autonomous inquiry into sensibility considered in abstraction from the understanding. But it is hard to see how spatiality, as the form of outer intuition, could be separated from the possibility of the "formal intuition", space itself as an object of intuition. And if it cannot, the footnote implicitly instructs us not to suppose that the thesis that space is the form of outer sense is meant to be intelligible independently of the Analytic.

independent of any involvement on the part of the understanding, is a ground for complaint.

Sellars's complaint is that "the characteristics of the representations of receptivity as such, which is what should *properly* be meant by the forms of sensibility, are never adequately discussed, and the so-called forms of sensibility become ever more clearly, as the argument of the *Critique* proceeds, forms of conceptual representations".[11] "Never adequately discussed" seems an understatement; so far as I can see, Kant never so much as mentions what Sellars thinks he should have meant by the forms of sensibility. It is perhaps implicit in the Aesthetic that Kant thinks of sensation as the matter of empirical intuition (A20/B34), and thereafter he occasionally speaks of sensation as the matter of perception or of empirical knowledge (e.g., A42/B59–60; A167/B209). But he never suggests that this matter has its *own* form as the matter it is, independently of its being formed into intuitions, perceptions, and empirical knowledge in the understanding-involving way that, as Sellars says, becomes increasingly clearly Kant's concern as the *Critique* unfolds.[12]

Sellars is convinced that a properly Kantian position requires forms of sense as such, forms of "sheer receptivity". Correctly in my view, he takes it that the Aesthetic does not consider such a topic. So something that should, he thinks, be fundamental to Kant's position is absent from the appropriate place in Kant's own presentation of it. (This conviction is reflected also in the other peculiarities Sellars finds in Kant's thinking: the counterpart to the mongrel conflation, and the "puzzling" abstractionist view of concept-formation.) One is bound to wonder whether Kant can have so egregiously missed what is required for his own thinking. Perhaps a properly Kantian conception of outer sense needs no form of sense as "sheer receptivity", but only space in the role that Sellars, rightly in my view, takes Kant to attribute to it: as the form of outer intuitability on the interpretation according to which intuition involves the understanding as well as sensibility. That is: perhaps a below-the-line conception of sensibility need not have the transcendental role that Sellars credits to it. That is what I am going to urge.

4. Sellars quotes from a passage in the section of the *Critique* headed "The Clue to the Discovery of All Pure Concepts of the Understanding" (the

---

11. *Science and Metaphysics*, p. 30.

12. Compare how one might think of bronze, say, as having its own form, independently of the forming of bits of it into statues or spearheads.

so-called Metaphysical Deduction), where Kant says: "The same function which gives unity to the various representations *in a judgment* also gives unity to the mere synthesis of various representations *in an intuition*" (A79/B104–5).[13] But as I have noted, Sellars reads Kant as holding that when we take an intuition to represent its object as a *this-such*, what goes in place of "such", at least in the case of intuitions at a certain basic level, need not yet be an expression of the corresponding concept as it might figure predicatively in a judgment. This means, I think, that Sellars cannot give the remark from the "Clue" its full weight.

Here I need to hark back to something I said in the first of these three essays, when I was trying to give the flavour of the Kantian idea that conceptual capacities have their paradigmatic actualization in judgment. If one judges, say, that there is a red cube in front of one, one makes a joint exercise of a multiplicity of conceptual capacities, including at least a capacity that would also be exercised in judging that there is a red pyramid in front of one and a capacity that would also be exercised in judging that there is a blue cube in front of one. And this joint exercise of these capacities is not simply their being exercised in a single act of judgment. That would be equally true of a judgment that there is a red pyramid and a blue cube in front of one. The capacities have to be exercised with the right togetherness. If the judgment is to be that there is a red cube in front of one, the two capacities I have singled out have to be exercised with a togetherness that is a counterpart to the "logical" togetherness of "red" and "cube" in the linguistic expression of the judgment, "There is a red cube in front of me".

We can connect this with the remark from the "Clue". This analogical specification of the mode of togetherness with which the two capacities I have singled out have to be exercised, if one is to be judging that there is a red cube in front of one, is a partial specification of the function that gives unity to the various representations in a judgment with that content, to put things in Kant's way.

In the first of these three essays, I used this conception of judgment as the basis for a parallel conception of the way in which perceptual, and specifically visual, experiences "contain" claims, as Sellars puts it in "Empiricism and the Philosophy of Mind". An ostensible seeing that there is a red cube in front of one would be an actualization of the *same* conceptual capacities that would be exercised in judging that there is a red cube in front of one,

---

13. For Sellars's citation, see *Science and Metaphysics*, p. 4.

with the *same* togetherness. This captures the fact that such an ostensible seeing would "contain" a claim whose content would be the same as that of the corresponding judgment.

As actualizations of conceptual capacities with the appropriate togetherness, the judgment and the ostensible seeing would be alike. They would differ only in the way in which the relevant conceptual capacities are actualized. In the judgment, there would be a free responsible exercise of the conceptual capacities; in the ostensible seeing, they would be involuntarily drawn into operation under ostensible necessitation from an ostensibly seen object.

But since the two kinds of conceptual episodes are alike in respect of being actualizations of the appropriate conceptual capacities with the appropriate togetherness, the "logical" point of the remark from the "Clue" applies to ostensible seeings just as it applies to judgments. Following Sellars's lead, I have exploited an analogy between judging and claiming, in order to offer a partial specification of the function that gives unity to the various representations in a judgment that there is a red cube in front of one: a conceptual capacity corresponding to "red" and a conceptual capacity corresponding to "cube" have to be exercised with a togetherness corresponding to the togetherness of "red" and "cube" in "There is a red cube in front of me". Now the same specification is equally and by the same token a partial specification of the function that gives unity to the various representations in an ostensible seeing that there is a red cube in front of one. We can recast the remark from the "Clue" to say: the function that gives unity to the various representations in an ostensible seeing is the same as the function that gives unity to the mere synthesis of various representations in an intuition.

Any ostensible seeing will have more specificity to its content than just that there is a red cube in front of one, even if its content includes that.[14] For my purposes here, I can ignore much of what makes this true. But it matters for my purposes that in an ostensible seeing whose content can be partly specified as that there is a red cube in front of one, the apparent red cube will be *placed* more determinately than just somewhere or other in front of one. From the standpoint of the subject of such an ostensible seeing, its content will be expressible by saying something like "There is a red cube *there*". Here we have to imagine a use of "there" that has a determinate significance by virtue of the subject's directing it in a specific way at the ostensible layout of the ostensibly seen environment. The same goes for

---

14. See "Empiricism and the Philosophy of Mind", §22.

a counterpart to such a use of "there" in a non-overt conceptual occurrence that is to be understood on the model of making a claim by uttering those words (such as an ostensible seeing would be in the picture Sellars gives in "Empiricism and the Philosophy of Mind").[15]

Imagine, then, an ostensible seeing whose content is (in part) that there is a red cube *there*. (To imagine an ostensible seeing in these terms, we have to imagine it from the subject's point of view.) And now suppose this ostensible seeing is not a merely ostensible seeing, but a seeing. In that case there *is* a red cube at the position the subject can mean by this kind of use of "there" in an overt expression of the content of the experience in question, or by its counterpart in the non-overt conceptual occurrence that the experience is. In the conceptual occurrence that the experience is, the red cube that there actually is, given that the experience is a seeing, is itself directly in the subject's view. It is in the subject's view as *that red cube*. We can put it like that if we imagine ourselves into the subject's point of view; we have to imagine this use of "that" as having a determinate significance by virtue of the same directedness at the (ostensible) layout of the (ostensibly) seen environment that we imagined as giving "there" a determinate significance, when we imagined "there" being used in specifying the content of the occurrence considered as an ostensible seeing that . . . .

What I have arrived at here is a conception of a kind of representation (or at any rate *Vorstellung*) of an object that fits a standard Kantian characterization of intuitions: immediate sensible representations of objects.[16] The conception coheres with Sellars's insistence that intuitions in Kant's dominant sense belong above the line. "Immediate" in a characterization of intuitions on these lines does not mean "not involving the understanding"; the intuitions that this characterization fits are not intuitions in the sense Sellars thinks Kant also needs, operations of "sheer receptivity". Sellars offers a different and better gloss on "immediate" by urging that intuitions in the dominant Kantian sense are representations of *thises* (or *thats*); more fully, of *this-suches* (or *that-suches*), which makes it unavoidably clear that even though they are immediately of objects, such representations already involve the understanding.[17] The remark from the "Clue" points to how we

---

15. Compare the notion of *conversio ad phantasmata* that Geach borrows from Aquinas in *Mental Acts*, pp. 65, 72, 74.

16. See, e.g., A19/B33.

17. Compare *Science and Metaphysics*, p. 3.

can conceive intuitions in this sense as actualizations of conceptual capacities with a suitable "logical" togetherness.

An ostensible seeing is an actualization of conceptual capacities with a specific "logical" togetherness. What makes it an ostensible seeing, as opposed to a conceptual episode of some other kind, for instance a judgment, is that this actualization of conceptual capacities is a conceptual shaping of sensory, and in particular visual, consciousness. The remark from the "Clue" says that an intuition is characterized by the same "logical" togetherness. If an ostensible seeing is a seeing, then the conceptual shaping of visual consciousness that constitutes it, those very conceptual capacities actualized in visual consciousness with that very "logical" togetherness, constitute—looked at, as it were, from a different angle—an intuition: an immediate presentness of an object to sense. A seeing that . . . is a seeing *of an object*, at least if its content is of the sort that figures in the example I have been working with. To apply what Kant says in the "Clue" to my example: the function that gives unity to the various representations in a judgment whose content we can imagine capturing from the subject's viewpoint as that there is a red cube *there* (the function that unites the various conceptual capacities exercised in such a judgment), or (this comes to the same thing) the function that gives unity to the various representations in an ostensible seeing with that same content (the function that unites the various conceptual capacities actualized in such an ostensible seeing), is the same function that—in the sort of case in which there *is* an intuition; that is, in the sort of case in which the ostensible seeing is a seeing—gives unity to the mere synthesis of various representations in an intuition of *the red cube there* or *that red cube*, to speak again from an imagined occupation of the subject's viewpoint.[18]

Here the fact that, say, "cube" figures in a specification of the content of an intuition—the intuition represents its object as that red *cube*—reflects the

18. How can something describable as a seeing that there is a red cube *there*, an intuition of *that* red cube, be a conceptual episode, given the characteristic Kantian association of concepts with generality (see, e.g., A320/B377)? There is no problem in the idea of a general conceptual capacity, an actualization of which is indicated by the fact that a particular experience can be described in those terms (where the description indeed exploits the particularity of a subject's experiential situation). This capacity (a capacity to mean determinate places by utterances of "there" or non-overt counterparts, and to mean determinate objects by utterances of "that . . ." or non-overt counterparts) is not restricted to the particular actualization of it we are imagining.

fact that for one to be the subject of such an intuition is in part for there to be actualized in one's sensory consciousness the very same *conceptual* capacity—possession of the concept of a cube—whose exercise would partly determine the predicative element in the content of a judgment whose content we could specify, with that imagined occupancy of the subject's viewpoint, in the form "That is a red cube". In fact the actualization of the relevant conceptual capacity in the intuition *is* an actualization of it in a conceptual occurrence whose content is, so to speak, judgment-shaped, namely a seeing (a seeing that . . .) whose content is that there is a red cube *there*—as we can put it with the same imagined occupancy of the subject's viewpoint. This seeing that . . . , in describing which we explicitly place an expression for the concept in question in a predicative position, is the very same conceptual occurrence—an actualization of the same conceptual capacities with the same "logical" togetherness—as the intuition.

So when we say that an intuition represents its object as a cube, the word "cube" does not signal a merely proto-conceptual contribution of the understanding to the constitution of the intuition, as it can in Sellars's Kant. Sellars insists, rightly in my view, that intuitions in the dominant Kantian sense already involve the understanding. I have been expressing this by speaking of intuitions not as *conceptual* shapings of sensory consciousness but as shapings of sensory consciousness *by the understanding*. That was to make room for the fact that in Sellars's reading, although the understanding, the faculty of concepts, is operative in the constitution of intuitions, concepts proper are not, at least in the case of intuitions at a certain basic level. But with the different reading I have arrived at, I can drop the circumlocution, and speak of intuitions, just like seeings that . . . , simply as *conceptual* shapings of sensory consciousness. Visual intuitions *of objects* simply are seeings that . . . , looked at as it were from a different angle. There is no opening here into the abstractionist picture of the formation of basic empirical concepts that Sellars finds in Kant.

In the passage in the "Clue", Kant speaks of "the mere synthesis of various representations" in an intuition. The insertion of "mere synthesis" implicitly differentiates the unity of an intuition from the unity of a judgment. It is plausible that this is connected with a passage Sellars also quotes, from just before the remark I have been considering, in which Kant speaks of synthesis as "the mere result of the power of imagination, a blind but indispensable function of the soul" (A78/B103). Sellars might cite this in support of his view that Kant envisages intuitions that are only proto-conceptual, even though they already involve the synthetic powers of the under-standing, so that they can be a source from which concepts proper can be derived. But these remarks of Kant's are perfectly intelligible on the different reading I am giving. The point is simply that it does not take cogni-tive work for objects to come into view for us. "Mere synthesis" just hap-pens; it is not our doing, unlike making judgments, deciding what to think about something. This is quite consistent with holding that objects come into view for us in actualizations of capacities that are fully conceptual, ca-pacities whose paradigmatic mode of actualization is in the exercise of cog-nitive responsibility that judging is.

5. I am following Sellars in taking it that we can express the content of a Kantian intuition by a phrase such as "that red cube". We might suppose that conceptual occurrences whose content can be given like that, with a phrase that is less than a whole sentence, are essentially potential ingredi-ents in some more extensive conceptual goings-on—say, in the judgment that that red cube is too big to fit in the box. (As before, in order to make sense of this use of "that", we have to imagine ourselves into the viewpoint of the subject of a specific case of the kind of conceptual occurrences in question.)

I do not want to dispute this suggestion. But the point that matters for my purposes is that these conceptual occurrences, whose content we can express with mere phrases, can also be conceived in a way that equips them—the very same conceptual occurrences—with judgment-shaped contents: specifically, for my example, the judgeable content that there is a red cube *there*. (Again, we have to imagine ourselves into the subject's viewpoint in order to deal with this use of "there".) The other thought—that intuitional content is essentially a fragment of judgmental content—would imply that the ability to have objects come into view for one is es-sentially dependent on the ability to make judgments, and that is indeed an implication of the position I am finding in Kant. But the point I am stressing yields not just that but also something more radical: that an actu-alization of the capacity to have objects come into one's view is itself al-ready an actualization of the capacity to have occur in one's life occur-rences with the sort of content that judgments have, not just an element in such an actualization.

So far as that goes, we might suppose the capacity to be a subject of actu-alizations of conceptual capacities with judgmental content just happens to be, but might not have been, sometimes actualized in the shape of intuitions: occurrences in which objects come into view, literally in the case of visual intuitions. But this cannot be Kant's view; that would fly in the face of his insistence that intuitions are indispensable if thought is to be contentful at all.[19] Kant's view must rather be something like this: the very idea of a conceptual repertoire is the idea of a system of capacities that allows, as it were at the ground level, for actualizations in which objects are immediately present to the subject.

This suggests a new twist to the non-traditional empiricism that, in Essay 1, I found in Sellars's discussion of the metaphor of foundations of knowledge, in "Empiricism and the Philosophy of Mind". Sellars's picture there is already deeply Kantian, and we can now see how to make it even more so.

As I pointed out, Sellars does not dispute the empiricist thought that everything else in a world view depends on perceptual knowledge, in a logical dimension in which we are moving when we relate beliefs to their credentials. He transforms the empiricist picture by adding another logical dimension in which a different kind of dependency is traceable in the opposite direction. What he insists is that the very idea of perceptual knowledge, and more generally the very idea that perceptual experiences, whether knowledge-yielding or not, "contain" claims, so that they can be so much as putatively knowledge-yielding, depend in this other logical dimension on the fact that the claims "contained" in perceptual experiences have their places in a world view. This dependence of foundations, now at best awkwardly so called, on superstructure is a transcendental matter. The claim is that we can intelligibly credit perceptual experiences with objective purport only in virtue of how the conceptual apparatus that constitutes their objective purport fits into the world view that is, in the other logical dimension, grounded on the deliverances of experience. But the downward dependence, the dependence of superstructure on foundations, is still narrowly epistemological.

The new twist is that, with the conception of Kantian intuitions that I am urging, we can put into the picture a downward dependence that is not narrowly epistemological but, like the upward dependence that is already in Sellars's picture, transcendental, a matter of requirements for it to be intelligible that the picture depicts directedness at objective reality at all. Kant

19. See, e.g., A50–2/B74–6.

implies that thought without intuitions would be empty.[20] We can now see that his point is not—at least not in the first instance—to insist that concepts must be capable of figuring in, say, judgments that can be *grounded* in experiences (which, to play this role, would have to be conceived as possessing judgeable content, for instance as seeings that . . .). The transcendental requirement is that it must be intelligible that conceptual activity has a *subject matter*. And Kant's thought is that this is intelligible only because we can see how the very idea of a conceptual repertoire provides for conceptual states or episodes in which a subject matter for conceptual activity is sensibly present, plainly in view in actualizations of capacities that belong to the repertoire.[21]

Not, of course, that we cannot direct thought at objects that we are unable to bring into view, perhaps because they are too small or too far away. But thought so directed is carried to its object, so to speak, by theory. The ultimate credentials of theory must lie in experience. And we can make sense of the idea, which is so far epistemological in the narrow sense, that the ultimate credentials for theory lie in experience—we can make sense of experience as made up of, for instance, seeings that . . .— only because we can make sense of experience as bringing objects into view. Concepts, which make thought what it is, can intelligibly be what they are—thought can intelligibly be of the objective at all—only because we can see how there can be conceptual occurrences in which objects are manifestly there for thinkers, immediately present to their conceptually shaped sensory consciousness. But equally, there can intelligibly be such conceptual occurrences only because we can see how thought can also be related to its subject matter in a way that is mediated by theory; this is Sellars's upward dependence applied to the relation between intuitions and world view.

That last remark opens into a topic I have so far passed over in silence. Kant's "Clue" is only a clue, to the discovery of the so-called pure concepts of the understanding; when he makes the remark I have been exploiting, we are still waiting for the transcendental deduction of the "pure concepts".

20. This is implicit in the remark "Thoughts without content are empty, intuitions without concepts are blind" (A51/B76).

21. This corrects the picture I gave, meaning it to be Kantian, in *Mind and World*. There I took it that "object", in the Kantian idea that intuitions are of objects, just meant "objective somewhat", including, for instance, states of affairs. I now think it means something much closer to what "object" means in the standard translations of Frege.

So even supposing I am on the right track in the conception of intuitions I have elicited from the "Clue", Kant's thought must be that work still needs to be done for us to be entitled to the idea of an immediate presentness of objects to subjects in intuition. We still need to understand how the categories make experience possible.

This is a large and complex matter, which I cannot go into in these essays. (So far as I can see, the categories are in a similar way not explicitly present in the parallel region of Sellars's partial reading of Kant, which is what I am aiming to exploit and improve on.)[22] However, what I have already said yields a hint as to the direction in which this topic lies from the position we have reached. I have found a conception of intuitions suggested in the "Clue", and I have been importing that conception of intuitions into a variant of the picture Sellars gives when he reflects on the metaphor of foundations. In doing that, I have been tacitly pointing to a place for something on the lines of the categories. In order to be entitled to see conceptual activity as having objective purport, we have to see how actualizations of conceptual capacities include intuitions. But—the new version of Sellars's upward dependence—we can make sense of objects coming into view in intuitions only because we can see how objects fit into a view of the world. Something like the categories, and the principles Kant connects with them, would figure in giving substance to that thought.[23]

6. Sellars thinks the transcendental role of sensibility, in properly Kantian thinking, is to supply manifolds of "sheer receptivity" to guide conceptual representations. At one point he suggests that Kant needs this picture if he

---

22. But see his paper "Some Remarks on Kant's Theory of Experience".

23. Sellars says "there is an important sense in which one has *no* concept pertaining to the observable properties of physical objects in Space and Time unless one has them all—and, indeed, as we shall see, a great deal more besides" ("Empiricism and the Philosophy of Mind", §19). "As we shall see" points forward to the discussion of the metaphor of foundations, where the claim becomes that one has no concept of the observable unless one knows a great deal about the world. We can put Sellars's thought here in Kantian terms: acquiring one's first conceptual capacities is necessarily acquiring many conceptual capacities, interlinked in such a way that the totality amounts to a conceptual repertoire that exemplifies the necessary forms of the understanding. It comes to the same thing to say that acquiring one's first conceptual capacities is necessarily acquiring a world view that conforms to the associated principles of pure understanding. (Of course this allows divergence from Kant over what these forms and principles are.)

is to "avoid the dialectic which leads from Hegel's *Phenomenology* to nineteenth-century idealism".[24] This remark is instructive.

Sellars is invoking Hegel as a bogeyman: as someone who, by failing to acknowledge any external constraint on thought, makes it unintelligible how what he is picturing can be directed at what is independently real, as it must be if it is to be recognizably thought at all. But this takes no account of the fact that Hegel thinks he finds his notion of Reason, moving freely in its own sphere, adumbrated precisely in Kant's attempts to characterize the interpenetration of sensibility and understanding, in the first and third *Critiques*.[25] Hegelian Reason does not need to be constrained from outside, precisely because it includes as a moment within itself the receptivity that Kant attributes to sensibility.

Now perhaps the conception of Kantian intuitions that I have arrived at is a way to begin bringing this difficult conception down to earth. Sellars's idea is that for thought to be intelligibly of objective reality, the conceptual representations involved in perceptual experience must be guided from without. And indeed they are, I can say. But there is no need for manifolds of "sheer receptivity" to play this guiding role. In a way we are now equipped to understand, given the conception of intuitions adumbrated in the passage from the "Clue", the guidance is supplied by *objects* themselves, the subject matter of those conceptual representations, becoming immediately present to the sensory consciousness of the subjects of these conceptual goings-on.

Sellars's own imagery for expressing his sense of the need for external constraint—his talk of guidance and the like—actually fits this constraint by subject matter better than it fits Sellars's candidate, constraint by "sheer receptivity".

24. *Science and Metaphysics*, p. 16. See also p. 29, where, in connection with Kant's failure to distinguish what he supposedly needs the forms of sensibility to be from "the 'forms' of that which is represented by the intuitive conceptual representations which are 'guided' by receptivity", Sellars says that "no sooner had [Kant] left the scene than these particular waters were muddied by Hegel and the Mills, and philosophy had to begin the slow climb 'back to Kant' which is still under way". Presumably the idea is that Hegel tried to do everything in terms of what is above the line, without the transcendentally needed guidance by "sheer receptivity", whereas the Mills reverted to an empiricistic version of the Myth of the Given, trying to do everything ultimately in terms of what is below the line.

25. I have learned here from Béatrice Longuenesse, "Point of View of Man or Knowledge of God: Kant and Hegel on Concept, Judgment and Reason".

Any faithful student of "Empiricism and the Philosophy of Mind" must be made uneasy by finding Sellars, in *Science and Metaphysics*, saying that states or episodes below his line *guide* states or episodes above it. This seems dangerously close to a lapse into the Myth of the Given, by Sellars of all people.[26]

At one point, speaking of the operations of the understanding in perception, in the guise of the productive imagination, Sellars is led to say, even more poignantly, that the transcendentally posited manifold of non-conceptual sensory impressions "is an independent factor which has a strong voice in the outcome".[27] This runs the same risk of seeming to lapse back into the idea of the Given. But even apart from that, this image of voice is difficult to cash out. When the manifold of "sheer receptivity" is playing the role Sellars tries to capture here with the image of voice, it is not speaking to *us*; that is a natural metaphor for Sellars's own thought, which I discussed in Essay 1, that when it is playing that role it is not apperceived. When a manifold of "sheer receptivity" does speak to us, on this natural interpretation of the image, it is no longer playing its transcendental role. To whom or what, then, is it supposed to speak when, in playing its transcendental role, and hence not being apperceived, it is having its say in the outcome of the operations of the understanding in perceptual experience? Perhaps to the understanding at its work? But if the manifold of "sheer receptivity" speaks to our understanding but not to us, we have an awkward separation of our understanding from ourselves, as if the understanding were a distinct cognitive subject within a person, doing its work as it were behind our backs.

But suppose we take it that the external constraint Sellars sees to be required is exerted, in intuition, by objects themselves, the subject matter of the conceptual representations involved in perception. Now the image of

---

26. Starting here, one can see how Brandom's conception of observational claims and knowledge, in chapter 4 of *Making It Explicit*, might be represented, not as radically non-Sellarsian, but as a charitable reading of Sellars's basic intentions. On this view, Sellars's own wish to keep sensory consciousness in the picture is a vestige of an archaic and risky philosophical outlook, which he himself undermines in his attack on the Myth of the Given. A hygienic replacement is the bare idea of reliable differential responsive dispositions. On this view, sentience is a mere detail of the causal connection between the responses and what they respond to; taking it to have more philosophical importance than that merely courts pre-Sellarsian dangers, as Sellars himself surprisingly does in *Science and Metaphysics*. I agree with Brandom that Sellars's thinking needs a charitable reading; but I am offering a way to preserve Sellars's Kantian thought that sensibility is transcendentally important, without running the risks that Brandom rightly wants to avoid.

27. *Science and Metaphysics*, p. 16.

voice fits more easily. A seen object as it were invites one to take it to be as it visibly is. It speaks to one; if it speaks to one's understanding, that is just what its speaking to one comes to. "See me as I am", it (so to speak) says to one; "namely as characterized by *these* properties"—and it displays them.

Of course this comparison of images cannot settle the question raised by Sellars's invocation of Hegel. After all, in "Empiricism and the Philosophy of Mind", Sellars himself exploits an image in which conceptual representations in perception are "evoked" or "wrung" from us *by objects*. His transcendental thought is that we can be entitled to this image of external constraint—a version of the idea Kant expresses by saying objects are what prevent our cognitions "from being haphazard or arbitrary" (*Critique of Pure Reason*, A104)—only if we acknowledge that the conceptual representations we want to think of in those terms are guided by "sheer receptivity".

Sellars's thinking here is bound up with a doctrine of his about the relation between "the scientific image" and "the manifest image", which he puts in "Empiricism and the Philosophy of Mind" by saying: *speaking as a philosopher*, I am quite prepared to say that the common-sense world of physical objects in Space and Time is unreal—that is, that there are no such things."[28] According to this doctrine, the red cubes and so forth that are, apparently, immediately present to us in intuitions do not really exist. So they cannot be what guide our conceptual representations in perception from outside. Presumably we must suppose that our conceptual representations are guided by the items that the scientific image substitutes for these merely apparent objects—swarms of colourless particles or whatever. But this real guidance cannot have the immediacy of the guidance by red cubes and the like that figures in the manifest image. So if that apparent immediate guidance by objects is to figure in the transcendental project of showing how it is that our conceptual activity is intelligibly conceptual activity at all, directed, as that requires, towards objective reality, then we have to reconceive it—transcendentally, or speaking as philosophers—as mediated guidance by genuinely real, non-sensible objects. If we want to conceive this mediated guidance by real objects as immediate guidance by something real, it can only be as guidance by the sensory goings-on out of which the productive imagination constructs the red cubes and the like that figure in the manifest image as the immediate objects of intuition.

---

28. §42. See "Philosophy and the Scientific Image of Man". I am indebted to Anders Weinstein for insisting on the relevance of this aspect of Sellars's thinking.

Sellars is committed to this as a reading of Kant's distinction between appearances, as immediate objects of intuition, and things in themselves.[29] Here I think his often wonderful attunement with the spirit of Kant's thinking deserts him. This Sellarsian picture cannot accommodate Kant's insistence that the things in themselves that matter for his thinking about empirical knowledge are the very same things that make their appearance in intuition.[30] I think it comes to the same thing to say: Sellars's idea that the red cubes and so forth of common sense do not really exist is philosophically misguided. I cannot properly justify these beliefs in these essays, but I hope to have begun on making it plausible that there is an alternative to what Sellars represents as compulsory.

It might be tempting to defend Sellars on these lines. If we do not acknowledge a transcendental need for guidance by "sheer receptivity", then we face a dilemma. On one horn, our attempt to make sense of conceptual activity as having objective purport degenerates into an "idealistic" fraud; the so-called

29. See chapter 2 of *Science and Metaphysics*.

30. See, e.g., Bxxvii, where Kant speaks of "the distinction, which our Critique has shown to be necessary, between things as objects of experience and those same things as things in themselves". When we speak as philosophers, we do not start to speak of a new range of objects, genuinely real as the objects of the manifest image were not. We speak of the same objects, under a special mode of consideration in which we abstract from the way in which the objects figure in our world view. Sellars reads Kant as a scientific realist manqué; in Sellars's view, had Kant only been sophisticated about the possibilities for scientific concept-formation, he would have cast the objects of the scientific image in the role of things in themselves. But for Kant, objects as they appear in the scientific image would be just another case of objects as they appear, with a transcendental background for that conception just as necessary here as anywhere. Sellars's attempt to be responsive to Kantian transcendental concerns goes astray in his idea that an appeal to science could do the transcendental job; here Sellars's scientism is seriously damaging.

I here correct the two-worlds picture of Kant that I presupposed in *Mind and World*. But note that what Kant insists on, in passages like Bxxvii, is an identity of things as they appear in our knowledge and "those same things as things in themselves"; not "those same things as they are in themselves". (This latter wording pervades, e.g., Henry E. Allison's non-two-worlds reading, in *Kant's Transcendental Idealism*.) Things in themselves are the very things that figure in our knowledge, but considered in abstraction from how they figure in our knowledge. That is not to say: considered as possessing, unknowably to us, other properties than those they appear as possessing in our knowledge of them. With this latter construal of things in themselves, the non-two-worlds reading might as well be a two-worlds reading. The picture still involves two realms of fact, one knowable by us and one unknowable by us; it does not undermine the damage this does to say that the same objects figure in both.

reality towards which we see our so-called conceptual activity as directed is a mere projection of the activity. On the other horn, we fall into an impossible transcendental realism, which we can make vivid by coalescing the image of objects speaking to us with an image of Richard Rorty's; on this horn, we picture objects as speaking to us in the world's own language.[31]

But this dilemma does not threaten the position I am urging.

I do not picture objects as speaking to us in the world's own language. Objects speak to us, in the metaphor that fits the position I am urging, only because we have learned a human language. We can play with the image of objects speaking to us in a language we know, say English, as I did a moment ago. But, less fancifully put, the point is that objects come into view for us only in actualizations of conceptual capacities that are ours. To entitle ourselves to this, we must acknowledge whatever we need to acknowledge for the conceptual capacities to be intelligibly ours. The fantasy of conceptual capacities that belong to the world itself is not to the point.

That does not land me on the other horn of the dilemma, according to which the so-called objects can only be projections of our thinking. Objects come into view for us in actualizations of conceptual capacities in *sensory* consciousness, and Kant perfectly naturally connects sensibility with receptivity. If we hold firm to that, we can see that the presence of conceptual capacities in the picture does not imply idealism, in the sense in which Sellars means invoking idealism to frighten us. If we conceive subjects as receptive with respect to objects, then, whatever else we suppose to be true of such subjects, it cannot undermine our entitlement to the thought that the objects stand over against them, independently there for them.

---

31. See, e.g., *Philosophy and the Mirror of Nature*, p. 298: "successfully representing according to Nature's own conventions of representation." For a Sellarsian formulation close to this imagery, see "Empiricism and the Philosophy of Mind", §34.

Intentionality as a Relation

1. Sellars shows us how to understand visual experiences as ostensible see-ings, occurrences in a subject's visual life that "contain" claims about an ostensibly visible region of objective reality. That they "contain" claims is the same fact as that they are conceptual occurrences, actualizations of conceptual capacities with a suitable "logical" togetherness. In that respect they are like judgments. But they are unlike judgments in the way in which they "contain" their claims. Judgments are free exercises of conceptual capacities with a suitable togetherness. But in an ostensible seeing whose content includes that of a given judgment, the same conceptual capacities are actualized, with the same togetherness, in a way that is ostensibly necessitated by the objective reality that is ostensibly seen. A visual experience is a case of being under the *visual impression* that things are thus-and-so in the ostensibly visible environment.

   This picture of visual experiences as conceptual shapings of visual consciousness is already deeply Kantian, in the way it appeals to sensibility and understanding so as to make sense of how experiences have objective purport. But Sellars thinks that to be fully Kantian the picture needs a further element. He thinks this idea of conceptual shapings of visual consciousness is something we can entitle ourselves to only by means of a transcendental postulation, according to which these conceptual shapings of visual consciousness are guided by manifolds of "sheer receptivity": occurrences in visual consciousness that are not conceptually shaped. Only so, Sellars thinks, can we legitimately take perception to yield conceptual representations of objective reality. If we do not acknowledge that the conceptual goings-on in perception are guided by "sheer receptivity", then however we work towards purporting to equip ourselves with an object of perceptual awareness, the supposed object can be no better than a projection of our mental activity.

This is what Sellars implies by invoking the idealism that Hegel made room for, as a pitfall awaiting Kant if he fails to credit sensibility with the role Sellars thinks it must have.

In holding that a properly Kantian view requires this guidance by "sheer receptivity", Sellars commits himself to taking a dim view of some features of the first *Critique*. The problems in Kant's own exposition, as Sellars sees them, come to a head with Kant's thesis that space is the form of outer sense. What space informs is outwardly intuitable phenomena, and it becomes increasingly clear as we progress through the *Critique* that outer intuition involves the understanding as well as sensibility. Focusing on space as informing outer intuitability, Kant fails to discuss what, according to Sellars, ought to be a crucial topic for him, the form of the manifolds of "sheer receptivity" that Sellars thinks must guide conceptual representations of outer reality in perception. Sellars says Kant does not "adequately" discuss this supposedly crucial topic, but really he does not discuss it at all.

Now obviously this mismatch between what Kant wrote about forms of sense and what Sellars thinks he ought to have written should give us pause. By itself, however, this carries little weight. No doubt the mismatch gives Sellars pause too, but he self-consciously claims to see better than Kant what Kant ought to have written. His thought is that there must be guidance by "sheer receptivity" if we are to be entitled to the basically Kantian idea that, by conceiving sensibility as shaped by the understanding, we make it intelligible how sensory consciousness can be directed towards objective reality, and thereby how thought in general can have objective purport. If Sellars is right about that, then he is right that, in failing to discuss forms of "sheer receptivity", Kant overlooks something crucially required by fundamental features of his own thinking. So the real question is whether Sellars is right about the necessity for guidance by "sheer receptivity".

In the second of these three essays, I began urging that Sellars is wrong about that. Kant conceives intuitions as representations in which objects are immediately present to subjects. From a remark in the section called "The Clue to the Discovery of All Pure Concepts of the Understanding", I elicited this suggestion: intuitions are conceptual occurrences that exemplify exactly the "logical" togetherness, on the part of actualizations of conceptual capacities in sensory consciousness, in terms of which we can make it intelligible that ostensible seeings "contain" claims about the objective environment. In fact, visual intuitions just are the actualizations of conceptual capacities, with the requisite togetherness, that constitute those ostensible

seeings that are seeings. If an ostensible seeing that . . . is a seeing that . . . ,
it is itself an intuition, at least if the content of the ostensible seeing deals
with an ostensible object—as in the case of an ostensible seeing that there is
a red cube at a position in the ostensibly visible environment that one can
single out as *there*.

Sellars thinks the conceptual representations in perception must be
guided by manifolds of "sheer receptivity", because he thinks that only so
can we make it intelligible to ourselves that conceptual occurrences in perceptual experience—and thereby ultimately thought, conceptual activity, in
general—are constrained by something external to conceptual activity. And
as he sees, we need such external constraint in our picture if we are to be
entitled to take it that conceptual activity is directed towards an independent reality, as it must be if it is to be intelligible as conceptual activity at all.
But I suggested that once we understand how objects can be immediately
present to conceptually shaped sensory consciousness in intuition, we can
take this need for external constraint to be met by perceived objects themselves. The transcendental task is entitling ourselves to see conceptual activity
as directed towards a reality that is not a mere reflection of it. To discharge
that task, we need not see conceptual representations in perception as externally constrained by anything except the relevant elements of the very
independent reality towards which we are in the course of entitling ourselves to see conceptual activity, in general, as directed. There is a kind of
circularity here, but not one that should make it look as if the putatively
constraining objects can only be projections of what we are trying to see as
conceptual activity—in vain, if we could not do better than this. The actualizations of conceptual capacities that we are focusing on when we do this
transcendental work are shapings of *sensory* consciousness, and thus of what
Kant describes, with an obvious appropriateness, in terms of receptivity.
That ensures that the objects we are entitling ourselves to see as present to
subjects in intuition are genuinely independent of the subjects.

Sellars himself talks of conceptual representations evoked by perceived
objects, in "Empiricism and the Philosophy of Mind". But he would relegate
the appropriateness of such talk to the manifest image, and he would urge
that we need to give it a transcendental vindication by showing how it cor-
relates with the scientific image. Otherwise the putative objective purport
that figures in the manifest image would be a mere illusion; the apparently
perceived objects—such things as red cubes—do not really exist. Now of
course there are familiar supposed grounds, of a scientific sort, for denying

independent reality to the immediate objects of perception, and attributing it only to their counterparts in the scientific image. I think these grounds are unconvincing, but I am not going to consider them in this essay.[1] What I am going to discuss is a different and I think more interesting feature of Sellars's thinking: a different way to understand why, for Sellars, guidance by the immediate objects of intuition cannot itself figure in transcendentally vindicating the very idea of objective purport.

2. In the original version of "Empiricism and the Philosophy of Mind", Sellars implies that seeings are the veridical members of the class of ostensible seeings.[2] For the reprinting in *Science, Perception and Reality*, he adds a couple of footnotes suggesting that if an ostensible seeing is to be a seeing, not only must it be veridical, but in addition the subject must know that the viewing circumstances are normal.[3]

Now it was surely wrong to imply that veridicality is all it takes for an ostensible seeing to be a seeing. Consider a case in which someone is screened off from a red cube by a successful *trompe l'oeil* painting in which an indistinguishable red cube is depicted as being precisely where the unseen red cube actually is. Here we have a veridical ostensible seeing that is not a seeing. But Sellars's attempt to correct this mistake, in the added footnotes, seems unhappy. Surely one might have occasion to say: "I now realize I was seeing a red cube, although at the time—because I thought the circumstances were abnormal—I did not realize it." Here what is perfectly intelligibly claimed is that the case was one of seeing, even though the subject did not know that the viewing circumstances were normal. What matters is that the circumstances should be normal, not that the subject should know they are.

Sellars's first thought would have been better put by saying that an ostensible seeing is essentially an ostensible *seeing*. His mistake was just to forget that being non-veridical is not the only way an ostensible seeing can be merely ostensible. Sellars's second thought poses a risk that is definitely avoided if we correct his first thought in that way; the invocation of normality

1. Finding them unconvincing does not require me to debunk the scientific image, but only to question its claim to exhaust reality.

2. §7; compare §22.

3. §22 (pp. 151, 152 in *Science, Perception and Reality*). I am grateful to Paul Coppock for drawing my attention to these footnotes.

encourages supposing we can build up to the notion of seeing by adding conditions to an independent notion of visual experience.

I extracted from Kant's "Clue" the idea that if an ostensible seeing that . . . is a seeing that . . . , the very actualization of conceptual capacities that accounts for its "containing" its claim also constitutes—at least if the content of the claim deals with an ostensible object—its being an intuition, in which an object is immediately present to the subject. Now we debar ourselves from this notion of immediate presentness of objects to subjects if we let it seem that a seen object would have to figure in the content of a conceptual occurrence that is a seeing of it as, for instance, occupying a position at the outer end of a causal chain that generates the subject's current experiential situation in some suitably designated way. And Sellars's second thought suggests just that. It suggests that seeings that . . . would need to "contain" not just claims about the environment but also claims to the effect that the subject's experience is "normally" related to the ostensibly seen environment (this being part of what the subject is supposed to know in enjoying an experience of the relevant kind). That introduces a mediation that would threaten our ability to take these same conceptual occurrences to be intuitions, immediately of objects, as the remark from the "Clue" suggests we should be able to.

This connection of immediacy with an absence of extra conceptual content matches an element in Gareth Evans's account of perceptually demonstrative thoughts.[4] Evans says demonstrative thoughts in the most basic sense are carried to their objects by an information-link that connects the objects to the subjects, rather than by a thought of the link. (Of course the counterpart I have arrived at is compatible with insisting, as Evans does, that thought can go directly to its object like this only against the background of a richly situating self-consciousness on the part of its subject.)

And we can take this correspondence with Evans further. The actualizations of conceptual capacities that constitute ostensible seeings can amount to intuitions, cases of having objects immediately present to one, only if the ostensible seeings are seeings. Of course merely ostensible seeings are ostensible *seeings*, so that—at least if their content deals with ostensible objects—they ostensibly constitute intuitions. But the mere appearance of an intuition is just that; it is not an actual intuition. I have been following Sellars in connecting the immediacy of intuitions with their being "representations

4. See chapter 6 of *The Varieties of Reference*.

of *thises*".[5] Now if I put the point that merely ostensible seeings afford mere appearances of intuitions in terms of this connection between intuitions and demonstratives, it amounts to this: Kant's conception of intuitions embodies a version of Evans's thesis that perceptual demonstrative content is *object-dependent*. If one is under the illusion of being perceptually confronted by an object, then one is liable to a counterpart illusion that there is available to one, for employment in conceptual activity, content expressible by a perceptual demonstrative reference to the supposed object—the content one might think one could express, in such a situation, by using a phrase such as "that red cube". This is just what the immediacy of intuitions comes to; if there can be conceptual shapings of sensory consciousness in which objects are immediately present to subjects, then illusions that objects are present to one in that way, which obviously can happen, are at the same time illusions about the contents of one's conceptually shaped consciousness.

This imputation of an illusion of content is often found counterintuitive (to use an indispensable term in spite of its awkwardness in this context). But the remark from the "Clue" makes it doubtful that this complaint has any substance. In a merely ostensible seeing that there is, say, a red cube at a position one can mean by a use of "there", there are *actualized* in one's visual consciousness conceptual capacities corresponding to the presence of the words "red", "cube", and "there" (in a use that exploits one's experiential situation) in a verbal expression of the experience's content. None of that conceptual content is an illusion. In the language of the remark from the "Clue", there is a function that does indeed give unity to the various representations in the content of the ostensible seeing, or rather this part of its content (since any actual ostensible seeing will have more to it). The content in question is the same as the content of a judgment the subject might express by saying "There is a red cube *there*". What is illusory is just the appearance that the same function also gives unity to a synthesis of the same representations in an intuition. The relevant function—the "logical" togetherness with which the relevant conceptual capacities are actualized— certainly *seems* to give unity to a synthesis of the representations in an intuition; that is to say that there *seems* to be a red cube immediately present to the subject. But since there is no such red cube—since the ostensible seeing is merely ostensible—this seeming intuitional unity is a mere semblance of

5. *Science and Metaphysics*, p. 3.

an intuitional unity; that is to say that there *merely* seems to be a red cube immediately present to the subject.

3. Exploiting the way Sellars suggests we should understand the immediacy of intuitions, I have arrived at a notion of object-dependent conceptual content expressible in demonstrative reference. But the notion I have arrived at is radically alien to Sellars. This yields a way to bracket Sellars's doctrine that the objects of the manifest image do not really exist, but still have an explanation for his inability to countenance the transcendental role I have suggested we can attribute to this conception of intuitions.

The point is that the picture depicts intuitions as, *qua* conceptual occurrences of a certain kind, *related* to objects. The idea that there is only an illusion of content in certain situations simply makes vivid the relational character of the conceptual occurrences that are intuitions. The idea is that for a conceptual episode to possess intuitional content just is for it to stand in a certain relation to an object; so if there is no object suitably related to a conceptual episode, then there is no such relation, and accordingly no such content. (Of course there is still a conceptual episode, an ostensible perceiving.) But it is central to Sellars's thinking that elements in the conceptual order can stand in content-involving or semantical relations only to elements in the conceptual order, not to elements in the real order. He thinks this "non-relational character of 'meaning' and 'aboutness'" is "the key to a correct understanding of the place of mind in nature".[6]

4. How can meaning and aboutness be non-relational? In expounding this Sellarsian thought, it is easiest to begin with the semantical character of elements in language, in the sense in which language is a repertoire for overt linguistic acts.

By saying what an expression means or stands for, we capture the expression's potential for making it the case that a linguistic act in which it occurs has a specific directedness towards extra-linguistic reality.[7] In this context, the thesis we are concerned with is that such semantical statements do not relate the expressions they deal with to elements in extra-linguistic reality.

6. *Science and Metaphysics*, p. ix.

7. For "means" in this role, see "Empiricism and the Philosophy of Mind", §31; for "stands for", see chapter 3 of *Science and Metaphysics*.

On the face of it, the forms ". . . means —" or ". . . stands for —" are relational. If the expressions that figure on the right-hand sides of statements of
such forms were used in the way they are used in ordinary (non-semantical)
discourse, we could take that appearance at face value; we could suppose
that the expressions refer to certain elements in extra-linguistic reality, those
towards which ordinary uses of them enable linguistic acts to be directed, so
that the statements could be taken to assert relations between these elements in extra-linguistic reality and the expressions mentioned on their left-
hand sides. But according to Sellars the expressions on the right-hand sides
of these statements are not used, at any rate not in that ordinary way. And
they are not exactly, or not merely, mentioned either. If they were merely
mentioned, it would be possible to understand what semantical statements
say without thereby knowing what determinate directedness towards objective reality is said to be enabled by the expressions that the statements deal
with, in linguistic acts in which those expressions occur; but that is not possible. In Sellars's view, the expressions that figure on the right-hand sides of
these semantical statements are neither ordinarily used nor ordinarily mentioned, but *exhibit* their own propriety-governed use. We can understand this
as a special kind of use, differentiated from using words in general in that it
does not serve, for instance, to refer to an object; or alternatively as a special
kind of mention, differentiated from mentioning words in general in that
there is a presupposition that it is addressed to people who understand the
expressions mentioned.[8]

How can a statement that relates an expression only to another expression
serve to determine an intentional character associated with the first expression, a role it plays in enabling linguistic acts it occurs in to be determinately
directed towards elements in extra-linguistic reality? As I said, the expression on the right-hand side of a specification of significance is supposed to

---

8. For a special kind of use, see, e.g., "Empiricism and the Philosophy of Mind", §31:
"not *mentioned* but *used*—used in a unique way; *exhibited*, so to speak." For a special kind of
mention, see, e.g., "Being and Being Known", p. 55, where Sellars initially says, of the
statement " 'Mensch' signifies [another variant for "means" or "stands for"] *man*", that it
"says, in effect, that the German word 'Mensch' has the same use as the English word
'man' "; then notes that on that account one could know what the statement of significance says without thereby knowing what "Mensch" means; and finally suggests that "this
can be remedied by interpreting [the statement of significance] as presupposing that the
word 'man' is in the hearer's vocabulary", so that it amounts to " 'Mensch' (in German)
has the same use as *your* word 'man' ".

exhibit its own propriety-governed use. If we were to formulate the relevant proprieties explicitly, we would be saying that there *ought to be* certain relations between, on the one hand, uses of the expression in question, considered now as elements in the real order (not the conceptual order), and, on the other hand, other elements in the real order, which can be, unlike the first set of parties to these relations, entirely extra-linguistic.[9] That is: these proprieties require a certain determinate relatedness to extra-linguistic reality on the part of occurrences in the real order in which speakers make ordinary uses of the expression that figures on the right-hand side of a semantical statement. By virtue of the non-ordinary use to which the expression is put there, the content of that requirement—a certain determinate relatedness to extra-linguistic reality—is reflected into what the statement says about the expression mentioned on its left-hand side, even though the statement relates that expression only to another expression. This is how a statement that affirms a relation between expressions is supposed to be able to capture the contribution made by the expression mentioned on its left-hand side to the intentional character, the directedness towards extra-linguistic reality, of linguistic acts in which the expression figures.

Sellars instructs us to model non-overt conceptual episodes on linguistic acts, and the structure of this account of meaning carries over into how he conceives the intentional character ("aboutness") of unexpressed thought. A conceptual episode's being intentionally directed towards an element in the real order is analogous to, say, a linguistic episode's containing an expression that functions as a name of an element in the real order. According to Sellars, this "aboutness" must not be conceived as a relation between an element in the conceptual order and an element in the real order. There are no semantical relations between the orders; aboutness, like meaning, is non-relational. But the content of the relation, wholly within the conceptual order, that is affirmed by a statement of aboutness is partly constituted by relations that would ideally relate conceptual episodes considered as elements in the real order to other elements in the real order.

9. The linguistic terms of these relations that there ought to be are what Sellars calls "natural-linguistic objects". See "Truth and 'Correspondence' ", p. 212: "although we may, indeed must, know that these linguistic objects are subject to rules and principles—are fraught with 'ought'—we abstract from this knowledge in considering them as objects in the natural order. Let me introduce the term 'natural-linguistic object' to refer to linguistic objects thus considered."

5. Why does Sellars think we must thus explain away the appearance that there are semantical relations between the conceptual order and the real order? His remarkable paper "Being and Being Known" suggests an answer.

Sellars there aims to motivate his non-relational conception of intentionality by discussing two versions of the opposing idea that intentionality can be relational. He formulates the opposing idea like this: "intellectual acts"—the "conceptual episodes" of "Empiricism and the Philosophy of Mind"—"differ *not* in their intrinsic character as acts, but by virtue of being directly related to different relata."[10]

He finds the first version of this conception in an inheritance, on the part of Cartesian philosophy, of some scholastic apparatus. "For the Cartesian", Sellars says, "the immediate relatum is an item having being-for-mind ('objective' reality). Thus the thought of a golden mountain is a thought which is related to a golden mountain *qua* having being-for-mind, being for the mind that is thinking of it."[11] "Content" is a natural label for something seen as having "objective" being *in* a thought. Using the term in that way, Sellars suggests that "the Cartesians postulated a domain of contents to mediate between the intellect and the real order".[12]

The second version Sellars identifies as the position of "the extreme realists of the early decades of the present century". In this version, the immediate relata of conceptual episodes are elements of the real order, not contents that mediate between conceptual episodes and elements of the real order. Philosophers in the Cartesian tradition had thought they needed those mediating contents in order to handle cases where the supposed real-order target of a conceptual episode does not exist; instead, in this version of the relational conception, the real order is expanded so as to include, for instance as "subsistent", the non-existent objects "which had puzzled previous philosophers into the theory of contents".[13]

Sellars urges, reasonably enough given how he sees them, that each of these options has drawbacks. The mediating function of "contents" becomes

10. "Being and Being Known", p. 41. The terminology of "intellectual acts" reflects the fact that "Being and Being Known" is a discussion of how to interpret Aquinas. But the issues are exactly those raised by "Empiricism and the Philosophy of Mind" and *Science and Metaphysics*.

11. "Being and Being Known", p. 41.

12. "Being and Being Known", p. 42.

13. Both quotations in this paragraph are from p. 42.

problematic, as the Cartesian tradition succumbs to a tendency towards scepticism and idealism; and in any case the language of "objective" being that Descartes inherits from scholastic philosophy merely labels the supposed relation between thought and objects, and does nothing towards explaining it. But the only alternative so far in view, extreme realism, is unsatisfactory just because of its extremism.

What seems to force a choice between these unattractive options is the assumption that conceptual episodes differ only extrinsically, in being related to different objects. This brings the assumption into doubt. And Sellars says, surely correctly, that the assumption—"the notion that acts of the intellect are intrinsically alike regardless of what they are about"[14]—is odd anyway, even apart from the awkward choice it confronts us with.

At this point Sellars writes: "But what is the alternative? In general terms it is to hold that acts of the intellect differ intrinsically *qua* acts in a way which systematically corresponds to what they are about, i.e. their subject-matter."[15] This "alternative" is Sellars's non-relational view of meaning and aboutness. Acts of the intellect—conceptual episodes—differ intrinsically, *qua* acts, in their intentional character. If we were allowed to understand intentional character as consisting in a relation to the extra-conceptual order, we could put that thesis—that intentional character is the intrinsically differentiating character of a conceptual episode—by saying that conceptual episodes differ intrinsically *in* being about what they are about. But according to Sellars, intentional character is non-relational. So the intrinsic differences between conceptual episodes cannot be differences *in* their subject-matter; they can have to do with subject-matter at all only by *systematically corresponding* to differences in subject-matter. The systematic correspondence is the reflection into statements of significance—which, Sellars insists, set up relations only between elements in the conceptual order, not across the boundary between the conceptual order and the real order—of relations ideally required, relations there ought to be, between conceptual episodes considered as elements in the real order and other elements in the real order.

Here, then, Sellars recommends his position by eliminating alternatives. But as my paraphrase of the argument has brought out, there is a possibility he does not consider, even to reject it: namely, that conceptual

14. "Being and Being Known", p. 42.
15. "Being and Being Known", p. 43.

episodes might differ intrinsically, not in a way that *systematically corresponds* to what they are about, but *in* being about whatever they are about. He assumes that anyone who wants to say intellectual acts differ only in what they are about, as opposed to differing in some way that systematically corresponds to differences in what they are about, will admit to supposing that intellectual acts do not differ intrinsically at all. (That was his formulation of the alternative to his non-relational conception.) He simply does not consider that someone might want to say a difference in what they are directed towards can itself be an intrinsic difference in intellectual acts. (That is just how it is with intuitions on the conception I have extracted from Kant's remark in the "Clue".) So the argument from exhaustion of possibilities is inconclusive; it depends on a tendentious formulation of the alternative to Sellars's position, according to which the alternative includes not just the idea that intentional directedness is relational but also—what Sellars assumes—that being related in the relevant way to an extra-conceptual item cannot be intrinsic to an intellectual act.

And it is not just the last step of the argument that looks unsatisfactory in this light. Sellars's incomplete conception of the possibilities shapes his reading of the two other positions he considers. The prospects for positions on those lines look different once we query Sellars's assumption.

Consider again the apparatus Descartes inherits from scholastic philosophy. Crediting intellectual acts with "content" is, as Sellars sees, just another wording for the idea that elements of the real order have "objective" being in them. But that in turn can be, as Sellars does not see, just another wording for the idea that they have an intrinsic character that consists in their being immediately related to elements of the real order. So conceived, "content" does not *mediate* between the intellect and the real order, as in Sellars's reading. Rather, crediting intellectual acts with "content" is a way to express the thought that goes missing in Sellars's argument, that an unmediated relatedness to elements in the real order can be an intrinsic character of an intellectual act.

It is true that the scholastic terminology does no more than label the relatedness in question. But the apparatus need not preclude a vindicating explanation—perhaps on the lines of the one I am suggesting we can find in Kant. (This would require that when we set about entitling ourselves to the scholastic terminology, we focus primarily on intuitions, in which real objects are actually present to subjects, rather than such intellectual acts as the thought of a golden mountain.) It need not be the apparatus itself that drives Cartesian reflection towards scepticism and idealism.

I think a Kantian rehabilitation of the scholastic-Cartesian apparatus would point to a version, purged of its extremism, of the twentieth-century realism that is the other option Sellars considers. In discussing this option, Sellars strangely implies that Russell's theory of descriptions belongs with a distinction between existence and subsistence, as another device for including non-existent objects in the real order, where they can be relata for intellectual acts.[16] But surely the point of the theory of descriptions is exactly to avoid an apparent need for non-existent real objects as relata for intellectual acts. In cases in which a relational conception of intellectual acts would require them to stand in relations to possibly non-existent objects, Russell instead takes their content to include *specifications* of objects. If no objects answer to the specifications, that does not threaten the contentfulness of the acts. There are indeed cases for which this Russellian strategy is unsatisfying, cases for which one wants to keep the idea of a relational intentionality in play even though the putative object of such intentionality may not exist. But one beauty of the idea that there can be illusions of relationally intentional content is that it enables us to gratify this quasi-Meinongian motivation without needing to postulate relations to merely subsistent objects. An illusion of a relation to an ordinarily real object does the work that seemed to require an actual relation to a merely subsistent object.[17]

6. I have brought out how Sellars's attempt to justify his non-relational conception of intentionality turns on the assumption that intentionality could be relational only if how a conceptual episode is directed at objective reality were not intrinsic to it. Reasonably enough, Sellars finds the idea that conceptual episodes are intrinsically alike, whatever they are

---

16. "Being and Being Known", p. 42: "Thus non-existent objects . . . found their place in the real order by means of a distinction between existence and subsistence and such other devices as Russell's theory of descriptions."

17. Sellars also ignores the difference between Russell's earlier conception of judgment as a relation to a state of affairs, which may or may not be existent, and his later conception of judgment as a multiple relation to objects and properties. Here again, the point of the later conception (unsatisfactory as it certainly is) is to avoid the Meinongian commitment that the earlier conception incurs, to non-existent states of affairs as real relata for false judgments.

about, unprepossessing.[18] But so far from justifying the assumption that a relational conception of intentionality would commit us to that idea, Sellars does not even identify it as an assumption. This looks like a blind spot.

We can describe the blind spot in another way. In "Being and Being Known", Sellars formulates his conception of intentionality in terms of the Thomistic notion of the intellectual word. In this terminology, the intrinsic character of intellectual acts consists in their being (second) actualizations of intellectual words, and their intentionality is determined by the semantics of the intellectual words in question. Sellars reads this as a version of his own standard conception, according to which unexpressed thought is to be understood on the model of linguistic acts, literally so called—performances of overt speech. And his account of the semantics of intellectual words fits the familiar pattern. A statement of the meaning of an intellectual word affirms a relation only within the intellectual order, not between the intellectual order and the real order, but nevertheless contrives to capture an intentional directedness towards the real order, because what it says is partly constituted by an ideally required relatedness between elements in the real order. So we can formulate the possibility Sellars does not consider in terms of the semantics of intellectual words. The missing possibility is that a statement of the semantical character of an intellectual word might relate the word, as an element in the intellectual order, to an element in the real order, towards which intellectual acts in which the word figures are intentionally directed. I shall put this by saying that the semantics of the language of the intellect might be Tarskian.

This would be a counterpart to the thought that the semantics of ordinary words might be Tarskian, which is ruled out by Sellars's doctrine that meaning is non-relational. Sellars occasionally discusses Tarskian semantics for ordinary words, but his discussions are quite unsatisfactory, and we can see this as a symptom of the same blind spot.

---

18. At p. 63 of *Science and Metaphysics*, Sellars is happy to "take for granted that the concept of a diaphanous act . . . is unsatisfactory". The concept of a diaphanous act is the concept Sellars finds in the views to which, in "Being and Being Known", he represents his own position as "the alternative": the concept of an act that differs from other acts in what it is intentionally directed towards, but not intrinsically. See *Science and Metaphysics*, p. 34.

Sometimes he suggests that the very idea of word-world relations as they figure in Tarskian semantics is "Augustinian", in the sense that fits the opening sections of Wittgenstein's *Philosophical Investigations*.[19] But this is simply wrong. It is perfectly congenial to Tarskian semantics to say that the notions of such word-world relations as denotation and satisfaction are intelligible only in terms of how they contribute towards capturing the possibilities for "making moves in the language-game" by uttering whole sentences in which the relevant words occur. These relations between words and elements in the extra-linguistic order should not be conceived as independently available building-blocks out of which we could construct an account of how language enables us to express thoughts at all.[20]

In other places Sellars suggests that proponents of relational semantics conceive the word-world relations that they take semantical statements to affirm in terms of "ideal semantical uniformities". This is an allusion to those propriety-governed genuine relations, between linguistic acts considered as elements in the real order and other elements in the real order, that figure in his picture as partly constitutive of the content of semantical statements.[21] Here Sellars is reading Tarskian semantics in the light of his own understanding of the possibilities. Statements of those "ideal semantical uniformities"—which are not themselves semantical statements, though they enter into the determining of what semantical statements say—are the closest his view can come to the idea of statements that are both semantical and deal with relations to elements in the real order. So Sellars takes it that proponents of relational semantics mistakenly think these statements of "ideal semantical uniformities" *are* semantical statements. This is to assume

19. For a suggestion in this direction on Sellars's part, see "Empiricism and the Philosophy of Mind", §30. Compare Brandom's contemptuous remarks about "a supposed word-world relation of reference", *Making it Explicit*, pp. 323–5.

20. A way of putting this is to say that Tarskian semantics can perfectly well accommodate the point Sellars makes about truth, directing it against Carnap, at pp. 100–102 of *Science and Metaphysics*. (Carnap tends to be teamed with Tarski in Sellars's discussions of semantics; see, e.g., *Science and Metaphysics*, p. 83: "semantics of the Carnap-Tarski type.") Sellars's point does not tell against doing semantics in terms of relations; rather, it is a way of saying why the derivability of conclusions conforming to "Convention T" is a good adequacy condition on a relational semantical account of a language. For a clear statement of the point that there is nothing "Augustinian" about Tarskian semantics, see Donald Davidson, "In Defence of Convention T".

21. See *Science and Metaphysics*, pp. 86–7; the same suggestion is made at p. 112. The "uniformities" in question here are those described at pp. 75–7.

that his opponents are working within a dimly grasped version of his structure, and misconstrue the significance of its elements.[22]

But that is not what is meant by saying that statements of, for instance, the form ". . . denotes —" relate words to objects. The point is rather this. First, the expression that figures on the right-hand side of such a statement is used in an ordinary way, not in the peculiar way that figures in Sellars's account of semantical statements. So we can see the statement as itself affirming a relation between the expression mentioned on the left-hand side and whatever element in the real order can be mentioned by a standard use of the expression on the right. Second, and crucially, the ideality or normativity that is relevant to such a statement is not that of the "ideal semantical uniformities" that figure in Sellars's own picture of the semantical. "Denotes" expresses a relation between elements of the linguistic order and elements of the extra-linguistic order, the very idea of which is—to borrow a Sellarsian phrase—fraught with "ought",[23] in a way that reflects what ensures that this conception of semantics is not "Augustinian". The very idea of such relations makes sense only in the context of how they enter into determining the conditions under which whole sentences are *correctly* or *incorrectly* asserted. The normativity expressed by those uses of "correctly" and "incorrectly" is reflected back into the content of such concepts as that of denotation.[24]

Sellars holds that we should understand non-overt conceptual episodes on the model of overt linguistic acts. So if it were acceptable to understand the semantics of intellectual words in Tarskian terms, that would be because our analogical understanding of intellectual words can exploit its being acceptable to understand the semantics of ordinary words in Tarskian terms. But Sellars's blind spot obscures the very idea that the semantics of intellectual words might be Tarskian, except as an expression of the unprepossessing conception in which intellectual acts have no intrinsic character. This helps

22. See *Science and Metaphysics*, p. 86: "It is a mistake to suppose, as Carnap does, that semantical statements in *his* sense, i.e. statements which involve such expressions as 'denotes' or 'designates', are semantical statements in the sense that they formulate (ideal) semantical uniformities."

23. See, e.g., "Truth and 'Correspondence'", p. 212.

24. Another consideration Sellars brings to bear against "semantics of the Carnap-Tarski style" connects this region of his thinking with his doctrine about the manifest image and the scientific image; he objects to a relational semantics for the language of the manifest image, on the ground that it would commit one to the reality of the objects of the manifest image. See "The Language of Theories", p. 109, n. 3.

to make it intelligible that the idea of relational semantics for ordinary words does not come into Sellars's thinking in the authentic form in which I have just sketched it.[25]

7. At the beginning of these three essays, I spoke of a structural feature of Sellars's thinking that, I suggested, makes a fully Kantian vision of intentionality inaccessible to him. I have now come close to uncovering what I meant. Sellars cannot see how a determinate intentional directedness can be both a relation to an element in the real order and an intrinsic character of a conceptual occurrence, and this corresponds to an inability to see how denoting, say, can be a relation that relates elements of the conceptual order to elements of the real order.

Why does Sellars not contemplate the possibility I am urging?[26] I do not mean to suggest that his blind spot is superficial.

It helps to compare two ways of interpreting the idea that our thought of meaning and aboutness is fraught with "ought".

On Sellars's interpretation, the content of a statement of significance is a reflection, into a statement of a relation within the conceptual order, of relations that there ought to be, according to the proprieties that constitute a linguistic practice, between two sets of elements in the real order, one of which comprises linguistic items considered in abstraction from the practical proprieties in virtue of which they are meaningful at all. The "ought" with which meaning and aboutness are fraught gets into the picture as a sentential operator, in whose scope there occur specifications of relations that would ideally hold between linguistic items so considered and other

---

25. This has a damaging effect on the thinking of some people who have been influenced by Sellars. Rorty, for instance, sees that the Tarskian semantics Davidson envisages for natural languages involves word-world relations, and concludes that Davidsonian semantical talk, so far from being fraught with "ought", is not even coherently combinable with a way of talking about language that is fraught with "ought". See "Pragmatism, Davidson and Truth". This misses the fact that the very idea of the word-world relations in question, for instance denotation, is itself already "ought"-laden, in a different way from any that comes into view in Sellarsian semantics. Rorty's reading of Davidson looks like a descendant of Sellars's blind spot.

26. It is not that Sellars cannot see how something as natural as sensory consciousness could be shaped by conceptual capacities, our possession of which is what elevates us above mere nature. (That is the supposed difficulty I tried to deal with in *Mind and World*.) Sellars has, and exploits, the idea of conceptual shapings of sensory consciousness.

elements in the real order. The content of the "ought" with which some fact about significance is fraught—what it is that, according to the "ought" in question, ought to be the case—can be factored out from the statement of significance and specified in terms that are not themselves meaning-involving.[27]

Contrast the Tarskian conception. Here denoting, say, is a relation, itself fraught with "ought", between an element in the linguistic or conceptual order and an element in the real order. There is no suggestion that to a statement of what some expression denotes there corresponds an "ought" whose content could be factored out, so that the "ought" in question could be seen as a separable determinant of the semantical character of the expression. The "ought" with which a statement of what some expression denotes is fraught reflects how the expression's denoting what it denotes enters into determining conditions for the correctness of assertions. The normativity that the "ought" conveys is an aspect of the expression's meaning, its impact on the significance of sentences it occurs in. This normativity is not something pre-semantical that could figure in constitutively explaining what meaning is from outside the semantical.

So I can formulate a structural feature of Sellars's thinking like this: he cannot see how semantical thinking could be "ought"-laden except by taking it to be fraught with "oughts" that can be seen as determining significance from outside the semantical. He thinks there must be proprieties of (what is in fact) linguistic practice, formulable in non-semantical terms, that underlie and constitute the semanticity of linguistic expressions.

Kant suggests an understanding of thought's being of the objective that centres on the immediate presentness of objects to conceptual consciousness in intuition. I have suggested a reading in which this immediate presentness is relational. Sellars wants to exploit the Kantian idea of a transcendental role for sensibility, but for him the idea that intuitional content might be understood in terms of a relation between the conceptual order and the real order is not an option. Now the contrast I have drawn between two ways of understanding fraughtness with "ought" suggests that we can see this as reflecting a general conception of what it takes to execute Kant's transcendental project. For Sellars, our entitlement to see elements in the

---

27. See, e.g., p. 92 of *Naturalism and Ontology*: "The rule governed uniformities . . . which constitute a language (including our own) can, in principle, be exhaustively described without the use of meaning statements. . . ."

conceptual order as intentionally directed towards elements in the real order has to be transcendentally secured from outside the semantical, from outside the conceptual order. We have seen this structural feature of Sellars's thinking operative in connection with the "ought" with which our thought of meaning and aboutness is fraught, but the idea that the transcendental work needs to be done from outside the semantical has a more general application. Given a conviction to that effect, a transcendental role for sensibility can only be the sort of thing Sellars envisages, a matter of conceptual activity being guided by "sheer receptivity". On this view, we cannot spell out a transcendental role for sensibility in terms of the immediate presence of objects to intuitionally structured consciousness, as in the reading of Kant that I have recommended. That would be already a case of conceptual directedness towards the real, so it could not figure in a vindication, from outside, of the very idea of conceptual directedness towards the real.

How can there be a semantical relatedness, itself fraught with "ought", between the conceptual order and the real order? It might be the beginning of an answer to say: this "ought"-laden relatedness to the real order must be itself embraced within the conceptual order. I have deliberately given that formulation a Hegelian ring, in order to suggest that what I have been representing as Sellars's blind spot, his inability to contemplate the possibility that intentionality might be relational, is part of a package with his conviction that to give philosophical reflection about intentionality a Hegelian shape is to abandon objectivity rather than to vindicate it.

We now have a variety of ways of describing this structural feature of Sellars's thinking. One is that it reflects his conviction that Hegel merely muddies the Kantian waters.[28] Against this, I have urged that if we see intuition in the way Kant proposes, we can take perceived objects themselves to supply the external constraint on conceptual goings-on for which Sellars thinks we need to appeal to "sheer receptivity". A non-sheer receptivity is operative in intuition so conceived, and that is enough to undermine the threat of "idealism", the threat that the supposed objects of these conceptual shapings of consciousness can only be projections of our conceptual activity. At any rate there is nothing against this reading of the transcendental role of sensibility except the putative reasons yielded by scientism for denying

28. See *Science and Metaphysics*, p. 29.

genuine reality to the objects that, speaking within the manifest image, we say are immediately present to us in intuition, and hence for refusing to allow that they themselves provide the transcendentally needed external constraint on conceptual activity. Discounting such scientism, we can refuse to be frightened by Sellars's invocation of Hegel. I am encouraged in this by the availability of another way to describe Sellars's idea that there must be guidance by "sheer receptivity": it reflects his blind spot for the Tarskian approach to the semantical.

It may seem a dizzying project to embrace relatedness to the real order within the conceptual order. But Tarskian semantics points to a sober interpretation. It is crucial to a proper understanding of Tarskian semantics that we have to *use* the words on the right-hand sides of semantical statements. (Contrast Sellars's conception of the way words figure on the right-hand sides of statements of meaning.) Sellars himself holds that unexpressed thought is to be understood on the model of linguistic acts. Exploiting that, we can apply the same point to unexpressed thought: we have to *use* the words that figure in specifications of what non-overt conceptual episodes are intentionally directed towards. In statements of meaning and aboutness, we relate the conceptual order to the real order, mentioning elements of the real order by making ordinary uses of the words on the right-hand sides of these statements. But we affirm these relations without moving outside the conceptual order—without doing more than employing our conceptual capacities.

How can our minds get into relations to elements in the real order simply by acquiring suitably shaped conceptual contents? That is just what we are enabled to find unmysterious by putting intuitional content, understood in the way Kant indicates, at the centre of our picture of the conceptual.

8. I began these three essays by suggesting that Sellars's thinking is especially instructive towards understanding Kant, and thereby finding intentionality unproblematic. I can now end by giving that suggestion a somewhat more determinate shape. The point is that the key question for understanding Kant, and thereby seeing how to become comfortable with intentionality, is just the question Sellars brings into focus: can the transcendental project be acceptably executed from within the conceptual order, or does it require a sideways-on point of view on the directedness of the conceptual at the real?

In the first of these three essays, I distinguished transcendental philosophy as such from a conception of it as requiring the sideways-on perspective. Sellars's position exemplifies this more specific conception, according to which the transcendental project needs to be undertaken from outside the thought whose objective purport it seeks to vindicate. Correctly in my view, Sellars fails to find anything answering to this conception of transcendental philosophy in Kant's Aesthetic; and he contrives to find this kind of thing in the Analytic only by ignoring Kant's insistence that appearances, things as they appear, are the same things that can also be conceived as things in themselves. The very idea of transcendental philosophy is a Kantian invention, and we can hardly suppose there really is none in the *Critique of Pure Reason*. The fate of Sellars's reading constitutes a powerful argument that the thought Hegel tries to capture with the image of Reason as subject to no external constraint—the rejection of a sideways-on standpoint for philosophy—is already Kant's own thought.

It is common for people not to see so much as a possibility that intentional directedness might be a relation to objects; this shows in the resistance or incomprehension typically encountered by Evans's work. Often this is combined with taking for granted the idea that conceptual activity is intentionally directed towards the world. Now Sellars is special in being responsive to the Kantian thought that we need a transcendental exercise in which we show our entitlement to the very idea of objective purport. He is also responsive to the more specific Kantian thought that this transcendental exercise must centre on intuition, so that we can exploit the receptivity of sensibility. But he is unresponsive to the Hegelian conceit of incorporating receptivity within Reason, and I have tried to display this as a blindness to a more soberly describable possibility. Given his conviction that the transcendental exercise must be undertaken from outside the conceptual, Sellars's responsiveness to Kant gives him no alternative but to construe the transcendental role of sensibility in terms of guidance by "sheer receptivity".

Suppose we agree with Sellars that it is an insight on Kant's part that the receptivity of sensibility must play a transcendental role. Reflecting on the context Sellars supplies for that thought, we can see that, aside from minor details, the conviction that Kant is right about the significance of sensibility presents us with a quite simple choice: either Sellars's picture of guidance by "sheer receptivity", or the idea I have recommended, that the guidance

Sellars thinks we need to credit to "sheer receptivity" can be displayed, in the course of the transcendental project, as exercised by the immediate objects of perception themselves.[29] I hope to have made it plausible that there is more to be said for the second option than Sellars allows.

29. The only alternative, at this level of generality, is to deny a transcendental role to sensibility altogether. Brandom's *Making It Explicit* is the most worked-out attempt I know to take this non-Kantian path and still purport to accommodate intentionality. In chapter 4, where Brandom undertakes to deal with empirical content, he deliberately refrains from attributing a transcendental role to sensory consciousness, thus denying himself the resources for a Kantian notion of intuitions. (The same fact about Brandom's thinking is reflected in his non-central placing of the situations that permit "strong de re ascriptions", in chapter 8.) In his chapter 8, Brandom undertakes to provide for the "representational character" of thought and language, without a transcendental exploitation of anything on the lines of intuitions, by appealing to the idea of a specification by A of what B's thought is about in which A takes responsibility for the way the object is specified. In "Replies", he claims that this apparatus legitimates an idea of word-world relations. I think this cannot work. See *Science and Metaphysics*, pp. 82–7, where Sellars shows, I think, that if we start with the idea that word-world relations are impossible or at least problematic (as Brandom does), then considerations about substitution inferences, of the sort Brandom exploits, cannot get us any closer to vindicating semantic relations between the conceptual order and the real order.

PART II

Kantian Themes in Hegel and Sellars

Hegel's Idealism as Radicalization of Kant[1]

1. Robert Pippin has urged that we should understand Hegel by appreciating how his thinking is both inspired by and critical of Kant.[2] I am going to sketch an approach to Hegel on these lines. To begin with, I shall simply appropriate Pippin's execution of that project. I shall note some divergences from Pippin towards the end.

2. In Hegel's view, Kant expresses a fundamental insight when he centres his account of the objective purport of experience on the transcendental unity of apperception. In the *Science of Logic*, Hegel writes (p. 584): "It is one of the profoundest and truest insights to be found in the *Critique of Pure Reason* that the *unity* which constitutes the nature of the *Notion* is recognized as the *original synthetic* unity of *apperception*, as the unity of the *I think*, or of self-consciousness." Pippin's reading of Hegel pivots on this passage, which he quotes at p. 18 of *Hegel's Idealism* and frequently harks back to.

Hegel is alluding to the first *Critique*'s Transcendental Deduction.[3] There, especially in the second-edition version (the "B Deduction"), Kant almost

1. This is a lightly revised version of a paper that was first published in Italian translation, as "L'idealismo di Hegel come radicalizazzione di Kant". I would have liked to revise it more drastically, especially towards the end. But the English version is to appear with a response by Sebastian Rödl, and I have resisted the temptation to shift the target.

2. See especially *Hegel's Idealism: The Satisfactions of Self-Consciousness*. I shall follow Pippin in focusing on Hegel's response to Kant's theoretical philosophy. I believe this does not preclude finding truth in the thought that Hegel's response to Kant cannot be fully understood without reconstructing his view of all three of Kant's *Critiques*, but I shall not try to substantiate that here.

3. The understanding of Kant, and especially of the B Deduction, that I shall express in this section and the next is the product of working through the first *Critique* with James

achieves an idealism that is authentic by Hegel's lights. (Hegel puts the Deduction in this light in *Faith and Knowledge*.)

Kant explains experience's possession of objective purport—its comprising what at least present themselves as intuitions, sensory states that are immediately of objects—in terms of the idea that intuitions are informed by the categories, the pure concepts of the understanding.[4] In the so-called Metaphysical Deduction, the "Clue to the Discovery of All Pure Concepts of the Understanding", he says (A79/B104–5): "The same function which gives unity to the various representations *in a judgment* also gives unity to the mere synthesis of various representations *in an intuition*; and this unity, in its most general expression, we entitle the pure concept of the understanding." So another way of describing the Deduction is to say Kant explains the objective purport of experience in terms of its exemplifying logical unities that are characteristic of judging. About judging, Kant says (B141): "I find that a judgment is nothing but the manner in which given [cognitions] are brought to the objective unity of apperception. This is what is intended by the copula 'is'. It is employed to distinguish the objective unity of given representations from the subjective." It is through this connection between judging, apperception, and intuition that we can understand his claim, a couple of pages earlier (B139), in a section titled "The Objective Unity of Self-Consciousness": "The transcendental unity of apperception is that unity through which all the manifold given in an intuition is united [into] a concept of the object. It is therefore entitled *objective* . . . ."[5] Instead of "concept" here, I think one might say "conceptually shaped awareness".

From what I have said so far, it might seem that Kant undertakes to explain the objective purport of intuitions—their being immediately of objects—in terms of a supposedly antecedent understanding of the objective purport of

---

Conant and John Haugeland, though they are of course not responsible for any defects in my presentation of it.

4. Intuitions, in the sense in which they are spoken of here, cannot stand opposed to concepts. Pippin (*Hegel's Idealism*, p. 30) says that Kant, at B160, "takes back, in a sense, his strict distinction between intuition and understanding". This risks being misleading. In the sense of "intuition" that is relevant to a remark such as the one in my text, there should never have even seemed to be such a strict distinction. (See Sellars, *Science and Metaphysics*, pp. 2–8, and my elaboration of Sellars in Essay 2 above.) As we shall see, however, Pippin's point is different.

5. "Into" for Kemp Smith's "in": the German is "in einen Begriff" (accusative), not "in einem Begriff" (dative). See Aquila, *Matter in Mind*, p. 136.

judgment—its being answerable to its subject matter. That would leave a question about how to understand the supposed starting point of the explanation, the objective purport of judgment. But I think the idea is rather that by invoking the unity of apperception we enable ourselves to make sense of the objective purport of intuitions and the objective purport of judgments *together*. The Deduction elaborates the idea of a subjectivity that is both intuitionally in touch with objective reality and able to make judgments about it. We are helped to make sense of its having each of those capacities by seeing it as also having the other. (For some elaboration of this, see Essays 1, 2, and 3 above.)

Why would this seem promising to Hegel? Judging is at the centre of the treatment of objective purport in general. And judging is making up one's mind about something. Making up one's mind is one's own doing, something for which one is responsible. To judge is to engage in free cognitive activity, as opposed to having something merely happen in one's life, outside one's control. This is the core of Kant's point when he describes the understanding—which is "the faculty of apperception" (B134n.)—in terms of *spontaneity*. See, e.g., A50/B74; and spontaneity is the main theme of the opening section of the B Deduction. (For a helpful treatment of relevant passages, see Pippin, "Kant on the Spontaneity of Mind".)

Pippin sees the apperceptive character of judging as one case of a general truth, that taking oneself to be φ-ing (for a range of mentality-implying substitutions for "φ") is partly constitutive of what it is to be φ-ing.[6] I think this is correct for the kind of mentality Kant is concerned with. But it is best seen not as clearly acceptable in its general form, with the application to judging derived as a special case, but rather as owing its very justification to the case of judging. The general claim holds because the capacity to judge is essentially apperceptive, and is inextricably bound up with the capacity for any mental directedness towards the objective—for instance, the capacity to have intuitions.

Kant sometimes writes as if any instantiation of the kind of unity that enables directedness at objects reflects *activity* on the part of apperceptive spontaneity. (See, e.g., B129–30.) But this is an overstatement. It requires him, awkwardly, to contemplate exercises of freedom that are unconscious. (See B130: "all combination, be we conscious of it or not, . . . is an act of the

---

6. See Pippin, *Hegel's Idealism*, p. 21: "my implicitly 'taking myself' to be perceiving, imagining, remembering, and so on is an inseparable component of what it is to perceive, imagine, remember, and so on."

understanding." Compare A78/B103: "Synthesis in general . . . is the mere result of the power of imagination, a blind but indispensable function of the soul, without which we should have no knowledge whatsoever, but of which we are scarcely ever conscious.") What he needs is only that the kind of unity in question is the kind that is characteristic of judgment. Not all instances of that kind of unity need to be seen as resulting from free cognitive activity. Intuitions just happen, outside the control of their subjects. But their unity is intelligible only in the context of apperceptive spontaneity.[7] And it is this, rather than the mysterious idea that freedom is exercised in intuitions themselves, that underlies the correctness of saying that intuiting is like judging in being apperceptive, that intuitions are at least implicitly self-conscious.[8]

Kant's account of objective purport centres, then, on self-conscious intellectual activity. And it is obvious how this could seem to point towards a Hegelian idealism, according to which the very idea of objectivity is to be understood in terms of the freely self-determining operations of a self-conscious intelligence.

3. It is not just in the centrality it accords to judgment that Kant's Deduction comes close to a Hegelian idealism.

---

7. On p. 26 of *Hegel's Idealism*, Pippin implies that subjects judge the content of their experience. (Even if we consider "a subject's experience of the 'internal flow' of his own mental states", we have to suppose, he says, that "such a subject is judging *that* such states are 'flowing' in that order".) This makes judging fundamental in a way that loses the possibility of using judgment and intuition to cast light on each other. The right point is just that the unity of intuitions is the same as the unity of possible judgments.

8. That is, *able* to be accompanied by the "I think" of apperception, though not necessarily accompanied by it (see B131). Note that for something to be implicitly self-conscious in the relevant sense, the "I think" must be in the subject's repertoire; the point of "implicitly" is just that it need not *actually* accompany every one of "my representations". Kant's point is not met if the very possibility of explicitly accompanying a "representation" with "I think" is yet to be provided for, in an explicitation such as is envisaged only in chapter 8 of Brandom, *Making It Explicit*. Whatever we have at the earlier stages of Brandom's progression, it is not even implicitly self-conscious in the relevant sense; that is, not apperceptive. Brandom claims a Kantian affiliation and a Hegelian inspiration, but in this respect—that he depicts a possibility of explicit self-consciousness as emerging after conceptuality has supposedly long been already on the scene, rather than being a condition for the presence of conceptuality at all—his thinking diverges radically from Kant, and precisely on a point on which Kant was a source of inspiration for Hegel, as the passage from the *Science of Logic* that I quoted at the beginning shows.

The B Deduction is framed to avoid a certain objection. Kant wants to establish that experience has its objective purport by virtue of being informed by the pure concepts of the understanding. The objection is that that ensures only thinkability. But a condition for objects to be thinkable is not thereby a condition for them to be capable of being given to our senses. Indeed (the objection goes on), the Transcendental Aesthetic has already supplied an independent condition for objects to be able to be given to our senses: they must be spatially and temporally ordered. For all Kant can show, objects could satisfy that condition for being present to our senses without conforming to the requirements of the understanding.[9] We can refuse to count a state of a subject as an *intuition*, a case of having an object available for *cognition*, unless the state has categorial unity. But if we do not answer the objection, the requirement that intuitions have categorial unity looks like mere subjective imposition, superadded to the requirement for things to be present to our senses, and nothing to do with the things themselves. Here "the things themselves" means things as given to our senses. The objectivity that threatens to go missing from the idea of a categorially ordered world is the objectivity Kant wants, not what he seeks to reveal as a mirage, the idea of a taking in of things apart from the conditions of our taking things in at all. On these lines, the prospects look poor for the claim Kant is aiming at, that the pure concepts of the understanding have genuinely objective validity.

Kant organizes the B Deduction so as to forestall this objection. The essential move is to deny that the Transcendental Aesthetic offers an independent condition for objects to be given to our senses. We can connect the way our sensibility is formed, the topic of the Aesthetic, with the unity of space and time as (objects of) "formal intuitions" (B160n.). Those formal intuitions are cases of the combination of a manifold into a single intuition, and as such they come within the scope of the guiding principle Kant states at the beginning of the Deduction (B129–30). What he actually says there is that all combination, all representation of something as complex, results from activity on the part of apperceptive spontaneity. And as it stands, that is what I described as overstatement; I urged that intuitions are not outcomes of intellectual activity. But a corrected version of the claim will suit

---

9. See A89–91/B122–3 (in the preamble to the Transcendental Deduction, common to both editions). This passage sets out a version of this stage of the potential objection, in the course of explaining why the task of a Transcendental Deduction (showing "how *subjective conditions of thought* can have *objective validity*") is so difficult.

Kant's purpose just as well: no combination is intelligible except in a context that includes the ability to engage in free intellectual activity. Capacities that belong to apperceptive spontaneity are actualized in intuitions. That goes in particular for the pure intuitions of space and time. So the formedness of our sensibility, the topic of the Aesthetic, cannot after all be fully in view independently of apperceptive spontaneity. The unity constituted by conformity to the requirements of our sensibility, which is the unity of the pure formal intuitions of space and time, is not a separate unity, independent of the unity that consists in being informed by the categories.[10] On these lines it seems, at least, that the objection does not arise, and Kant takes himself to be entitled to claim that the categories apply to "whatever objects may *present themselves to our senses*" (as, at B159, he puts what he is going to show). He takes himself to have averted the threat that figured in the objection, that categorial requirements take on the look of mere subjective imposition.[11]

The threat is that Kant's position is only a subjective idealism. Against this, he aims to show that the requirements of the understanding are not just subjective requirements but requirements on objects themselves. As he

---

10. See B144–5, where Kant is setting out what he is going to do in the second part of the Deduction: "In what follows . . . it will be shown, from the mode in which [omitting Kemp Smith's "the"] empirical intuition is given in sensibility, that its unity [that of the mode in which empirical intuition is given in sensibility] is no other than that which the category . . . prescribes to the manifold of a given intuition in general." He is going to argue that there is only one unity, common to the Aesthetic and the Analytic; not two separate and independent unities.

11. See Pippin, *Hegel's Idealism*, pp. 27–31. This is the context in which Pippin makes the remark I cited in n. 4, that Kant here "takes back, in a sense, his strict distinction between intuition and understanding" (p. 30). My point there was that intuitions of empirical objects involve the understanding, in a way that the Deduction is aimed at making clear; in that sense there should not have seemed to be a "strict distinction". But the "strict distinction" Pippin means is not one that would be violated by supposing that understanding enters into the constitution of intuitions, but a distinction between the topics of the Aesthetic and the Analytic—between conditions on experience required because our knowledge is sensible and conditions required because our knowledge is discursive. And Kant's organization of his book—first the Aesthetic, then the Analytic—can certainly make it look (as he acknowledges in the footnote at B160–1) as if there are two independent sets of conditions, as if the pure intuitions of space and time are independent of the synthetic powers of the understanding. This is what Pippin means to say Kant "takes back". But rather than say Kant here takes something back, it would be more charitable to say he tells us he never intended to give such an appearance.

puts it at B138 (before he has finished entitling himself to this claim): "The synthetic unity of consciousness is . . . an objective condition of all knowledge. It is not merely a condition that I myself require in knowing an object, but is a condition under which every intuition must stand in order to become *an object for me.*" Or, in the prefatory matter to the Principles of Pure Understanding (A158/B197): "the conditions of the *possibility of experience* in general are likewise conditions of the *possibility of the objects of experience . . . .*" The requirements of the understanding first come into view as subjective conditions. That is the guise in which they appear when we conceive them as requirements of the understanding. But on reflection it is supposed to emerge that they are equally conditions on objects themselves. This conception, with its equipoise between subjective and objective, between thought and its subject matter, is—at least in aspiration—what Hegel would recognize as an authentic idealism.[12]

4. So why is it no better than an aspiration? Why does Kant's conception not succeed in being the idealism, not merely subjective, that it aspires to be?

In the second part of the B Deduction, Kant extends into the terrain of the Transcendental Aesthetic conditions that first come into view as constitutive of spontaneous self-conscious thought. (See Pippin, *Hegel's Idealism*, p. 31, where Pippin speaks of Kant as "extending, or trying to extend, his account of conceptual conditions 'into' the manifold of intuition itself".) Kant's aim is to reveal thereby that that is only the guise in which such conditions first appear—that the conditions are objective no less than subjective.

But given how Kant conceives the role of sensibility in his picture, the extension into the terrain of the Aesthetic can reach only as far as the fact that our sensibility has forms, and not to the specific forms it has: its spatiality and temporality. The most Kant might be able to claim universally, about sensibility as such, is that any sensibility—at any rate any sensibility that

---

12. One might be tempted to describe it as an objective idealism. But that phrase is well suited to characterize a counterpart to subjective idealism, which misses the Hegelian equipoise by conceiving its transcendental conditions as primarily objective, where subjective idealism conceives them as primarily subjective. In that role the phrase figures in Hegel's critical response to Schelling, and generally to the kind of idealism in which the real world is seen as an emanation from a world-soul; see Pippin, *Hegel's Idealism*, p. 61. The idealism of whose possibility Kant's Deduction gives a glimpse achieves genuine objectivity, but it is neither subjective nor objective.

partners a discursive intellect in yielding empirical knowledge—would allow the formation of pure intuitions, reflecting the way the sensibility is formed as the formal intuitions of space and time reflect the way our sensibility is formed. But in his picture it remains a sort of brute fact about us—given from outside to the unifying powers of apperceptive spontaneity, and not determined by their exercise (not even in the extended sense of being intelligible only in a context that includes their exercise)—that the pure intuitions that reflect the forms of our sensibility are intuitions of space and time.

In the Aesthetic, Kant tries to ground *a priori* knowledge on the way our sensibility is formed. But in view of the brute-fact character, as he depicts it, of the spatiality and temporality that our sensibility requires, which persists even after, in the B Deduction, he has done the most he can towards embracing those requirements within the scope of apperceptive spontaneity, it is problematic how he can conceive this knowledge as both *a priori* and genuinely objective. In representing those requirements as given from outside to the unifying powers of our apperceptive spontaneity, he makes it look like a kind of contingency that any world *we* can take in through our senses must be spatially and temporally ordered—even if he can say it is not a contingency that the world of any experience must be ordered in a way that fits the requirements of some sensibility or other. The harshest way to put this criticism is to say that though the Aesthetic purports to ground *a priori* knowledge that is objective, in the only sense we can make intelligible to ourselves, what it puts in place is indistinguishable from a subjectivistic psychologism.[13] Whatever is the case with the requirements that reflect the discursiveness of our intellect (and we shall need to reconsider them), the requirements that reflect how our sensibility is formed—the requirements of spatial and temporal ordering—look like subjective imposition. Transcendental idealism, which is just this insistence that the apparent spatiality and temporality of our world derive from the way our sensibility is formed, stands revealed as subjective idealism.

And the rot spreads. Before we considered transcendental idealism in this light, Kant's extension of apperceptive unity into the territory of the Aesthetic seemed to forestall the objection that he cannot represent the

---

13. This is what Hegel famously says about Kant's idealism, in a much maligned section of his *Lectures on the History of Philosophy*. See Pippin, *Hegel's Idealism*, p. 264, n. 5, and the partial defence of Hegel he cites there, in his chapter 5.

requirements of the understanding as more than subjective imposition. But what seemed to be a demonstration that the pure concepts of the understanding have objective validity depends essentially on how *our* sensibility is formed. Kant makes this clear at B148–9: "The pure concepts of the understanding . . . extend to objects of intuition in general, be the intuition like or unlike ours, if only it be sensible and not intellectual. But this extension of [the] concepts beyond *our* sensible intuition is of no advantage to us. For as concepts of objects they are then empty, and do not enable us to judge of their objects whether or not they are possible. They are mere forms of thought, without objective reality, since we have no intuition at hand to which the synthetic unity of apperception, which constitutes the whole content of these forms, could be applied, and in being so applied determine an object. Only *our* sensible and empirical intuition can give to them [sense and meaning *(Sinn und Bedeutung)*]."

If we allow ourselves—as Kant encourages—to play with the idea of sensibilities formed otherwise than ours, we can suppose they would generate pure intuitions that reflect their ways of being formed as the formal intuitions of space and time reflect ours. And perhaps we can imagine that beings endowed with such sensibilities might construct their own transcendental deductions of the objective validity of categorial thinking, each exploiting—as Kant's Deduction does—the thought that the unity of the mode in which empirical intuition is given in their sensibility is no other than that which the category prescribes to the manifold of a given intuition in general (compare B144–5). But this fancy is no help when we set out to vindicate the objective validity of categorial thinking for ourselves. What that requires is averting the threat that categorial requirements turn out to be merely subjectively imposed on objects as they are given to *our* senses.

That was the threat that seemed to be averted when Kant noted that the unity of the formal intuitions of space and time is itself a case of the objective unity of apperception.

But now it appears that in the context of the transcendental ideality of space and time, the very idea of objects as they are given to our senses has to be seen as reflecting a subjective imposition. And if that is right, the most Kant can claim to have established is that there is no *extra* subjective imposition involved in demanding that a world empirically knowable by us conform to the requirements of the understanding. But the subjective imposition that he thus shows we do not add to when we move from considering the requirements of sensibility to considering the requirements of the understanding—the subjective imposition involved in requiring a world knowable by us to be spatially and temporally ordered, as transcendental idealism has us conceive that requirement—infects the whole package of requirements. The Deduction seemed to show that what Kant brings into view in the first instance as requirements of the understanding, and so as subjective conditions, are equally also objective conditions, conditions on objects themselves. But that depends on its being acceptable to gloss "objects themselves" with "objects as they are given to our senses". And if the relevant characteristic of objects as they are given to our senses—their being spatially and temporally ordered—reflects a subjective imposition, the promise of a proto-Hegelian equipoise between subjective and genuinely objective was illusory. Kant's whole construction is dragged down, by the transcendental idealism about space and time that is at its foundation, into being a subjective idealism.

This makes it urgent to reconsider the idea that pertaining to things as they are given to our senses is as much objectivity as we can intelligibly want in requirements of the understanding. If there are conditions for it to be knowable by us how things are, it should be a truism that things are knowable by us only in so far as they conform to those conditions. And Kant wants it to seem that if we hanker after an objectivity that goes beyond pertaining to things as they are given to our senses, we are hankering after something that would violate that truism. But it is equally truistic that a condition for things to be knowable by us must be a condition for a possibility of our *knowing* how things are. And if some putative general form for states of affairs is represented as a mere reflection of a fact about us, as the spatial and temporal order of the world we experience is by transcendental idealism, that makes it impossible to see the relevant fact about us as grounding a condition for our *knowing* any instance of that form. Transcendental idealism ensures that Kant cannot succeed in depicting the way our sensibility is formed as the source of a condition for things to be *knowable* by us.

By arguing that the requirements of the understanding pertain to things as given to our senses, Kant gives the appearance of showing that those requirements have objective validity. But it is after all not recognizable as objective validity, because the requirements credited to our sensibility are not recognizable as conditions for it to be *knowable* that things are spatially and temporally ordered thus and so. To say that the requirements of the understanding pertain to things as given to our senses is not, as Kant needs it to be, just another way of saying that the requirements of the understanding pertain to things themselves, in the only construal we can intelligibly give to such a claim. Wanting a different conception of objectivity is not chafing at a supposed limitation imposed by the truism that things are knowable by us only in so far as they conform to the conditions of our knowing them. Kant handles what should be that truism so as to depict it as imposing a real limitation, as a truism could not do. According to transcendental idealism, our capacities to know things reach only so far, and beyond that boundary there is something we cannot know: namely, whether things themselves are really spatially and temporally ordered. If we cannot know whether things themselves are really spatially and temporally ordered, that undermines the possibility of recognizing as knowledge the supposed knowledge we are supposed to be able to achieve within the boundary. That in turn ensures that the Deduction cannot succeed in vindicating a genuine objectivity for the requirements of the understanding.[14]

5. I may have seemed to be simply assuming that it would have been a good thing for Kant to achieve a Hegelian equipoise between subjective and objective. But my account of the debilitating consequences of his failure to do so should have dissolved any such appearance. Looking at Kant like this suggests that a successful critical idealism would have to be speculative in a Hegelian sense.

Kant's attempt to secure objective validity—pertinence to something we can genuinely conceive as objects themselves—for the requirements of the understanding founders, because although he manages to represent the unity of our formal intuitions, *qua* intuitions, as a case of a kind of unity that can be understood only in terms of its role in free intellectual activity, nevertheless something else remains outside. That is a way of putting the thesis that space and time are transcendentally ideal.

We can conceive that "something else", which Kant still conceives as given from outside to our apperceptive spontaneity, as the matter of our formal intuitions. Kant conceives that matter as having its own form, prior to the unity that informs the formal intuitions. It is because the pure matter

14. It should be clear that this objection cannot be dismissed as depending on an unwarranted "two-worlds" reading of Kant on appearances and things in themselves. I have formulated the objection in a way that does not contradict Kant's identification of "things as objects of experience" with "those same things as things in themselves" (Bxxvii). That identification does nothing to dislodge the fact that Kant makes the spatial and temporal organization of things as objects of experience into a mere reflection of a fact about us.

of our outer sensibility is as it is, reflecting the formal character of our outer sensibility, that the result of unifying that matter into an intuition is a pure intuition of *space*, and similarly with our inner sensibility and the pure intuition of time.

What goes wrong in Kant's attempt at the equipoise is that the requirements that derive from the form of our sensibility are only partly embraced within the scope of the kind of unity effected by apperceptive spontaneity. The obvious conclusion is that nothing that enters into our ability to relate cognitively to objects must be left out. The insight that is fundamental to critical philosophy is that conditions for the possibility of our knowing things are not derived from independent conditions on things themselves. If we are to accommodate that insight while conceiving the conditions in such a way that they are genuinely recognizable as conditions of our knowing things, we need to bring the conditions entirely inside the sphere of free intellectual activity.[15]

From this viewpoint, we can see how Kant deserves the praise he receives from Hegel—for instance, in the passage I quoted from the *Science of Logic*—for his reaching towards an idealism balanced between subjective and objective. That is what animates his attempt to put the objective unity of self-consciousness at the centre of his picture. But he is to be blamed—though no doubt not as severely as Hegel does—for not realizing that he cannot have what he aims at without bringing everything relevant to our ability to direct our minds at objects within the scope of the unity of spontaneous self-consciousness.

15. Henry Allison usefully characterizes transcendental idealism in terms of a distinction between "conditions of the possibility of knowledge of things" and "conditions of the possibility of the things themselves". See *Kant's Transcendental Idealism*, p. 13. Transcendental, or pre-critical, realism rejects the distinction by seeing conditions of the possibility of knowledge as derivative from autonomous conditions of the possibility of things. Allison's claim is that if we try to reject the distinction while retaining the basic critical thought that knowledge cannot be thus understood in terms of a pure passivity, we inevitably fall into a subjectivistic phenomenalism. But this reflects Allison's assuming that any attempt to reject the distinction while remaining critical could only be a symmetrical counterpart to transcendental realism, taking "subjective" conditions to be autonomous as such where transcendental realism takes "objective" conditions to be autonomous as such. What goes missing is the Hegelian alternative, which is inspired by how Kant wants to think of the requirements of the understanding: that the relevant conditions are inseparably both conditions on thought and conditions on objects, not primarily either the one or the other. See my remarks about Allison in *Mind and World*, p. 43, n. 18.

I hope the way I have let this conception emerge from considering Kant has done something towards making it conceivable that we need that Hegelian conception if we are to preserve Kant's critical insight. But if the idea is to be credible, it is crucial to stress that what I am criticizing Kant for leaving outside the scope of the unity of apperception is only what I have suggested we can conceive as the matter of our formal intuitions. The problem is not with Kant's conception of empirical intuitions. The problem arises because he frames that conception within the claim that space and time are transcendentally ideal. A Kantian conception of empirical intuitions—intelligibly of objects by virtue of exemplifying unities of the kind characteristic of judgment—almost succeeds in showing how the very idea of objective purport can be understood in terms of free intellectual activity. (This is easier to see if we correct what I described as a tendency on Kant's part to overstate the extent of spontaneous *activity*.) What spoils things is that when we widen the picture to take in transcendental idealism, it turns out that the "objects" that we have contrived to see empirical intuitions as immediately of, thanks to the fact that the intuitions have a kind of unity that must be understood in terms of apperceptive spontaneity, are after all, in respect of their spatiality and temporality, mere reflections of another aspect of our subjectivity, one that is independent of apperceptive spontaneity. If we can contrive not to have transcendental idealism framing the picture, we are not subject to this disappointment. Discarding the frame is just what we need in order to arrive, at least from this angle, at a Hegelian radicalization of Kant. In the resulting picture, the objects of empirical intuitions are both genuinely objective and such that the very idea of our getting them in view requires an appeal to apperceptive spontaneity.

There is a temptation to accuse Hegel of reconstruing objective reality as a precipitate of utterly unconstrained movements of the mind, and to suppose that seeing the matter of our pure intuitions as external to the spontaneity of the understanding immunizes Kant against any such downplaying of the world's independence. (See, e.g., Michael Friedman, "Exorcising the Philosophical Tradition", especially at pp. 439–44.) But this is exactly the reverse of the truth. Kant frames his attempt to vindicate objective validity for the categories within transcendental idealism about space and time. And so far from ensuring a common-sense realism about objective reality, that is just what ensures that it is not really objective validity that he contrives to establish for the categories. The way to protect the common-sense conception of empirically accessible reality as independent of us, while retaining the critical insight, is precisely to see our way to discarding that frame.

This is important for a feature of Hegel's relation to Kant that I have not so far mentioned: his rejection of the sharp boundary between understanding and reason. In Kant understanding is conditioned by sensibility, whereas reason is unconditioned. Now the conditionedness in question is the very thing that spoils Kant's attempt at a non-subjective idealism. What it means to say, in this context, that understanding is conditioned by sensibility is precisely that the scope of apperceptive spontaneity does not include the matter that is united into our formal intuitions of space and time. The point is not about the way empirical thinking is beholden to the independent reality disclosed in experience. That is not, just as such, an infringement on the freedom of apperception. It constitutes what we might conceive, rather, as the medium in which that freedom is exercised. Hegelian talk of the pursuit of knowledge as the unconditioned activity of reason rejects the frame in which Kant puts his attempt at such a conception, not the conception itself. Such Hegelian talk does not manifest "a tendency to distance rational thought from sensible experience and to minimize the empiricist elements in Kant's own conception".[16]

6. I have followed Pippin in considering the B Deduction, and in particular its second part, as a Kantian inspiration for Hegel. But I have diverged from some aspects of Pippin's treatment. I hope saying something about this will sharpen the picture. I shall consider two main issues.

First, Pippin does not isolate the specific reason why the Deduction fails—the fact that for Kant the matter that is united into our formal intuitions cannot be embraced within the scope of apperceptive spontaneity. By the same token, he does not pinpoint how the Deduction almost succeeds.

He rightly singles out the attempt to extend the unity of apperception into the sphere of the Aesthetic as Kant's closest approach to a Hegelian po-

---

16. Friedman, "Exorcising the Philosophical Tradition", p. 440. Of course I do not deny that rejecting the frame, and hence making room to see the pursuit of knowledge as the unconditioned activity of reason, has substantial consequences for Kant's outlook. Notably, objective validity for "ideal" requirements can spread into the terrain of the Transcendental Dialectic of the first *Critique*. Requirements that Kant can see only as regulative—as meeting subjective needs of ours rather than characterizing objective reality itself—can be seen as objectively valid. See Pippin, *Hegel's Idealism*, p. 68.

sition. But he does not make the crucial point that the extension can embrace only the unity that constitutes the form of our pure intuitions. Rather, he considers the extension, without specifying its limits, as a proto-Hegelian *lapse* on Kant's part from his more characteristic position.[17] And he sees the results of this supposed lapse, taken all together, as if they exemplified an idealism that ought to be, just as such, congenial to Hegel. Thus, when he defends the claim that the tendency of the Deduction is idealistic, what he points to is the fact that, according to Kant's own claims for it, the Deduction shows objective validity for the categories only in relation to objects of human experience.[18]

But in the first place, the extension of apperceptive unity to include the unity of our pure intuitions is not a lapse. It is, as Kant sees, crucial to such success as the Deduction can claim. It is not inconsistent with the Aesthetic. At most it corrects a misleading impression that could have been given by the fact that Kant starts with the Aesthetic. (He has to start somewhere.)

And, in the second place, the idealism involved in claiming objective validity for the categories only in relation to objects of human experience is the idealism of the whole package. As I have urged, it degenerates into subjective idealism because of the transcendental idealism about the matter of our formal intuitions that persists even when Kant corrects the impression that their unity is independent of apperception. This is exactly not an idealism Hegel would applaud. To find the germ of a Hegelian idealism in the Deduction, we have to note, as Pippin does not, the limits of Kant's extension of apperception into the territory of the Aesthetic. That is what opens up the prospect of a proper idealism, achievable by overcoming those limits.

Hegel claims, in "Glauben und Wissen", that the "inner unity" of the activity of the transcendental imagination, for Kant, "is no other than the unity of the intellect [*Verstand*] itself" (*Faith and Knowledge*, p. 89). Pippin

17. See the passage at *Hegel's Idealism*, p. 30, which I discussed in earlier notes. Compare p. 37: "If . . . Hegel is right that Kant's own case for the apperceptive condition of any possible experience undercuts his strict separation between concept and intuition, ..."

18. See *Hegel's Idealism*, p. 32; and (particularly disquieting) p. 267, n. 23, where Pippin argues that the Deduction's reliance on pure intuitions "necessarily idealizes the argument". The thrust of that note is that the Deduction involves a commitment to *transcendental* idealism. But if I am right, that is exactly why it goes wrong in Hegel's view, not a way of identifying the feature of it that will have struck Hegel as pointing in the right direction.

says this "would provoke a vigorous denial by Kant". In spite of the B Deduction passage Hegel approves of, Pippin says, "the predominant Kantian position is clearly that the intellect *cannot* produce unity within experience 'on its own,' that the form and matter of intuition are required" (*Hegel's Idealism*, p. 77). This belongs with Pippin's suggestion that the near success of the Deduction depends on a lapse from Kant's basic thinking, in a Hegelian direction. But as I have insisted, the extension of apperceptive unity to the unity of the pure intuitions is quite consistent with Kant's basic thinking. And, given how transcendental imagination figures in the second part of the B Deduction (in a way that culminates in the claim that the unity of the formal intuitions of space and time is a case of the apperceptive unity that characterizes intuitions in general), Hegel's remark, so far from being something Kant would deny, is a close paraphrase of Kant's own programme for the second part of the Deduction—to show that the unity of "the mode in which empirical intuition is given in sensibility" (which he goes on to spell out in terms of the activity of the transcendental imagination) "is no other than that which the category . . . prescribes to the manifold of a given intuition in general" (B144–5). Of course matter is required for any instance of such a unity, but Kant's hopeful thought is that the unity belongs to form—including the unity of the formal intuitions of space and time, which is "produced" by transcendental imagination. This is the very reason the Deduction comes as close as it does to succeeding. Here Hegel reads Kant more perceptively than Pippin does.

Pippin's unfortunate focus on the whole package, instead of isolating transcendental idealism as the ingredient that spoils it, is reflected in his describing the "transcendental skepticism" to which Kant is vulnerable and which Hegel must avoid in such terms as this (*Hegel's Idealism*, p. 277, n.1): "since the phenomenal world was 'conditioned' by our conceptual scheme, had we a different scheme, there would be a different (phenomenal) world; hence the thing-in-itself problem." But Kant's idealism degenerates into subjective idealism not because of relativity to "our conceptual scheme" but because it contains a subjective idealism about spatiality and temporality, a subjective idealism that reflects their being conceived precisely as external to apperceptive unity, and so external to anything one could call a "conceptual scheme".

At B145 Kant calls the need for categorial unity "a peculiarity of our understanding". Pippin cites this (*Hegel's Idealism*, p. 33) as if it puts the requirements of the understanding on a level in Kant's picture with those that derive from the way our sensibility is formed. But the context makes it clear that Kant means a peculiarity of our understanding *qua* discursive, finite, dependent on sensibility—not *qua*, specifically, human.

The point here can perhaps be expressed by means of an admittedly difficult counterfactual: by Hegelian lights, Kant's Deduction would have worked if Kant had not attributed brute-fact externality to the spatial and temporal form of our sensibility. In that case, the Deduction would have succeeded in showing how what first comes into view in the guise of the capacity of a finite understanding can be reconceived as the unlimited freedom of reason.

7. I can work into my second divergence from Pippin by reverting to the suggestion that Kant's Deduction points towards a proper idealism, which would be achieved by overcoming the limits in Kant's extension of apperceptive spontaneity into the territory of the Aesthetic. In these terms, the needed alteration to Kant is in one way quite simple, though of course very far-reaching. I do not believe Pippin's conception of Hegel's commitments, as inheritor of a Kantian legacy, fits well into this picture.

Pippin notes that a Hegelian understanding of the objectivity of conceptual determinations, arrived at through appreciating how Kant's approach is nearly but not quite successful, can have no place for an analogue to Kant's Schematism or the second part of the B Deduction (*Hegel's Idealism*, p. 38). But he takes it that the descendant of Kantian categories, in this new environment, is Hegelian Notions (plural), which stand to ordinary empirical concepts in a descendant of the relation in which Kantian categories stand to ordinary empirical concepts (see *Hegel's Idealism*, p. 258, and p. 305, n.6). This belongs with the fact that he repeatedly glosses Hegelian talk of the self-determination of the Notion in terms of a development undetermined by experience (see pp. 93, 100, 145, 146, 250). This strand in Pippin's reading culminates in the suggestion that, even after the *Logic*, Hegel has an "unresolved problem" of specifying the distinction between Notions and ordinary concepts: "So many . . . concepts are clearly as they are because the world is as it is, and cannot possibly be considered categorial results of thought's pure self-determination, that Hegel's project cries out for a more explicit, clear-cut account of when and why we should regard our fundamental ways of taking things to be 'due' wholly to us, in the relevant Hegelian sense."[19] And it belongs with this that according to Pippin Hegel has a "problem of 'returning' to the empirical world", a reappearance of "Kant's infamous *Übergang* problem" (*Hegel's Idealism*, p. 259).

But if we see Hegel's idealism as the result of changing Kant's outlook only as required in order to overcome the limits in his extension of the scope of apperceptive spontaneity, this suggestion of undischarged obligations looks unwarranted.

The picture is rather on these lines. "The Notion" (singular) is conceptuality as such, properly understood. Conceptuality as such is categorial, in a more or less Kantian sense that we can gloss in terms of apperceptive spontaneity. Conceptual capacities are essentially such as to be exercised in judgment. Hegelian talk of "the Notion" does not allude to special non-empirical concepts about which an issue would arise about how they relate to ordinary empirical concepts. That is just what goes wrong in Kant's treatment of the idea of the categorial; it is because Kant sees things like this that he needs to appeal to something external to apperception in the second part of the B Deduction and the Schematism.[20]

Talk of "the free movement of the Notion" fits, for instance, the evolution of empirical inquiry. (This is the right instance to begin with if we approach Hegelian thinking from Kant's Deduction.) And empirical inquiry is guided by experience. Kant already almost incorporates experience, as a guide for empirical inquiry, within the freedom of apperceptive spontaneity. As I suggested earlier, if he had not treated the spatial and temporal form of our sensibility as a brute-fact externality, he could have depicted the independent layout of the world we experience as the medium within which the freedom of apperceptive spontaneity is exercised. With the shift that takes us from Kant to Hegel, we can say that the spatiality

---

19. *Hegel's Idealism*, p. 258. Pippin suggests that a "table of Notions" (transcendentally argued for, rather than just borrowed from the existing state of logic, as Hegel complains Kant's "table of categories" is) would meet this need.

20. At p. 211 of *Hegel's Idealism*, Pippin writes, in connection with Book II of the *Logic*, of "a conflation of an argument for the necessity of 'mediation' in general (conceptual activity, *überhaupt*) with a case for *essential* mediation, the determinate categorial conditions required for there to be determinate 'thought objects'". On the interpretation I am urging, this is not a conflation but a way of making the needed alteration to Kant. The idea that there are two separate topics here is a vestige of the Kantian conception of the categorial.

and temporality of our experience are no more an infringement on the freedom of apperception than are the specifics of the spatial and temporal layout of the world as we experience it, in the conception Kant almost manages. And now the conception Kant almost manages is genuinely available to us.[21]

Here again, Hegelian rhetoric can give the impression that he is representing reality as a precipitate of wholly unconstrained movements of the mind. I have tried to discourage that impression with the image of a medium within which freedom is exercised. What figures in Kant as the receptivity of sensibility does not disappear from the scene, but is reconceived as a "moment" in the free self-determination of reason.[22] If we see things like this, there should not seem to be an *Übergang* problem. There should not seem to be a need to "return" from the standpoint of Absolute Knowledge to the empirical world. The standpoint of Absolute Knowledge is a standpoint at which we understand that the pursuit of objectivity is the free unfolding of the Notion. It is not a standpoint at which we have somehow removed ourselves from the empirical world. If the case of the pursuit of objectivity that we are considering is empirical inquiry, we are

21. At p. 105 of *Hegel's Idealism*, Pippin writes, in connection with the *Phenomenology*: "Clearly, [Hegel] cannot be talking about *any* concept used in knowledge claims when he refers to the necessary inherence of the Notion in consciousness. The enterprise of the *PhG* cannot be to show that our doubts about the objectivity of any concept can be overcome." This last claim is obviously right. But it does not follow that talk of the Notion cannot be talk of conceptuality as such. Doubts about the objectivity of this or that concept are addressed within what consciousness, in the *Phenomenology*, is taught to conceive as the free unfolding of the Notion. The business of the *Phenomenology* is to educate consciousness into conceiving the pursuit of objectivity in those terms, not to anticipate the results of the activity that we are to conceive in those terms. (Except perhaps in the second-level application to itself that I consider later.)

22. Pippin gives expression to this conception in at least two places. At p. 68, he describes the Hegelian rethinking of Kant's distinction between reason and understanding by saying: ". . . reason's 'self-legislation,' as Kant called it, can be viewed as constitutive of the possibility of objects if . . . it can be shown that what Kant thought was an independent intuitive condition was itself a moment of Reason's self-determination." Again, at p. 87 he speaks of "Hegel's assertion that receptivity must be considered as somehow a moment in a subject's progressive self-understanding". These passages strike me as fundamentally right. I do not see how Pippin squares them with the idea that the unfolding of the Notion is not guided by experience. That idea looks like a vestige of the Kantian reflective dualism that spoils the Transcendental Deduction.

already engaged with the empirical world in enjoying Absolute Knowledge.[23]

It is important to be clear—as perhaps Hegel himself is not—that experience as I am speaking of it here, with guidedness by experience conceived as a "moment" in the free unfolding of the Notion in empirical inquiry, is not experience as it figures in the *Phenomenology*. There we have a series of attempted conceptions of mindedness, the progression through which is supposed to reveal finally that what they are attempted conceptions of is properly conceived as the free movement of the Notion. "Experience" is a label for what befalls these attempted conceptions, successively found unacceptable by their own lights in a way that propels "consciousness", the recipient of the *Phenomenology's* education, into improvements. If this is a case of the free movement of the Notion, it is at a second level: the free movement of the Notion of the Notion. The *Phenomenology* educates "consciousness" into seeing its *ordinary* intellectual activity (theoretical and practical) as the free movement of the Notion, by chronicling a series of, as we might put it, efforts on the part of the Notion to come to explicitness, as that whose free movement ordinary intellectual activity is. Perhaps at the second level we can see this philosophical journey as itself a case of the pursuit of objectivity—objectivity about the pursuit of objectivity—and so apply its results to itself. But it is a good idea to avoid conflating the levels.[24]

---

23. At p. 246 of *Hegel's Idealism*, Pippin suggests that "self-consciousness about the spontaneity of Notional determination . . . appears to be the *extent* of [Hegel's] resolution". I think that is exactly right. What I am objecting to is Pippin's thought that such a "resolution" leaves work to be done, on the lines of coming up with a "table of Notions".

I say there *should* not seem to be an *Übergang* problem, or a problem of returning to the empirical world, because it is not clear that Hegel gets his own drift clear enough to be definitely immune to such problems. But my claim is that if we see his enterprise in the light I am recommending, he need have no such problems.

24. "Experience" reveals each of the successive conceptions, short of Absolute Knowledge, as inadequate by its own standards. Pippin registers, at p. 106 of *Hegel's Idealism*, the essential point here, that each of these efforts at conceptions of objectivity embodies its own criterion of objectivity. This makes mysterious, at least to me, his procedure on the next page (one of the places where he gets Notions, in the plural, into the picture), where he argues that "the question of the adequacy of any potential Notion . . . can only be understood relative to other possible Notions". As far as I can see, the question of adequacy always arises, in the experience of "consciousness" at a given stage, from within a candidate conception of objectivity, which emerges as inadequate in the light of *its own* criterion. There is

8. As I said, this angle on Hegelian thinking points to a way of arriving at it that is in one sense very simple: just eliminate the externality that vitiates Kant's Deduction. Of course, as the lengths I have needed to go to indicate, such a move cannot be executed in as short a space as it takes to describe it. In any case, for whatever reasons, Hegel does not give a presentation that starts from Kant. But there is reason to think a route from Kant's Deduction is at least one course Hegel's thinking takes; here I follow Pippin, even if I dissent from him over the details of the route. This recommends keeping in mind the "simple" route to a Hegelian position as we try to understand the more complex progressions Hegel himself offers.[25]

---

no need for this invocation of relativity to other conceptions of objectivity. Pippin goes on (p. 107): "Such a Notion is necessary for there to be experience; there *is* experience, and the question of legitimacy thus can only arise relative to other possible Notions." But this use of "experience" (meaning experience of ordinary objects) is what I am urging is foreign to the *Phenomenology*. There is no need to *assume* that there is the experience that is relevant to the *Phenomenology*. It happens in the course of philosophical reflection.

25. The destination of the "simple" route looks much like what I set out in my *Mind and World* (as improved and corrected by Essays 1, 2, and 3 above). Wolfgang Carl suggested (in conversation) that what I presented in *Mind and World* was what a Strawsonian reading of Kant's Transcendental Deduction should have looked like, whereas what Strawson offers as a reading of the Deduction is a better fit, in aim and orientation, to the Refutation of Idealism. (See Strawson, *The Bounds of Sense*.) I had already suggested (*Mind and World*, p. 111) that Strawson's Kant, who was my Kant in that work, was closer to Hegel than Kant.

In "Some Pragmatist Themes in Hegel's Idealism: Negotiation and Administration in Hegel's Account of the Structure and Content of Conceptual Norms", Brandom gives a very different picture of Hegelian thinking. He cites the passage from the *Science of Logic* that I began with, and claims to be following Pippin's lead as I have. But Brandom's own thinking is remote from Kant's in just the respects that the "simple" route exploits. He undertakes to recast Kant's thinking about spontaneity and receptivity in a way that omits the very idea of intuitions, conceived as episodes in sensory consciousness that are directly of objects. See *Making It Explicit*, pp. 712–3, n. 10, and see chapter 4 for Brandom's attempt to do without intuitions. Unsurprisingly, then, Brandom's reading of Hegel does not make contact with the details of what happens in the B Deduction. In spite of Brandom's claim to take off from Pippin, he does not follow the methodological recommendation I state in the text.

Self-Determining Subjectivity and External Constraint

1. A stress on self-determining subjectivity is characteristic of German ideal-ism in general. Hegel takes this theme to an extreme with his talk of absolute knowing as the free self-realization of the Concept. Now my title is meant to point to an obvious question that such language raises. If a con-ception expressible in such terms is to fit subjective engagement with objec-tive reality, the free self-realization of the Concept had better itself embody a responsiveness to constraints that are in some sense external. Rather than disappearing from the scene, the external constraint that figures in a more ordinary conception of objectivity must be incorporated within what we are supposed to be shown how to conceive as self-determination. I am going to consider a specific exemplification of this thought, which I shall put in place by considering some features of the philosophy of Wilfrid Sellars.

2. By way of an intuitive gloss on the theme of subjective self-determination, we might speak of rejecting dogmatism, or acquiescence in anything merely given, in respect of the question what is properly author-itative in thinking. It is incumbent on thought to be responsive to reasons recognized as such, and nothing can count as a reason for a thinking subject unless its authority as a reason can be freely acknowledged by the subject.

Now this talk of refusing to acquiesce in the merely given should remind at least some people of Sellars's assault on what he calls "the Myth of the Given". And indeed at the beginning of his classic work "Empiricism and the Philosophy of Mind", Sellars explicitly aligns himself with Hegel, whom I have represented as taking the idealistic insistence on self-determination to an extreme. Sellars implies that his own attack on "the framework of givenness" corresponds to moves on the part of Hegel, "that great foe of 'immediacy'" (§1). Later Sellars imagines an interlocutor describing Sellars's reflections as "incipient *Méditations hégéliennes*" (§20).[1] It is clear that Sellars intends his campaign against the Myth of the Given to be understood as Hegelian, at least in spirit.

Sellars stresses how much comes within the scope of the Myth of the Given. He writes: "Many things have been said to be 'given': sense contents, material objects, universals, propositions, real connections, first principles, even givenness itself" (§1). But the body of "Empiricism and the Philosophy of Mind" is devoted to what Sellars casts as "a first step in a general critique of the entire framework of givenness" (ibid.), an attack on a specifically empiricistic version of the framework. One might expect at least a rough match with the first movement of Hegel's *Phenomenology*, and Sellars's stress on the partial character of his "first step" serves, in effect, to acknowledge how much more there is to Hegel's attack on immediacy than unmasking its pretensions in an account of empirical knowledge. Nevertheless, reflection about the temptation to appeal to givenness in connection with acquiring knowledge through experience is a good context in which to begin to think through the prospects for combining an idealistic affirmation of self-determination with making room for an idea of external constraint.

Any empiricism traces the credentials of empirical knowledge to experience. In saying that, I am not merely rehearsing a truism about the very idea of empirical knowledge; witness the idea, common to Donald Davidson (see "On the Very Idea of a Conceptual Scheme" and "A Coherence Theory of Truth and Knowledge") and Robert Brandom (see chapter 4 of *Making It Explicit*), that if there is anything that deserves to be called "experience", it figures not in the credentials of empirical knowledge but at most in its causation. That is a rejection of empiricism altogether. Sellars, by contrast, does not object to the very idea that the credentials of empirical knowledge are provided by experience. What he criticizes is a particular way of spelling out that idea—an empiricism entangled in "the framework of givenness", which he calls "traditional empiricism" (§38). According to traditional empiricism, experience yields a foundational level of knowledge, available to us in perception through the operation of capacities that we have at birth or develop in ordinary biological maturation, and in no way dependent on acculturation or acquired knowledge. In experience, on this picture, objective reality impresses itself on subjects immediately, to use the Hegelian term Sellars

---

1. I have improved Sellars's French.

invokes. Against this, Sellars urges that even the most basic perceptual knowledge is acquired in actualizations of conceptual capacities, and conceptual capacities are not at our disposal by virtue of mere biology, but accrue to us along with mastery of a language, which must embody a familiarity with rational linkages between one concept and another. These linkages include, crucially, materially sound inferential connections, and command of such connections is inseparable from having substantial knowledge of the world.

To elaborate this thought, Sellars focuses on what might seem the best case for the outlook he opposes—concepts that might seem suited to figure in the basic empirical judgments that, in the traditional empiricist picture, would be directly grounded in the supposedly immediate getting of the perceptual given. Consider, for instance, concepts of colours. Sellars argues that the very possession even of such concepts, and hence their availability to figure in acquiring empirical knowledge that is in one sense fundamental, depends on worldly knowledge. He exemplifies this by claiming that to have concepts of colours one must know what conditions are suitable for telling what colours things have by looking at them (§18). But that does not exhaust the point Sellars is making; the very idea of colours, as even apparent properties of things, makes sense only in the context of a rich battery of knowledge about how visible things impinge on perceiving subjects. So even in what might seem the best case for proponents of the given, Sellars rejects the immediacy that traditional empiricism attributes to the knowledge yielded by perception, and replaces it with a mediation by acquired conceptual capacities and worldly knowledge, knowledge that must be already in place for the perceptual knowledge that is in one sense fundamental to be so much as available to us.

3. It can be tempting to cast the empiricistic version of the Myth of the Given that is Sellars's primary target as an interpretation of the familiar Kantian duality of understanding and sensibility, spontaneity and receptivity. In this interpretation, sensory receptivity yields immediately given cognitions. Conceptual capacities, which belong to the spontaneous understanding, come into play only subsequently, in basic empirical judgments, conceived as directly warranted by those immediately given cognitions and in turn warranting the further reaches of a world view. And now it is a way of putting Sellars's point to say that this picture of how sensibility and understanding cooperate is hopeless. The supposed immediately given cognitions could not stand in the supposed warranting relations, in the first

instance to basic empirical judgments and thereby to an entire world view. When we conceive the operations of sensory receptivity as prior to and independent of any involvement of conceptual capacities, we debar them from intelligibly standing in rational relations to cases of conceptual activity. We ensure that they could at best be triggers or promptings to bits of conceptual activity, not justifications for them. In thus excluding the supposed immediate gettings of the given from rational relatedness to a world view, we in fact make it impossible to understand them as *cognitions* at all.

If one cannot see room for any other interpretation of the Kantian duality, one will suppose that the very idea of a cooperation between the spontaneity of the understanding and the receptivity of sensibility, the core idea in Kant's conception of empirical knowledge, is entangled in what Sellars calls "the framework of givenness". But just as Sellars's target can be expressed in those Kantian terms, so the thinking that he sets in opposition to it can be read as offering a different interpretation of the Kantian duality.

Sellars's key move here is to put forward a conception of experiences as "so to speak, making" claims, or "containing" them (§16). These wordings are self-consciously metaphorical, and Sellars notes that he incurs an obligation by offering them; this "verbal currency" needs to be put "on the gold standard" (§16). He discharges the obligation by offering a rational reconstruction of concepts of what he calls "thoughts"—that is, episodes that are like speech acts in that they need to be described in terms of propositional content, but unlike speech acts in being non-overt, or "inner". "Thoughts", so specified, include experiences conceived as "containing" claims, and Sellars makes it clear that his eye is still on experiences when he gives his rational reconstruction (see the retrospective remarks at §60). His aim is not to reject empiricism altogether, but to show the possibility of a non-traditional empiricism, an empiricism purged of the "framework of givenness". In Sellars's rational reconstruction, "thoughts", including experiences, figure in the first instance as posits in a theory constructed to explain overt behaviour, both linguistic and non-linguistic.[2] As is usual with posits, these posits come with a model, which enters essentially into how we are to understand the concepts of the posited items. The model in the case of "thoughts" is

---

2. In the first instance only, because the story is enriched, at the second stage, to account for the fact that a subject's own thoughts are known to her directly, not by way of arriving at a theoretical explanation for her own behaviour. See §59. But the details do not matter for my present purposes.

speech acts. So, somewhat as the particles that are posited to explain the behaviour of gases under pressure are modelled on, say, tiny bouncing balls, the posited non-overt propositional episodes are modelled on episodes in which propositional content is overt, for instance claims literally so called (§§56–9). That goes for experiences in particular. What Sellars does, then, is not exactly to cash out the metaphorical talk of experiences as "containing" propositional claims, but rather to tell us something about what kind of extended use of language is in question in such talk. Expressed claims are the model we need to exploit in grasping the concept of experiences.

Why is this move helpful? Why is it helpful to suggest that episodes in which propositional content is present but not expressed—experiences in particular—should be modelled on speech acts, in which propositional content is made explicit? Here it is illuminating to see Sellars's thought, at least as it applies to experiences, as an analogue to a thought of Kant's.

In the so-called Metaphysical Deduction of the Categories, the section of the first *Critique* called "The Clue to the Discovery of All Pure Concepts of the Understanding", Kant writes (A79/B104–5): "The same function which gives unity to the various representations *in a judgment* also gives unity to the mere synthesis of various representations *in an intuition*; and this unity, in its most general expression, we entitle the pure concept of the understanding." Kant is here claiming, in effect, that intuitions—cases of sensory consciousness of objects—have logical structures, and they are the same as logical structures possessed by judgments. That is why an inventory of the logical structures possessed by judgments can be a clue, a guiding thread, in arriving at an enumeration of the categories—the pure concepts of the understanding—in their guise as the logical structures of intuitions. And the remark yields a key to how, in the Transcendental Deduction, Kant undertakes to vindicate the "objective validity" of the categories. The idea is to display the categories as unities that can account for the objective purport of both empirical judgments and intuitions.

Kant's thought, then, is that we can make sense of how intuitions present objects to us by seeing intuitions as possessing logical structures. Now when we formulate the thought at that level of abstractness, it is obvious that it does not need the specific inventory of logical forms that Kant works with. Moreover, Kant's formulation envisages logic as enumerating forms of judgments rather than statements, and that frame, too, is obviously inessential. Kant's "clue" is that the kinds of unity in virtue of which multiple actualizations of representational capacities in sensory consciousness cohere into a single intuition, presenting objective reality to a subject, are the same as the kinds of unity in virtue of which multiple actualizations of representational capacities in discursive thinking cohere into a single judgment, in which a subject commits itself as to how things stand in objective reality. Sellars's play with the idea that speech acts can serve as a model for "thoughts", and in particular for experiences, expresses a corresponding idea. Sellars is inviting us to take it that the kinds of unity in virtue of which actualizations of representational capacities in sensory consciousness cohere into single experiences—and in virtue of which experiences at least purport to, and in the best case actually do, involve objective reality making itself available to us—are the same as the kinds of unity in virtue of which multiple meaningful uses of words cohere into single claims, in which subjects express commitments about how things stand in objective reality.

That is to say that when Sellars says experiences contain claims, he is putting forward a conception of experiences that is at least closely akin to Kant's conception of intuitions, as it is elaborated in the Analytic of the first *Critique*, and especially in the Transcendental Deduction. In "Empiricism and the Philosophy of Mind", Sellars does not line up his own thinking about experience with Kant's. But the Kantian character of his thought becomes explicit in Sellars's Kant book, *Science and Metaphysics: Variations on Kantian Themes*, which he describes (p. viii) as a sequel to "Empiricism and the Philosophy of Mind". In the Kant book Sellars, among much else, reframes his fundamental moves from "Empiricism and the Philosophy of Mind" by way of a reading of Kant's first *Critique*. He rightly insists that, at least by the time we get to the "clue" and the Transcendental Deduction, it is clear that what Kant is considering under the label "intuitions" is not those supposed immediate givens that figure in the empiricistic version of "the framework of givenness"—operations of sensory receptivity conceived as prior to and independent of any involvement of the understanding—but episodes of sensory receptivity already structured by the understanding. Intuitions as they figure in the Transcendental Deduction are, *qua* intuitions, cases of sensory receptivity in operation, but Kant's "clue" is that they are unified by kinds of unity that also unify judgments. For idiosyncratic reasons that we need not go into here, Sellars thinks the representational capacities that are actualized with the relevant kinds of unity in the most primitive Kantian intuitions are only proto-conceptual, not yet fully conceptual—not yet susceptible of being exercised in judgments (*Science and Metaphysics*, pp. 4–7). But he distances himself from this feature of the view he finds in Kant. In Sellars's own thinking, which he now explicitly presents as Kantian in inspiration, experiences are actualizations in sensory consciousness of capacities that are conceptual, cohering into unified experiences by way of unities of the kind that constitute the singleness of judgments, which are, equivalently, unities of the kind that constitute the singleness of claims.

So we can understand Sellars's image, in which experiences make claims or contain propositions, as a variant on Kant's conception of intuitions as categorially unified.

4. In Kant's account of intuitions—which I am claiming corresponds to Sellars's conception of experiences—the note of self-determination is sounded when Kant invokes the spontaneity of the understanding. We can consider two glosses on this connection of the understanding with an idea of freedom. First, the paradigmatic mode of actualization of conceptual capacities, in the relevant sense, is in judging, which is freely responsible cognitive activity, making up one's mind. Second, and more abstractly, concepts constitute norms for cognitive activity, and the core of the self-determination idea is that the authority of any norms at all, whatever activity they regulate, must be capable of free acknowledgment by the subjects who engage in the activity.

Kant himself sometimes seems to put an inappropriate weight on the first of those two glosses. He talks as if instances of the kind of unity in virtue of which intuitions are intelligibly of objects are like instances of the kind of unity in virtue of which judging is committing oneself as to how things are in that in both cases the unity is actively effected by a subject. For instance, in the Transcendental Deduction he says that any combination of a manifold, any representation of something as a complex unity, "be we conscious of it or not, . . . is an act of the understanding" (B130). That is to suggest that the unity exemplified by an intuition is brought about by an exercise of freedom, though one that we may not be conscious of.

Now the idea that we sometimes exercise freedom without being conscious of it is at best awkward. And in any case, the note of voluntary action does not fit well with the idea that intuitions are operations of the *receptivity* of sensory consciousness. It is really not up to us what we perceive, except in ways that are irrelevant to what Kant's words suggest. No doubt we can control our perceptual intake, for instance by turning our heads, but that is not exercising a freedom to unify "representations" into single intuitions.

Indeed, we had better acknowledge that, apart from such irrelevancies, what we perceive is not up to us. That seems to be required if we are to be able to see experience as taking in objective reality, and hence if we are to be able to satisfy an intelligible motivation for believing in the immediacies that are supposed to ground knowledge in traditional empiricism, even while we avoid the framework of givenness by insisting on conceptual mediation. It is a mistake to think Kant's "clue" implies that the unity of an intuition is itself brought about by free cognitive activity. Judging, one of the exemplifiers of the sorts of unity the "clue" concerns, is free cognitive activity, but enjoying intuitions, the other field for those sorts of unity, is not. The point is just that the sorts of unity that unite intuitions are the same as the sorts of unity that unite judgments. It must be intelligible that the representational capacities that are involuntarily drawn into operation in intuitions are susceptible of joint actualization with that kind of unity, and that is secured by their being capacities that can also be freely exercised in judging. This suffices to put in place the kinship Kant insists on between the objective purport of intuitions and the objective purport of judgments. He does not need to suggest that the forming of intuitions is itself an exercise of freedom, let alone one that takes place behind our backs.

This shifts the weight to the second of those two glosses on the invocation of freedom. In the thick of experience, the conceptual capacities we currently have are drawn into operation in a way that is not up to us. But for them to be intelligibly conceptual capacities in the relevant sense, capacities that belong to the spontaneity of the understanding, it must be that in having them drawn into operation we find ourselves answerable to the authority of norms for thought that constitute the content of the capacities. And this subjection to authority comes within the scope of the self-determination idea. So, though our experience at any time is determined, outside our control, by concepts we find ourselves with at the time, we have a responsibility over time to ensure that our acquiescence in the concepts we find ourselves with is not a matter of subjecting ourselves to an alien authority, exercised by dogma or tradition. I shall come back to some of the issues this raises at the end of this essay.

5. Exploiting Sellars and Kant, I have put in place the outline of a picture that promises to combine finding a place even in empirical cognition for the self-determining rationality of the cognitive subject—the spontaneity of the understanding—with acknowledging a sense in which empirical cognition

is constrained by objects themselves, presenting themselves to consciousness in intuition. At an abstract level, there is already something discernibly
Hegelian about such a picture, just to the extent that it can be described in
those terms. To move to something perhaps more specifically Hegelian, I
want now to take issue with a detail in Sellars's version of the picture that I
have so far omitted. The problem I want to bring out in this region of Sellars's thinking comes to a head in the fact that Sellars makes nothing of a
Kantian move that gives Hegel an opening. This region of Kant's thinking is
instructive about the Kant–Hegel relation anyway, independently of the
connection with Sellars, but Sellars's take on Kant is a good way into the
area.

In Sellars's reading, sensibility figures in two separable ways in an authentically Kantian account of empirical cognition. Sellars thinks Kant is
not as clear about this as he should have been. But according to Sellars,
Kant needs two distinct appeals to sensibility, and he should have clearly
distinguished them. First, intuitions, in the sense in which they figure in the
"clue" and the Transcendental Deduction, involve sensibility already shaped
by capacities that belong to the understanding. That is the feature of Sellars's Kant that I have been exploiting. But, second, Sellars thinks empirical
thinking must be "guided" by what he calls "sheer receptivity" (*Science and
Metaphysics*, p. 4)—that is, sensibility functioning independently of the understanding.

Sellars means this appeal to "sheer receptivity" to provide an interpretation of the thought that anything recognizable as empirical cognition
would need to be constrained by a reality external to cognitive activity.
That is an application, to the particular case of empirical thinking, of the
requirement of external constraint that is the second side of my topic. One
might think this intuitive requirement of external constraint is met by the
way in which the picture, even without the mention of "sheer receptivity",
incorporates the presence to consciousness of ordinary perceptible objects,
which is made intelligible by conceiving intuitions as cases of sensory receptivity shaped by the understanding. Does this not enable us to see how
objects themselves, by presenting themselves to sensory consciousness,
exercise a rational control over thinking about them? But that is not Sellars's view.

Sellars thinks the ordinary objects that seem to be present to consciousness in perceptual intuitions are strictly unreal. He thinks "scientific realism" requires this denial of reality to those constituents of, as he puts it,

the manifest image.[3] It cannot be those merely apparent ordinary objects that are the source of the required constraint from an external reality. What do really exist are the constituents of the scientific image that correspond to those merely apparent ordinary objects: swarms of elementary particles or something of the sort. Empirical cognition can be subject to genuinely external constraint only by way of impacts on our senses from those genuinely real items. Sellars puts this forward as an interpretation for Kant's distinction between phenomenal objects, constituents of the manifest image, and things in themselves, which Sellars identifies with constituents of the scientific image.

This part of Sellars's thinking is connected also with another feature of his reading of Kant. What we have so far is that for Sellars, the required external constraint on empirical cognition must be brought to bear by sensibility functioning independently of the understanding, not by sensibility shaped by the understanding so as to give rise to intuitions in the sense in which they figure in Kant's "clue" and the Transcendental Deduction, appearances of being sensorily confronted by ordinary—phenomenal—objects. And so far I have mentioned a "scientific realist" motivation for this feature of Sellars's thinking. But the "scientific realist" motivation converges with Sellars's reading of the thought Kant elaborates in the Transcendental Aesthetic, the thought that our sensibility brings its own forms, spatiality and temporality, to its cooperation with the understanding. As Sellars notes, what Kant discusses as the forms of our sensibility are certain formal features of how things are presented in intuitions, in the sense in which intuitions figure in the "clue" and the Transcendental Deduction—the sense according to which intuitions are already informed by the understanding. But in Sellars's view, that is a misstep on Kant's part. (See *Science and Metaphysics*, pp. 8, 28–30.) It shows that Kant does not properly appreciate what his own thinking requires. In Sellars's view, the point of the Aesthetic should be that our sensibility has its forms in its own right, independently of its cooperation with the understanding. So it is not only that particular cases of external constraint on empirical thinking are a matter of impacts from constituents of the scientific image on sensibility, supposedly understood independently of how it cooperates with the understanding to yield the manifest image. In addition, the form of intuitions as such, *qua* cases of our

---

3. See *Science and Metaphysics*, chapter 2. For the terminology of "manifest" and "scientific image", see "Philosophy and the Scientific Image of Man".

sensibility at work, is supposedly intelligible in isolation from the understanding.

Remarkably enough, in view of Sellars's hostility to "the framework of givenness", this picture, which Sellars thinks is the one Kant should have accepted, seems to cast the forms that our sensibility contributes to empirical cognition in the role of mere givens or immediacies, brutely alien to the understanding and shoving it around from outside. Where I say "shoving around", Sellars says "guiding", but that seems euphemistic by his own lights. Recall how he argues that rational input to the question what to think can come only from goings-on that already involve the understanding.

As I said, Sellars thinks Kant is misstepping by his own lights in failing to discuss forms our sensibility can be taken to possess in isolation from its cooperation with understanding. But this is hard to square with some striking remarks in the second-edition version of the Transcendental Deduction. There Kant explicitly insists on the very feature of the way he handles the formedness of our sensibility that Sellars thinks is a mere slip. He insists that our sensibility is not to be seen as having its forms independently of its interaction with understanding. As Kant in effect acknowledges, one might have gathered from the Transcendental Aesthetic that he takes the formedness of our sensibility to be intelligible before we bring the understanding into the picture (B160n.). That is just what Sellars thinks Kant's line ought to be. But in the second half of the B Deduction, Kant makes it clear that he wants us to realize the Aesthetic was not to be read as offering a self-standing account of the forms of our sensibility.

As long as it looks as if our sensibility has its forms independently of its cooperation with the understanding, it can seem that conformity to those forms ought to constitute an independent sufficient condition for presentness to our senses. And then when Kant urges that objects do not count as present to *intuition* unless what is given to the senses has categorial unity, it can seem that the requirement of categorial unity is no better than a subjective imposition, filtering out what human understanding can cope with from what is anyway present to our senses. That threatens Kant's aim of showing that the categories secure for intuitions a genuinely objective purport. In the second half of the B Deduction he responds to this threat by arguing, in effect, that the intelligibility of the topic of the Aesthetic presupposes the "formal intuitions" (B160n.), space and time. And in that these "formal intuitions" are themselves cases of the combination of a manifold into a single intuition, they come within the scope of the principle that drives the whole Deduction—that the unity of intuitions is not prior to and independent of the unifying capacities of the understanding. So the formedness of our sensibility is not, after all, independent of the understanding, and Kant takes himself to be entitled to claim that, rather than merely selecting, out of what is anyway there for the senses, what is conformable to the capacities of human understanding, the categories apply to "whatever objects may *present themselves to our senses*" (B159).[4]

As Hegel appreciatively, and I think accurately, describes Kant's move at this point: "Here [that is, in the second half of the B Deduction], the original synthetic unity of apperception is recognized also as the principle of the figurative synthesis, i.e. of the forms of intuition; space and time are themselves conceived as synthetic unities, and spontaneity, the absolute synthetic activity of the productive imagination, is conceived as the principle of the very sensibility that was previously characterized only as receptivity." (*Faith and Knowledge*, pp. 69–70.)

This move, which Hegel applauds as showing Kant at his most "speculative", makes it possible to take in stride the idea Sellars cannot countenance—that the external constraint on empirical cognition that is required for it to be intelligibly cognition at all is provided by the objects presented to us by intuitions, still conceived in the Kantian way, as actualizations of conceptual capacities in sensory receptivity. It is true that the objects presented to us by intuitions are in one obvious sense phenomenal. They make their appearance to us in experience. But with the Kantian move that Hegel applauds, we eliminate any implication that how they appear to us is partly a reflection of forms that our sensibility has as a matter of brute fact, independently of our capacity to take in objects—forms that our sensibility has immediately, as Hegel might say. And now to call these objects "phenomenal" need not seem to sound a disparaging note, as if we were saying "merely phenomenal, not genuinely real". The idea that our sensibility has its own forms need not seem to mesh with the "scientific realism" that induces Sellars to deny the reality of ordinary perceptible objects.

Kant's official doctrine about things in themselves is anyway out of line with Sellars's "scientific realist" reading of it. The official doctrine is that the

---

4. I owe the reading of the B Deduction that I sketch here to extended discussions with James Conant and John Haugeland.

things that present themselves to us in experience are the very same things that can also be conceived, by way of an abstraction from the idea of our powers to acquire knowledge of objects, as things in themselves (see *Critique of Pure Reason*, Bxxvii). "Things in themselves" and "things as they present themselves in experience" express two different ways of conceiving the same things. This is plainly inconsistent with Sellars's thesis that things as they present themselves in experience are unreal, mere appearances of things in themselves, which Sellars thinks Kant should have conceived as constituents of the scientific image.

But we do not need to saddle Kant with such a position about phenomena and things in themselves to find parts of his treatment of spatiality and temporality unsatisfactory in a related way. Though he does not suggest that phenomenal things are unreal, as Sellars does, Kant does tend to suggest something of the sort about the features of how they appear to us that he traces to the way our sensibility is operative in their appearing to us. He tends to suggest that those features, the spatial and temporal ordering of the world as we experience it, are mere reflections of the forms of our sensibility, for all we know not features of things themselves, or—worse—knowably not features of things themselves. That makes for a tenuousness in the sense in which access to objects by way of intuitions, as he conceives that, can be recognized as a subjective engagement with what is genuinely objective.

But when he takes the step Hegel applauds in that remark about the B Deduction, and displays the synthetic unity of apperception as the principle no less of the forms of intuition than of the pure concepts of the understanding (as Hegel puts it), Kant makes that strand in his thinking unnecessary. Now it should no longer seem that the forms of our sensibility are mere brute facts about the shape of our subjectivity, with the effect that the features of our world view that derive from the role of those forms in experience seem to be mere reflections or projections of our subjectivity. No doubt the very idea of a form of finite or human cognition is, just as such, the idea of something that characterizes a certain sort of subjectivity. But as the idea of a form of *cognition*, it should equally be the idea of something objective. Much of what Kant says about the forms of our sensibility makes it seem that in their case we cannot really exploit that two-sided character of the idea of forms of cognition. When Kant makes it look as if the forms of our sensibility are brute-fact features of our subjectivity, it becomes difficult to see how they could also be forms of the manifestness to us of what is genuinely objective. But when, in the move Hegel applauds, Kant puts the forms of our sensibility on a level with the categories, he takes a step towards making it possible to see the forms of our sensibility, no less than the categories, as genuinely forms of cognition—at once forms of subjective activity and forms of genuine objectivity with which that activity engages. (Of course a great deal would need to be said to spell out this hint.)

Reworked on these lines, a Kantian conception of intuitions combines subjective self-determination with objective constraint, and now in a way that does not require us to qualify the sense in which what exercises the constraint is objective reality. On these lines we can begin to make sense, in the context of empirical cognition, of Hegelian talk about a liberation from the opposition of consciousness. The objects of intuition are now conceived as fully objective even in respect of their spatial and temporal organization. But their otherness to consciousness, at any rate perceptual consciousness, is *aufgehoben*; not abolished, but situated in a larger story so that it no longer seems to threaten the self-determining rationality of the subject.

6. Richard Rorty has argued that the very idea of being answerable to objects in our thinking about them is a betrayal of the ideal of self-determination. (See, e.g., "Solidarity or Objectivity?".) In Rorty's view, aspiring to make oneself answerable to the world is a secular counterpart of subjecting oneself to the will of an authoritarian deity. Full human maturity requires liberation from dogmatic religion. Just so, Rorty urges that a proper affirmation of our independence requires us not to conceive ourselves as beholden to the world in our investigative activities. We should replace this ideal of answerability to the non-human with an ideal of answerability to our fellow human beings, in a context of free negotation between equals. In Rorty's slogan, the guiding image for our intellectual activity should be solidarity rather than objectivity.

Rorty is invoking a requirement that we think for ourselves, and that is a way of giving expression to the idealist insistence on self-determination that is one side of my topic. As I said, Hegel takes this insistence on self-determination to an extreme. So it might seem that when Rorty recommends substituting answerability to our fellow human beings for answerability to a reality that is largely non-human, at the centre of our picture of intellectual activity, he is promoting a fundamentally Hegelian conception. Indeed, Rorty cites Hegel as a forerunner when he applies the idea to empirical thinking in particular. He thinks Hegel belongs with Davidson, Brandom, and (in what must be by my lights a complete misreading) Sellars, as someone who would have no truck with the idea that experience mediates an answerability to the world. (See "The Very Idea of Human Answerability to the World", especially at p. 140.)

I have been sketching a picture in which objects occupy a position of authority over our thinking, in a presence to consciousness that is made intelligible by exploiting a version of Kant's conception of intuitions. Now it seems point-missing to suggest, as Rorty does, that this is to undervalue the freedom of the thinking subject. The authority of perceived objects is not like the pseudo-authority of the merely given—as if letting what is present to consciousness control one's thinking were like letting one's thinking be shaped by an uncritically inherited tradition. Intuitions are unities whose elements are actualizations of capacities belonging to the spontaneous understanding. For my purposes here, the point of this conception is to ensure that what is, if you like, given in intuition is exactly not a case of givenness in the sense in which acquiescing in the given conflicts with being in control of one's life. Emancipating our intellectual activity from the pseudo-authority of the merely given cannot be freeing ourselves from the authority of reasons. If we make sense of how a bit of the world might present itself to consciousness, as we can by exploiting Kant's conception of intuitions, modified to give full weight to the suggestion about sensibility that Hegel applauds, we make sense of how the world might afford us compelling reason to believe that things are a certain way. Taking it to be incumbent on us to form beliefs on such grounds involves no abdication of our responsibility for being in control of our own lives, no allowing ourselves to be enslaved by an alien force.

7. I want to end by considering a more sophisticated way to urge that something on the lines of solidarity, or at any rate communal being, must be basic in a picture of intellectual activity that is shaped to the fullest possible extent by the self-determination idea, as Hegel's is. I have been talking in terms of thought subjecting itself to the authority of objects. And the suggestion I want to consider is about how to understand this concession of authority to objects. The concession is dictated by the norms that constitute the content of concepts, empirical concepts in particular. Those norms are what give determinate shape to the ways in which we take it to be correct to let our thinking be controlled by its subject matter. So—the proposal goes—we need to inquire into the source of the normative authority of

concepts. And now, first, the self-determination idea requires that we take those norms to be laws we make for ourselves. And, second, we cannot spell out that image in terms of single individuals giving themselves the law. We can understand the authoritativeness of conceptual norms only as instituted by communal activity. Robert Brandom has worked to make this idea of norms as communally self-legislated more determinate (see *Making It Explicit*), but here I want to consider it only at the abstract level at which I have formulated it.

Cashing out the idea of rational self-determination in terms of an image of legislating for oneself goes back to Kant's appropriation of Rousseau. The image is fine, but we need to be careful about what it can amount to. When we say that rational norms are self-legislated by rational subjects, the point is that acknowledging the authority of those norms is not abandoning control of one's life to an alien power. But that is consistent with—and indeed requires—that we not pretend to make sense of the idea of a legislative act that confers authority on the norms of reason. If the legislative act is not already subject to the norms of reason, how can it be anything but arbitrary? But nothing instituted by an act that is arbitrary could be intelligible as the authority of reason. If self-legislation of rational norms is not to be a random leap in the dark, it must be seen as an acknowledgment of an authority that the norms have anyway. Submitting to that authority is not handing over control of the relevant areas of one's life to a foreign power. What controls one's life is still in oneself, in whatever it is about one that enables one to recognize that the norms are authoritative. But their authority is not a creature of one's recognition. Seen in this light, the self-determination idea is a version of the basic commitment of rationalism.

The norms that constitute the content of empirical concepts are determinations, responsive to the specifics of the world as it presents itself to us, of norms that are internal to thinking as such. So the external constraint I have been talking about, constraint by objects, is authorized from within the practice of thinking, by norms that are constitutive of the practice. No doubt this sketchy imagery needs elaboration, but it is not clear how something other than further elaboration of the idea of norms internal to thinking could cast more light on the source of this normativity. The self-legislation image does not help here. That cannot be its point, for reasons I have just sketched in connection with norms of reason in general. Fundamental norms for thinking cannot be seen as instituted by thinkers; as soon as one is a thinker, one is already subject to such norms. And there is a mystery in the idea that individuals who are not yet thinkers could convert themselves into thinkers by instituting norms that are constitutive of thinking as such. If they are not yet thinkers, how can we make sense of their being able to legislate such norms for themselves? There is indeed a sense in which the source of the norms is in us. But what the idea comes to is not that we confer authority on the norms in an act of legislation that brings them into being as authoritative, but just that they are constitutive of the practice of thinking, an activity in which we realize potentialities that are our own. We do not have a choice whether to be thinkers, but that does not imply that in submitting to the norms that thinking is anyway subject to, we abdicate any genuine freedom.

This picture is generically Kantian. Of course Kant's specific way of filling in its details is unsatisfactory by Hegel's lights. For one thing, thinking as such needs to be seen as essentially engaged with the objective, and Kant's most characteristic attempt to secure that, for empirical thinking, is shaky, though the "speculative" remarks in the B Deduction point in a more promising direction. For another thing, Kant simply takes over from current logic his inventory of the fundamental forms of thought, and Hegel has a familiar objection to that. In working out the self-determination idea, we must not take anything on trust from an established tradition.

Such considerations point towards an alternative way of spelling out the idea I described as generically Kantian—the idea that the specifics of the way empirical thinking concedes authority to its subject matter are to be traced to norms that are internal to thinking as such. From one point of view the step from Kant's version to one that might be attributed to Hegel is of course enormous. But even so, they are two versions of one basic conception. In particular, coming at the divergence from this angle uncovers nothing that recommends seeing it as Brandom does, with Hegel offering a communal version of the self-legislating image in response to a question Kant simply ignores, about the source of our being bound by determinate conceptual norms. (See Brandom, "Some Pragmatist Themes in Hegel's Idealism".)

Of course I am not denying that communal being is central to Hegel's thinking, and not central to Kant's. And I do not dispute that we can begin to say why it is central to Hegel's thinking by finding something right in the idea that the image of self-legislation does not work at the level of single individuals, but requires a communal context. But the point here is not, I think, that by representing legislating for ourselves as a complex communal performance we can somehow sidestep the dilemma that besets the idea of an act that, because it institutes fundamental norms, has to be seen as taking place in a normative void. The dilemma cannot be evaded, and the point is a different one. In the rationalistic image there is something in subjects that enables them to recognize the authority of norms of reason. And we can begin to see why communal being matters by seeing that we can bring that rationalistic idea down to earth—in one sense naturalize it—by taking it that the capacity to recognize the requirements of reason, still seen as authoritative anyway, not owing their authoritativeness to their being recognized, is acquired by initiation into suitable communal practices, rather than being an endowment built, perhaps supernaturally, into the make-up of human beings as such.

The idea that any actual take on what is a reason for what is a historically situated achievement, unintelligible except in the context of a community, is one side of a two-sided picture. If we focus too closely on that one side, we risk—naturally—a one-sided understanding (in something like the sense in which one-sidedness often figures in Hegel), with the most obvious pitfall being a variety of relativism. Starting from here, insisting that the requirements of reason are authoritative anyway is the needed corrective, the return from one-sidedness. If we start from the insistence that the norms of reason are authoritative anyway, the most obvious pitfall of one-sidedness is a pre-critical platonism, and now the stress on communal being is the needed corrective. Brandom's talk of norms as instituted at least encourages one of these kinds of one-sidedness. For a better understanding of Hegel, we need to see, of course in more detail than I can offer here, how to keep these two sides in balance.

ESSAY **6**

Sensory Consciousness
in Kant and Sellars[1]

1. If we understood Kant's theoretical philosophy, we would understand
how to think about the limits of intelligibility—the bounds of sense, in one
interpretation of P. F. Strawson's intentionally ambiguous title.[2] That would
put us within reach of an insight only glimpsed, I think, by Kant himself:
that those limits are not well conceived as a boundary, enclosing a territory
by leaving other territory outside it. But we can approach that connection
with the theme of boundaries and limits only by dealing with the details of
the first *Critique*, and some of that is all I will be doing here.

2. Sensibility is one of the "two stems of human knowledge" that Kant distinguishes in the Introduction to the *Critique* (A15/B29), in an image he
reverts to near the end of the work (A835/B863). In the first passage, the
other stem is understanding; in the second, it is "the whole higher faculty
of knowledge".

As Kant begins to explain how sensibility and understanding are related,
it can seem that sensibility is supposed to account, by itself, for *intuitions*,
while understanding accounts for *concepts*, which are, on this picture, simply
separate from intuitions. As he proceeds, however, it emerges that in his
view the spontaneous cognitive faculty that, in the guise of the understanding, is responsible for concepts also enters into the constitution of intuitions. That is how things are in his dominant conception of intuitions;

1. An ancestor of this essay was delivered to a Kant conference called "Thinking about
Boundaries and Limits", held in Kirkenes, Norway, in June 2006, under the auspices of
the Barents Institute and the Norwegian Kant Society, to both of which institutions I am
grateful. Thanks to James Conant for help and encouragement.
2. P. F. Strawson, *The Bounds of Sense*.

108

this is explicit by the time we reach the Metaphysical Deduction. (See A79/B104–5.)

But in holding that the higher faculty is partly responsible for intuitions, Kant is not dislodged from crediting them to sensibility as well, in that—in a standard Kantian metaphor—sensibility provides their material, though their form is due to the higher faculty. We might say he conceives an intuition—that through which a cognition is immediately related to an object (see A19/B33)—as *sensory consciousness of an object*.

I want to compare two answers to the following question: in a Kantian view, how should we conceive the *sensory* character of sensory consciousness of objects?

3. Though it is a stem of human knowledge, Kant is firm that sensibility alone does not yield cognition. Cognition requires thought, and sensibility is not a capacity to think. "[T]hrough mere intuition", he says, "nothing at all is thought, and the fact that this affection of sensibility is in me does not . . . amount to a relation of any such representation to an object" (A253/B309).[3] The reason "it is . . . correct to say that the senses do not err" is not that "they always judge rightly" but that "they do not judge at all" (A293/B350).

Given what I said about Kant's dominant conception of intuitions, it may be surprising that in the first of these passages he says *intuition* is insufficient for thought, and hence for (cognitive) relation to an object. But this is consistent with his holding, as I claimed, that the higher faculty enters into the constitution of intuitions. That need not imply—what would contradict what he says here—that intuitions as such involve the understanding, the capacity to think. If there is thought in an intuition, its content must have been articulated, analysed, into contents for determinate conceptual capacities. And the sheer occurrence of intuitions does not ensure that such analysis has been effected. We can say this even while we insist that the higher faculty is responsible for their form. We must suppose it is not in its guise as the understanding, the faculty of concepts, that the higher faculty does the informing that makes intuitions what they are. If, with Wilfrid Sellars, we connect intentionality with being conceptual,[4] we should say that

---

3. Kemp Smith inserts "[by itself]" where I have marked an ellipsis. This does not distort the thought, but the addition seems needless.

4. See Sellars's *Science and Metaphysics: Variations on Kantian Themes*, p. 23: "the intentional is that which belongs to the conceptual order."

apart from that work of articulation intuitions have at most proto-intentionality. An intuition as such is, as Kant says (A20/B34), of an appearance, by which he means, in this context, something (conceptually) undetermined—even though the higher faculty enters into the constitution of the intuition whose object it is.

But that is only a complication in the interpretation of the doctrine that sensibility alone does not provide for cognition.

A thought on these lines is operative in Sellars's attack on empiricist forms of the Myth of the Given. Sellars urges that if the deliverances of the senses are independent of conceptual capacities,[5] then receiving those deliverances cannot be knowing anything, and cannot ground the knowing of anything else, as traditional empiricism makes out that it does.

The *locus classicus* for Sellars's attack on the Given is "Empiricism and the Philosophy of Mind". There he does not invoke a Kantian provenance for his campaign. But elsewhere he stresses its Kantian inspiration. Here is a characteristic statement: "My thesis will be that sense is a cognitive faculty only in the sense that it makes knowledge possible and is an essential element in knowledge, and that of itself it knows nothing. It is a necessary condition of the intentional order, but does not of itself belong to this order. This thesis was first advanced by Kant, but can, fortunately, be separated from other, less attractive, features of the Kantian system".[6]

4. Kant introduces sensibility as "the capacity (receptivity) for receiving representations through the mode in which we are affected by objects" (A19/B33). He explains sensation *(Empfindung)* as "the effect of an object upon the faculty of representation, in so far as we are affected by it" (A19–20/B34). In the taxonomy of kinds of representation *(Vorstellung)* near the beginning of the Transcendental Dialectic (the *Stufenleiter*: A320/B376–7), sensation figures as "a perception [that is, a representation with consciousness] which relates solely to the subject as a modification of its state".

---

5. That is, of the higher faculty in the guise of the understanding. At *Science and Metaphysics*, pp. 4–7, Sellars attributes to Kant a conception of intuitions according to which the capacities operative in them are only proto-conceptual, and this could be taken as an acknowledgment of the complication I have just been discussing. But the complication does not figure in the version of Kantian thinking that Sellars himself endorses. Nothing in my essay will turn on this, and I shall ignore it from now on.

6. "Being and Being Known", p. 46. In *Science and Metaphysics*, Sellars deals with the main themes of his own philosophy through a reading of Kant.

Now Sellars has a distinctive interpretation for this conception of sensibility and sensation.

As Sellars understands the Kantian position, sensibility yields sensations, and sensations are inner episodes (or states)[7] *exhaustively* characterizable by descriptions that relate them solely to the subject as modifications of its state. They do not have intentional directedness. Sellars insists that "of" in, say, "a sensation of red" must not be assimilated to "of" in, say, "a thought of a man".[8] (It is more like "of" in "a sensation of pain".) And for Sellars an episode (or state) that is a sensation is *completely* describable—so far as concerns what it is for consciousness—by descriptions that use "of" only in that non-intentional way. As Sellars sees things, this is just a way of expressing the fundamental Kantian insight, that sensibility alone does not yield cognition, because it does not provide for thought.[9]

One might wonder whether, given this conception of sensations, it is appropriate to call them "representations", as Sellars does when he expounds Kant in *Science and Metaphysics*. But Kant himself classifies sensations as one of the varieties of representation in the *Stufenleiter*, even though he says they are perceptions that relate solely to the subject as modifications of its state. I shall come back to this.

Sellars holds that, in contrast with sensations, perceptual episodes and states exemplify intentionality. And he provides for this by maintaining that—to put the thought in Kantian terms—the understanding is involved in their constitution.

In "Empiricism and the Philosophy of Mind" he introduces a conception of a perceptual experience "as, so to speak, making an assertion or claim" (§16). Kant might have invoked judgment in offering a parallel image. But Sellars wants to express a Kantian thought by exploiting a view of his own: that the understanding acquires first actuality, the potential for the second actuality that consists in intellectual acts, when a subject is initiated into language. Later in the essay, he cashes out that "so to speak"—delivering on

---

7. In "Empiricism and the Philosophy of Mind", Sellars focuses on episodes. This is because his attention is on a certain reading of Ryle. But his concern is with vindicating a non-dispositional inner in general; states that cannot be reduced to dispositions should be just as important to him as episodes.

8. See, e.g., Part V of "Empiricism and the Philosophy of Mind"; compare the passage I cited from "Being and Being Known".

9. See the excellent treatment of Sellars on sensory consciousness in chapter 8 of Willem A. deVries, *Wilfrid Sellars*.

what he earlier acknowledged as a promissory note—by suggesting that thought about inner episodes with conceptual content uses episodes of overt speech as a model. The intentionality of unspoken thoughts is to be understood by analogical extension from the directedness at their subject matter of acts we can conceive as thinking-out-loud.[10] That is a picture of thought in general, but Sellars notes that it entitles him to the thesis he signalled as promissory when he was characterizing experiences in particular (§60). For Sellars, the intentionality of experiences is a case of the intentionality of acts of thinking.

In contexts in which he is aligning himself more directly with Kant, Sellars shifts the focus from experiences in that sense, items with propositional content, to intuitions. On Sellars's interpretation, intuitions, in Kant's dominant sense, have contents expressible by phrases of the form "this such".[11] Such a content is not the content of a claim. But it exemplifies intentionality, and it comes within the scope of Sellars's Kantian insistence that intentionality is not on the scene unless the understanding is. The intentional directedness of an intuition at reality—its being an intuition *of*, say, a pink cube—is to be explained by analogical extension from the way in which, given the presence of a demonstrative phrase, say "this pink cube", in a form of words uttered in a certain context, anyone who understands the utterance can identify a certain object as what the utterance is about. As before, this gives a specific shape, suitable for philosophy after the linguistic turn, to a Kantian thought about intentionality, now applied to intuitions in particular: that their intentionality is to be understood in terms of their being partly constituted by the spontaneous cognitive power that, in its guise as the understanding, is the faculty of concepts.

For Sellars, then, when one enjoys experiences, conceived as having propositional content, one engages in thinkings, and intuitions have contents that can be constituents of what is thought in thinkings about objects present to one in experience. But experiences and intuitions are not *just* thinkings (in a sense in which thinkings can have less than propositional content, so that intuitions too can count as thinkings). The immediate relation to an object that a cognition acquires through an intuition is a matter of

---

10. The first phase of the "myth of Jones": Part XV of "Empiricism and the Philosophy of Mind".

11. In his own voice Sellars sometimes calls these items "takings". See, e.g., "Some Reflections on Perceptual Consciousness", pp. 434–5. For intuitions as having content of the form "this such", see, e.g., chapter 1 of *Science and Metaphysics*.

the object's being—in some sense—*sensibly* present to the knowing subject. And when an experience, in the sense Sellars exploits in "Empiricism and the Philosophy of Mind", is a cognition, the state of affairs thanks to whose obtaining the experience is veridical is—in some sense—*sensibly* present to the knowing subject. Experiences and intuitions are not just thinkings, but also shapings of sensory consciousness.

Here we come to what is distinctive about Sellars's interpretation of the fundamental Kantian insight, that sensibility alone does not yield cognition. For Sellars, sensory consciousness in a strict sense, the primary product of sensibility, is populated by sensations, and sensations are exhaustively describable in a way that relates them solely to the subject as modifications of its state. So, as I noted, they lack intentionality, and they must be distinct from anything that has intentionality. The result is that Sellars has to conceive experiences and intuitions as *composites*: they must comprise *both* items whose character as thinkings provides for intentionality *and* items whose character as sensations provides for placement in sensory consciousness. A visual intuition, for instance, is a thinking of an object as a *this-such accompanied*, in a special way (I shall come back to this), by visual sensations. The sense in which an intuition is not just a thinking but also a shaping of sensory consciousness is that part of the composite that is an intuition is a thinking and another part is a shaping of sensory consciousness.

My question was this: in a Kantian position, how should we conceive the *sensory* character of sensory consciousness of objects? Sellars's answer is that, while sensory consciousness of objects is *of objects* by virtue of the presence of thinkings in the composite that philosophical reflection reveals it to be, it is *sensory* by virtue of the presence of sensations in that composite.

For Sellars, as I said, intuitions are thinkings—in a sense in which thinkings can have less than whole propositions as their contents—accompanied in a special way by sensations. The mode of accompaniment is a topic of some difficulty. In any plausible elaboration of a view on these lines, the thinkings that are one element in these composites would be *occasioned* by the sensations that are the other element. But this occasioning cannot be a causal connection of the sort in which it is a mere contingency that some specific cause has some specific effect—as if the sensations that occasion thinkings of things as green might just as well have occasioned thinkings of things as red. The nature of the sensations that constitute one element in an intuition must be more intimately connected than that with the intentional content of the thinking that is its other element. It is presumably at least in part with a view to capturing this intimate connection that Sellars, in *Science and Metaphysics*, represents the conceptual elements in perceptual consciousness as *guided* (not merely caused) by the sensational elements.[12]

Elsewhere he tries to capture the unity of the composite items he takes experiences to be with this remark: "visual perception itself is not just a conceptualizing of colored objects within visual range—a 'thinking about' colored objects in a certain context—but, in a sense most difficult to analyze, a *thinking in color* about colored objects."[13]

Sellars's most sophisticated treatment of the relation between the conceptual and sensational elements in experience is in "The Role of the Imagination in Kant's Theory of Experience". There he offers a reading of Kant on the productive imagination—a power that belongs both to sensibility and to understanding. The essential point in Sellars's reading is that the productive imagination, presented with a sensory manifold in which an object is made available to intuition, performs *two* tasks. As a power of the understanding, it generates a conceptual representation, partly expressible by, say, "this red pyramid facing me edgewise". And as a power to form images, it constructs out of materials contributed by sense (and imagination) a corresponding "image-model", which in the same case is "a point-of-viewish image of oneself confronting a red pyramid facing one edgewise" (p. 426). Each task influences the other. Importing the metaphor from *Science and Metaphysics*, we might say the image-model guides the conceptual representation. But the conceptual representation provides a "recipe" for the construction of the image-model—or better, a series of image-models, varying in their perspectival ("point-of-viewish") character as the actual or envisaged relative positions of the perceiver and the object change. Raw sensations, deliverances of sensibility independently of the higher faculty, presumably constrain the possibilities for image-models and so for the conceptual activity that stands in this complex relation to image-models. But what guides conceptual goings-on is not a mere aggregate of raw sensations but the result of a construction, with sensations included in its material, according to a recipe supplied by

12. See, e.g., pp. 16, 29.
13. "The Structure of Knowledge", p. 305.

the conceptual goings-on themselves. So in this picture the higher faculty enters into the constitution of what does the guiding as well as that of what is guided by it.[14]

5. The sensational element in visual intuitions would need to include, at least, sensations of *colour*. In the terms introduced in Sellars's reading of Kant on the productive imagination, a sensation of translucent pink would need to be included in the material for the image-model that combines with a conceptual representation to constitute an intuition of a translucent pink cube.

The character of the sensational element, so far as concerns its capacity to guide the conceptual element in the intuition in respect of the colour the cube is represented as having, would need to be more determinate than could be captured by describing it as a sensation of translucent pink. But that would need to be a correct, though incompletely determinate, description of it.

For Sellars, then, colour concepts (in some sense) must characterize the *sensational* component of visual intuitions. And this role for colour concepts is in one way fundamental. In Sellars's view, it is only because colour enters into the phenomenal character of visual sensations that colour figures in thoughts about perceptible objects.

This may seem surprising, because Sellars holds that the colour concepts that characterize colour sensations are derivative from concepts of colours as apparent properties of perceptible objects.[15] The present point is that he combines this, perfectly consistently, with holding that the primary place in reality for the phenomena of colour is at the level of sensation.[16]

Now it is a striking phenomenological fact that in visual sensory consciousness colour is inextricably connected with *shape*. The translucent pink, in the sensory consciousness of translucent pink that figures in seeing a translucent pink cube, is a *volume* of translucent pink with a perspectivally presented *cubic* shape. (Something similar goes for surface colours.) So in

14. I have imported the metaphor of guidance from *Science and Metaphysics* so as to bring out that the picture Sellars offers in "The Role of the Imagination in Kant's Theory of Experience" is not vulnerable to my objections, in Essay 2 above, against the way the metaphor figures in the earlier work.

15. See, e.g., "Empiricism and the Philosophy of Mind", Part XVI.

16. This is especially clear in his later work, but the idea is already operative in, e.g., "Philosophy and the Scientific Image of Man".

the Sellarsian picture colour naturally brings shape with it into the sensational part of the truth about visual intuitions. *Being of something cubic* has to be recognized as a manner of *sensing*.

Here too, the spatially sensational element in an intuition would need to have more determinacy than such a description captures. It would need to have features sufficient to make intelligible its guiding the conceptual representation that is the other element in the intuition, not just in the intuition's representing the seemingly seen object as cubic, but also in respect of, for instance, how the seemingly seen cube is represented as oriented to the viewer. But the unspecific characterization, "sensation of something cubic", will do to bring out the feature of Sellars's thinking I want to focus on here.[17]

Kant holds that space is the form of our outer sensibility. As Sellars notes, it becomes increasingly clear, as we progress through the *Critique*, that Kant's thought concerns an order that characterizes the objects of our outer *intuitions*, in the sense in which intuitions are partly constituted by the higher faculty.[18]

But Sellars thinks that in a properly Kantian picture, manners of sensing would have to include being of something cubic. And he insists that it would be a confusion to equate this spatial specificity of *sensations* with the spatial specificity exemplified in an *intuition's* being, say, of something cubic. That would be conflating the non-intentional "of" in descriptions of sensations with the intentional "of" in descriptions of thinkings, which include the intentionality-involving components of intuitions.

In Sellars's view, then, Kant needs a spatiality that informs the *sensational* element in our outer intuition. It must be distinct from the spatiality that informs the intentional content of our outer intuition. But this latter spatiality is the only spatiality Kant considers. Sellars thinks Kant could have explained a purely sensational spatiality by analogical extension from the spatiality of our outer intuition. But Kant does not do that. He does not equip himself with a purely sensational spatiality. In Sellars's view, that implies that he contrives, in effect, to miss the very point of the idea he is trying to express when he talks of space as a form of *sense*. As Kant

---

17. On the inextricability of colour and shape in sensory consciousness, see especially "Berkeley and Descartes: Reflections on the Theory of Ideas".

18. See *Science and Metaphysics*, pp. 28–30.

develops it, Sellars says, "the idea that Space is the form of outer sense is incoherent".[19]

To the extent that the spatiality of the sensational element in intuitions can be equated with the spatiality of image-models, Sellars's reading of Kant on the productive imagination puts him in a position to tone down this criticism. As we saw, Sellars conceives image-models as constructed according to recipes supplied by conceptual activity. There can be nothing wrong with their having formal properties, including spatial organization, that are intelligible only in terms of an involvement on the part of the higher faculty. But even in this sophisticated version of Sellars's picture, it is natural to think there must also be a spatial ordering at the level of the raw sensations that serve as material for image-models. How could there be, say, a blue spot at the apex of an imaged pyramid, presented in an image-model with the apex upward, if a sensation of blue were not related, in a purely sensational space, by an analogue of the "above" relation to sensations of colour that constitute the material for the parts of the image-model that present the lower parts of the imaged pyramid? So it still seems that a Kantian view, as Sellars understands it, requires a purely sensational spatiality. And Sellars still needs to accuse Kant of failing to appreciate what his own thinking requires.

6. But what is the alternative? (To echo a move often made by Sellars himself.)[20]

Our sensibility should be our version of something non-rational animals also have. What functioning sense-organs yield for a non-rational animal is not items exhaustively describable in a way that relates them solely to the animal as modifications of its state. Sensibility provides an animal with representations—awarenesses in some sense—of features of its environment. As such, the products of sensibility are characterizable not only in a way that relates them to the subject as modifications of its state, but also in a way that relates them to what they are representations of. It is true that

---

19. *Science and Metaphysics*, p. 8. DeVries writes (*Wilfrid Sellars*, p. 231) that "one reason (among many) that Sellars finds Kant so amenable" is that Kant "also [that is, like Sellars] believes that there is a kind of 'inner space-time' whose structure mimics physical space-time to a large degree". But the fact is that Sellars chides Kant for *not* arriving at such a conception; he thinks this is what Kant should believe, not what he does believe.

20. For a couple of examples, see "Empiricism and the Philosophy of Mind", §35, and "Being and Being Known", p. 43.

for Kant, since non-rational animals do not have a spontaneous higher faculty of knowledge, their sensory representations can be ordered only by association, and so cannot amount to cognitions in the demanding interpretation he places on that idea.[21] Thanks to the higher faculty that distinguishes us from non-rational animals, our sensory representations can have the status of cognitions, as theirs cannot. But the higher faculty is not needed for what sensibility yields to be representations. It is by virtue of the higher faculty that the representations we receive through sensibility are cognitions, but not that they are representations *überhaupt*.

This makes it open to question how faithful to Kant Sellars is in his understanding of what is yielded by sensibility as such.

In Sellars's view, which he takes to be Kant's, the whole truth about an item that is a sensation is captured by a characterization that relates it solely to the subject as a modification of its state. But Kant's explanations of the idea of sensation are compatible with the following different possibility.

Start with a representation acquired through sensibility. It may or may not be one that, because the higher faculty is operative in its constitution, has the status of a cognition—a perceiving that something is the case—or of something that makes cognition possible by putting the subject in immediate relation to an object—an intuition. In any case, if we characterize it as the representation it is, we do not relate it solely to the subject as a modification of its state.

But we can redescribe *that same item* in a way that abstracts from its being a representation, which, if it is a cognition or cognition-enabler, is its intentionality. And when we abstract from its representational character, we describe it—that very item—as the effect of an object on the faculty of representation, in so far as the subject is affected by the object: that is, as a sensation (A19–20/B34). Suppose we started with a cognition or cognition-enabler. Then what the abstraction enables us to describe as a sensation is not something that *accompanies* a thinking, a possessor of intentionality. It *is* a thinking, but it comes into view as the sensation it also is when we describe it in a way that abstracts from its intentionality.

In this picture, what provides for an intuition, say, to belong to sensory consciousness is not apportioned to an item other than one whose characteristics

---

21. He urges this in, among other places, a well-known letter to Marcus Herz (May 26, 1789).

provide for the intuition to be of an object, as in Sellars's picture. We can still say sensory consciousness contains sensations. But the intentionality of intuitions is accounted for by the fact that in intuitions *sensory consciousness itself* is informed by the higher faculty. The thinkings that provide for the intentionality of perceptual cognitions are not *guided* by sensory consciousness, as it were from without. They *are* sensory consciousness, suitably informed.

There is no backsliding here from what I described as the fundamental Kantian insight, that sensibility alone does not yield cognition.[22] Without the higher faculty, sensibility can yield at most the representations, merely associatively ordered and so not amounting to cognitions, that Kant allows to non-rational animals. If we are asked to contemplate an affection of an animal's sensibility through which it receives a representation, but we are not told whether the animal is a rational animal, we cannot tell whether what we are contemplating—the representation received through the mode in which the subject is affected—is even a candidate for being a cognition, or something that enables cognition in the way intuitions do. If it is a cognition or cognition-enabler, that is because its being what it is is not provided for by sensibility alone, but depends on its being informed by the higher faculty. So the fundamental Kantian insight is respected.

In describing an item that is a representation, and perhaps a cognition, as the sensation it may also be, we abstract from that about it in virtue of which it is the representation it is. Perhaps that can help towards making it intelligible—more intelligible, anyway, than it can be in Sellars's reading— that sensations figure as representations in the *Stufenleiter*.

7. Consider an intuition of a translucent pink cube. How might we redescribe it so as to abstract from its intentionality and display it as a case of sensation, thus placing it in sensory consciousness?

Here is a possibility: it is an instance of the kind of affection of sensibility that is characteristic of intuitions of translucent pink cubes.

---

22. I am defending what deVries calls "intentionalism in the treatment of sensations" (*Wilfrid Sellars*, p. 305, n. 20). He connects Sellars's rejection of this with "his Kantian distinction between sense and conception". But my point is that the reading of the Kantian distinction according to which sensory consciousness cannot itself be informed by intentionality is not compulsory. There is nothing un-Kantian about the position I am defending.

That may seem a cheat. But there can be nothing wrong with specifying sensational character indirectly, exploiting what we need to abstract from in order to describe an item as a mere modification of the subject's state.

To stay with such indirect specifications of sensational character is to diverge from Sellars. Not that Sellars disputes that such specifications are possible. But he thinks he is obliged to devise ways of describing sensations directly, not just in terms of the kinds of perception they figure in.[23] (He does this by introducing analogical uses of concepts of the proper and common sensibles, modelled on their uses for properties seemingly possessed by perceptible objects.) However, in the context of the alternative interpretation I am putting forward for a Kantian conception of sensory consciousness, there is no such obligation. On this view the sensory aspect of perceptual consciousness of objects is not secured by items that, by virtue of autonomous sensational properties, guide other elements in perceptions into having certain intentional contents. The relevant items *are* possessors of intentional content, but considered under an abstraction from their intentionality. So the indirect style of specification for their sensational character is perfectly legitimate.

But we can exploit the idea of abstraction in a different way. As before, we start with an intuition of a translucent pink cube. But we aim to redescribe it as a sensation by omitting from that specification anything whose presence reflects what we must abstract from in order to describe the item solely as a modification of its subject's state.

Obviously we may no longer describe it as an intuition. More interestingly, since for Kant (in the doctrine Sellars complains about) spatiality informs the intentionality of outer intuition, we must omit "a . . . cube" from the specification of what the item is of. (The article goes with the count noun.) But it is not so clear that "translucent pink" must go. If it does not, we are left with this: "a sensation of translucent pink."

On the surface, this matches Sellars's usual form for describing sensations of colour. However, according to Sellars "of" in "an intuition of a translucent pink cube" expresses intentionality, whereas "of" in "a sensation of translucent pink" does not. But if we reach "of translucent pink" by dropping "a . . . cube" from "of a translucent pink cube" in what was a specification of the intentional content of an intuition, why should "of" change its

---

23. See, e.g., "Empiricism and the Philosophy of Mind", §22 (last paragraph); §45 (third paragraph); and §61, item (2).

character? Why not suppose this form for describing sensations of colour exploits—in a vestigial form—the apparatus of intentionality?

Can "a sensation of translucent pink" describe a mere modification of a subject's state even if "of" signals intentionality in a vestigial form? There is no obvious reason why not. The point is precisely that the intentionality is vestigial. If spatiality is essential for intentional directedness at outer reality, then we abstract from outward directedness when we omit the specification of shape from the description of an intuition we began with. Why not suppose the result describes the item as a mere affection of sensibility?

It is in intuitions, with their non-vestigial intentionality, that we should locate the inextricable connection of colour with shape in visual consciousness. We reach these specifications of colour sensations by abstraction from specifications of intuitions in whose content we can acknowledge that colour and shape are indissolubly bound together. If we say that *qua* sensation the item we are concerned with is of colour and not of shape, we do not imply that we have given a complete characterization of an item in whose nature being of colour is somehow separated from being of shape.

That sensations of colour are mere affections of sensibility is a natural thought for Kant, given that he thinks the true home in reality of colours, which falsely present themselves as qualities of perceptible objects, is in these configurations of subjectivity. (See, e.g., B44.) Sellars has a version of this characteristically eighteenth-century thought. But even if we suppose—as I think we should—that the colours we seemingly see really are, in the best cases, qualities of the objects we seemingly see to have them, we can still find a point in the idea that sensations of colour as such—that is, characterized with the abstraction that makes "of" only vestigially indicative of intentionality—are mere affections of sensibility. Once we lift the abstraction, they come back into view as putative cognitions, or enablers of cognition, of objects with their colour qualities, which, on this account, the objects really have if the putative cognitions are cognitions. But the descriptions yielded by the abstraction omit the context that would be needed if the colours they mention were to be figuring in them as apparent qualities of external objects.

In this picture, spatial specificity figures in the complete truth about items that are visual sensations, but not in descriptions of their character as sensations. There is no need for the purely sensational spatiality whose absence from Kant Sellars complains about. And there is another respect in which this picture promises to line up more closely with Kant than Sellars can manage. In this picture, the idea of magnitude gets a grip on sensations, as such, only in the guise of intensive magnitude. (See the Anticipations of Perception.) For Sellars, the presence of that thought in Kant must be a mark of the same defect, in Kant's grasp of what his thinking requires, that Sellars finds in Kant's failure to provide for a purely sensational spatiality.

I have been suggesting that visual sensations in the sense Kant explains are not, *qua* sensations, of shape. This does not imply that access to spatial properties is not sensory. This restriction in what sensations as such can be said to be of is consistent with insisting that the *whole* content of visual experience, including what it reveals about spatial properties, is a matter of informing, by capacities that belong to the higher faculty, *of sensory consciousness*. An intuition of a translucent pink cube, with all its content, is an affection of its subject's sensibility. It is just that in order to describe it in a way that relates it *only* to its subject, as a modification of the subject's state, we have to omit its being of something cubic, since that characterizes outwardly directed intentionality.

8. In "Empiricism and the Philosophy of Mind", as I said, Sellars puts forward a conception of experiences on which they contain propositional claims. I used to take that to be a version of the thought I have attributed to Kant—that experience is sensory consciousness informed by the higher faculty.[24] That made it an urgent question for me why Sellars thinks he must *also* invoke sensations, conceived as a further element in experiences over and above their containing claims.

An implication of what I have urged here is that my question had a false presupposition. Sellars comes close to Kant in saying experiences contain claims. But all he can make of that idea is that experiences are composites, with claim-containing items accounting for their intentionality and sensations accounting for their sensory character. And this reflects his not arriving at what I take to be the authentically Kantian view. Sellars does not envisage claim-containing occurrences that are themselves shapings of sensory consciousness.

Sellars thinks a phenomenologically acute consideration of experiences in which one seems to see the red and triangular facing side of an object discloses a "descriptive core" consisting in "the fact that *something* in *some*

---

24. This was how I understood Sellars in Essays 1, 2, and 3 above.

way red and triangular is in *some* way present to the perceiver *other than as thought of*".[25]

It is implicit here that there are two kinds of presence: presence to thought and presence to sense. Sellars's talk of presence otherwise than as thought of distinguishes the sensational aspect of experiencing from the thinking that is its other aspect. He writes: "A scholastic might say that in perception (and ostensible perception) the relevant proper and common sensibles have *being for sense* as well as *being for thought*. Thus, when I see or ostensibly see something to be a pink ice cube, a pink cube has not only being for thought but also being for sense. The *somehow* presence of the pink cube could then be referred to as its being sensed."[26]

In this formulation, it is the *same* items that have being for sense and being for thought. This is not an identification of being for sense with being for thought. For Sellars, being for thought is a matter of intentionality, and being for sense is not. But he takes quite seriously the idea that what has being for thought, in the intentional component of an ostensible seeing of a pink cube, is the *something somehow* pink and cubic that he thinks is present to the perceiver otherwise than as thought of, the "descriptive core" of the experience.[27] On this view the conceptual element in perception miscon-strues sensed volumes of colour as occupants of public space endowed with sensible properties. What has being for thought in experience is, as in the scholastic formulation, the same thing that has being for sense.

It can seem unquestionable that whenever one ostensibly sees a pink cube, even if one's experience is a merely ostensible seeing, there is an actual sensory presence to one, something that cannot be accommodated by ac-knowledging that one is *thinking*, in whatever way, of a pink cube. That is what Sellars is supposing when he takes it to be clear that over and above the intentionality in an ostensible seeing of a pink cube, there is sensing in the of-a-pink-cube manner—that *something somehow* pink and cubic is present to one *otherwise than as thought of,* in no matter what mode of thought. But this idea loses its seeming compulsoriness if thinkings of a pink cube can include items that are sensory consciousness informed by the higher faculty.

25. "The Structure of Knowledge", p. 310. He uses this kind of language in several places.

26. Ibid.

27. See the closing pages of "Some Reflections on Perceptual Consciousness", and "Foundations for a Metaphysics of Pure Process".

With this different conception of the possibilities for acts of thought, we can say that when one sees a pink cube, the pink cube has a being for thought that *is* being for sense. When one merely seems to see a pink cube, there merely seems to be an instance of that kind of being for thought. That is, there merely seems to be an instance of the being for sense that that kind of being for thought is.

Not that there merely seems to be visual *Empfindung*. By abstracting from intentionality, we can redescribe a merely ostensible seeing, no less than an actual seeing, as a mere affection of its subject's sensibility. *Qua* mere affection of sensibility, a merely ostensible seeing can be indistinguishable from the affection of sensibility there would have been if there had been an actual seeing. That leaves it unmysterious that there should seem to be an instance of the being for thought that is being for sense. That is the only kind of presence we need to countenance. Merely ostensible seeings seem— merely seem—to be instances of that kind of presence. That suffices to accommodate their phenomenology. There is no need for a kind of presence of which they are actual instances.

In this picture, there is only one task for the productive imagination where Sellars's reading has two. The productive imagination generates representations with conceptual content partly expressible by phrases of the form "this such". So far, this matches Sellars's reading. But there is no extra task of effecting constructions in sensibility, Sellars's image-models. The conceptual representation partly expressible by, say, "this pink cube" already belongs to sensibility no less than to the understanding. An episode or state with content expressible like that is itself a shaping of sensory consciousness. What the productive imagination generates is a unity involving both sensibility and understanding—not an amalgam, however intimately bound together, of components that belong severally to sensibility and understanding.

9. Why is Sellars convinced that Kantian thinking must be understood his way? I shall end by mentioning some explanations. Each would need a great deal of discussion.

First, Sellars is influenced by a disputable interpretation of the idea, in itself plausible, that to have its objective purport conceptual activity must be constrained from outside itself. This part of his thinking is encapsulated in the following passage: "it is only if Kant distinguishes the radically non-conceptual character of sense from the conceptual character of the synthesis of apprehension in intuition . . . and, accordingly, the *receptivity* of sense from the *guidedness* of intuition that he can avoid the dialectic which leads from Hegel's *Phenomenology* to nineteenth-century idealism."[28]

Second, Sellars's thought about perception must be understood in the context of his project of a stereoscopic vision, combining the scientific and the manifest images of man-in-the-world. Sellars thinks due respect for the scientific image requires us to displace colours from their manifest-image status as real qualities of external objects. His conception of the sensational aspect of experience is, in part, a concession, by way of compensation, to the phenomenological basis for the manifest-image conception of colours. (He envisages an ultimate integration of sensation into the scientific image, conceptually enriched as needed.)[29]

As a ground for thinking the philosophy of perception must take the shape Sellars gives it, and for reading Kant as adumbrating a view on those lines, this stands or falls with the project of a stereoscopic vision. That is a large issue. But as I have already indicated, I see no good reason to say external objects are not coloured. And I add: not just when we delineate the manifest image, but when we say how things really are. This does not deny science the respect it is due.[30]

As I noted, Sellars's attitude towards the manifest-image conception of colours matches something in Kant. But that does not justify reading Kant as Sellars does. We can bypass questions about secondary qualities and still see a point in conceiving experience as sensory consciousness informed by the higher faculty. We do Kant better service, not by denying him that conception, on the ground that the result would underwrite the view he takes of secondary qualities, but by relieving him of that view, on the ground that it has no basis apart from a misconstrual of what science can teach us.

Third, it is plausible that Sellars's thinking is shaped by a dualism of rationality and animal nature. That would account for the absence, from his inventory of possibilities, of the idea that the higher faculty—what distinguishes us from other animals—might inform the deliverances of our sensibility, a capacity we have by virtue of being, simply, animals. But one great

28. *Science and Metaphysics*, p. 16. I consider this part of Sellars's thinking in Essays 2 and 3 above.

29. See "Philosophy and the Scientific Image of Man", and "Foundations for a Metaphysics of Pure Process."

30. See my papers "Values and Secondary Qualities" and "Aesthetic Value, Objectivity, and the Fabric of the World".

beauty of the position I am representing as authentically Kantian is its immunity to such dualisms. It exemplifies a frame of mind in which they are seen as mere prejudice.

Fourth, Sellars has a conception of thought's bearing on objects—as we can put it so as to leave everything open—that would imply that no idea of being for *thought* could accommodate the *presence* to us that characterizes the phenomenology of our perceptual experience when we see something, and seems to characterize it when we seem to see something. It would make no difference if we singled out a kind of thought supposedly distinctive of ostensible seeing. For Sellars, thinking has its subject matter in the mode of *signifying*, and he holds that signifying must not be understood in relational terms.[31] But a genuine *presence* of an object to a subject would be a relation between the object and the subject. So for Sellars, it could not be captured by any idea of being for *thought*. I believe this reflects a mistake on Sellars's part. But that is a topic for a different paper.[32]

31. See, e.g., *Science and Metaphysics*, p. ix, where Sellars says that appreciating "the non-relational character of 'meaning' and 'aboutness'" is "the key to a correct understanding of the position of mind in nature". He uses the language of signifying in, for instance, "Being and Being Known".

32. There is a first shot, not quite in this context, in Essay 3 above.

Conceptual Capacities
in Perception

1. Our perceptually based beliefs are intelligible as manifestations of rationality. We can make sense of them by putting them in an explanatory nexus with perceptual experience. If someone has a perceptually based belief, she believes something because her experience reveals to her, or at least seems to reveal to her, that things are as she believes them to be. And that "because" introduces an explanation that depends on the idea of rationality in operation.

I think crediting our perceptual experience with this rational significance is a fundamental insight of empiricism. I have argued that, in order to accommodate it, we need to conceive our perceptual experience as an actualization, in sensory consciousness, of conceptual capacities.[1]

This conception of our perceptual experience bears a resemblance to Kant's conception of empirical intuitions. In the first *Critique* (especially clearly in the Transcendental Deduction), Kant conceives empirical intuitions as configurations in sensory receptivity that are categorially structured. For Kant, intuitions belong together with judgments in this respect: what makes their objective purport possible is that they have categorial unity. To put a Kantian thought in a contemporary idiom, the content of intuitions is of the same general kind as the content of judgments. And of course the content of judgments is conceptual.

This echo of Kant brings out a connection with the theme of creativity.[2] Kant introduces the understanding, the seat of conceptual capacities, by contrasting it with the receptivity of sensibility. He describes the understanding as "the mind's power of producing representations from itself, the

---

1. See *Mind and World*, and Essays 1, 2, and 3 above.
2. This essay was written for a conference with creativity as its overarching theme.

spontaneity of knowledge" (A51/B75). Even more directly, he says that concepts are "based on the spontaneity of thought" (A68/B93). So his conception of empirical intuitions links their objective purport, their serving to make objects immediately present to us, with a capacity he attributes to us for spontaneous self-determination in thought.

I shall come back to this. But first I am going to spend some time elaborating the conception of perceptual experience that credits this role to the spontaneous understanding. The main task is to explain the relevant idea of conceptual capacities. That will require first saying something about the idea of rationality.

2. I said that perceptually based belief is linked to experience by an explanatory nexus that depends on the idea of the workings of rationality. The notion of rationality I mean to invoke here is the notion exploited in a traditional line of thought to make a special place in the animal kingdom for rational animals. It is a notion of responsiveness to reasons *as such*.

That wording leaves room for responsiveness to reasons, though not to reasons as such, on the other side of the division drawn by this notion of rationality between rational animals and animals that are not rational. Animals of many kinds are capable of, for instance, fleeing. And fleeing is a response to something that is in an obvious sense a reason for it: danger, or at least what is taken to be danger. If we describe a bit of behaviour as fleeing, we represent the behaviour as intelligible in the light of a reason for it. But fleeing is not in general responding to a reason as such.

For that idea to be appropriate in this connection, we would need to be considering a subject who can step back from an inclination to flee, elicited from her by an apparent danger, and raise the question whether she *should* be so inclined—whether the apparent danger is, here and now, a sufficient reason for fleeing. If what an animal does flows immediately from its natural motivational tendencies, with no room for this kind of reflection, its behaviour is determined by its nature. That is not to deny that its behaviour is voluntary; and an animal, *qua* producer of voluntary behaviour, is not to be simply identified with the motivational impulses that come naturally to it. But in this kind of case the distinction between the behaving animal and its motivational impulses has no particular importance. There is no particular point in saying it is the animal itself that determines what it does. In contrast, consider a person who steps back from an inclination to flee that comes naturally to her, and decides that the circumstance that elicits the inclination is a sufficient reason for fleeing. If she then acts on that reason, she is self-determining in her action.

This is only an example, to give the flavour of the conception of rationality I mean to appeal to. Obviously reasons for acting are not exhausted by circumstances of a sort that would naturally prompt inclinations, when those circumstances are transformed into reasons, able to be responded to as such, for a subject who can raise the question whether that is what they are. And of course there are also reasons for belief.

Let me stress that what matters is the *capacity* to step back and assess whether putative reasons warrant action or belief. If someone actually steps back, of course that shows she has the capacity to do so. But if the capacity is present without being exercised, we have in view someone who can respond to reasons as the reasons they are. And rationality in the sense I am explaining may be actually operative even though the capacity to step back is not being exercised. Acting for a reason, which one is responding to as such, does not require that one reflects about whether some consideration is a sufficient rational warrant for something it seems to recommend. It is enough that one could.

Consider someone following a marked trail, who at a crossing of paths goes to the right in response to a signpost pointing that way. It would be absurd to say that for going to the right to be a rational response to the signpost, it must issue from the subject's making an explicit determination that the way the signpost points gives her a reason for going to the right. What matters is just that she acts as she does because (this is a reason-introducing "because") the signpost points to the right. (This explanation competes with, for instance, supposing she goes to the right at random, without noticing the signpost, or noticing it but not understanding it.) What shows that she goes to the right in rational response to the way the signpost points might be just that she can afterwards answer the question why she went to the right—a request for her reason for doing that—by saying "There was a signpost pointing to the right". She need not have adverted to that reason and decided on that basis to go to the right.

3. I find it helpful to connect the idea of conceptual capacities with this notion of rationality. I use the idea of conceptual capacities in a way that is governed by this stipulation: conceptual capacities in the relevant sense belong essentially to their possessor's rationality in the sense I am working with, responsiveness to reasons as such.

The primary context for the idea of responsiveness to reasons as such is *reasoning*: an activity in which someone explicitly considers what to believe or what to do, and takes reasons into account in determining her belief or her action. Capacities can be at work in operations of rationality, and so can be conceptual capacities in the sense of my stipulation, only in subjects who can exercise those capacities in reasoning. The ability to step back and assess whether putative reasons really are reasons, which I exploited when I introduced the idea of responsiveness to reasons as such, is part of the ability to reason. So to invoke reasoning is just to provide a label for the context in which I am putting the idea of responsiveness to reasons as such.

If an animal has in its repertoire behaviour appropriately conceived as fleeing, it must be able to discriminate (perhaps not very accurately) between situations that pose danger to it and situations that do not. But given my stipulation, this ability to discriminate does not suffice for having the concept of danger. Having the concept requires a subject who can respond to dangerousness as the reason it is. And that requires in turn the ability to take dangerousness into account in reasoning.

Now that I have introduced reasoning, I can put a point I have made already like this: cases in which one engages in reasoning do not exhaust the scope of one's responsiveness to reasons as such. Consider again the person who, without taking thought as to what to do, goes to the right in rational response to a signpost that points that way. Up to a point, her behaviour, unreflective as it is, is like going to the right on the part of an animal that has been trained to go to the right in response to objects with a certain shape. Such an animal has acquired an ability to discriminate between things that have that shape and things that do not. But as with the ability to discriminate between situations that pose danger and situations that do not, this does not suffice for having the concept of things that point to the right. Having the concept requires the ability to take something's falling under it into account in reasoning. Our rational subject has that ability, though she does not exercise it on the occasion we are considering, when she goes to the right without reasoning to a decision to do so. And the conceptual capacity that her possession of the ability entitles us to attribute to her, with the concept of things that point to the right as its content, is operative also in the unreflective response we are considering: a response, not involving reasoning, to a signpost's pointing to the right as a reason for going to the right. Conceptual capacities in the relevant sense are at work not just in reasoning but, in general, in responding to reasons as such, whether or not it takes the form of explicitly drawing conclusions from reasons in forming beliefs or in acting.

4. I have connected responsiveness to reasons as such, and hence conceptual capacities, with reasoning. That is to put the relevant notion of rationality in the context of a notion of *inference*, understood broadly enough to cover acting in consequence of practical reasoning as well as coming to believe something in consequence of theoretical reasoning. If someone believes something or acts in a certain way for a reason, she need not have reached her belief or her action by an inferential step. But I have so far considered only operations of rationality involving structures of a kind that *could* characterize theoretical or practical inferences, from reasons to beliefs or actions.

But my aim was to spell out how the idea of rationality is in play when we explain perceptual beliefs in terms of experience. And here the notion of inference gets no grip. When one acquires a belief in this way, one comes to believe that things are as one's experience reveals, or at least seems to reveal, that things are. The content that the explanation attributes to the experience is the same as the content of the belief explained, not a premise from which it would make sense to think of the subject as having reached the belief by an inferential step.[3]

This does not undermine the thought that these explanations make beliefs intelligible as results of the subject's rationality at work. And here too, this is rationality in the sense that separates rational from non-rational animals, the sense I have tried to capture in terms of responsiveness to reasons as such. (This is widely controverted, on the ground that it prevents us from accommodating the way non-rational animals come to know about things through their senses. It should be clear later why this is wrong.)

One can have an experience that reveals to one that things are thus and so without coming to believe that things are thus and so. One need not avail oneself of every rational entitlement one has. Consider a case in which one is misled into mistrusting one's experience. One does not believe it is revealing to one how things are, but in fact it is doing just that.

A belief-acquisition explicable as rational in the light of an experience is a case of rationality at work, even though, as I have urged, this mode of

---

3. This formulation leaves room for acknowledging that the experience has content over and above what is invoked in explaining the belief.

operation of rationality is not capturable by a structure that could characterize an inference. The belief is intelligible in terms of a rational entitlement to it supplied by the experience. And since having the experience constitutes a rational entitlement to belief whether or not one acquires the belief it entitles one to, that same rationality must be at work in one's having the experience at all, even if one does not acquire the belief it entitles one to. So, applying the stipulation to this case: if our notion of an experience is to be capable of playing the role it plays when we explain perceptually based beliefs as manifestations of rationality, we must understand having such an experience—being in possession of such an entitlement—as itself, already, an actualization of the conceptual capacities that would be exercised by someone who explicitly adopted a belief with that content.[4]

This is a kind of actualization of conceptual capacities whose members are cases of perceiving, or at least seeming to perceive, that things are thus and so. When we explain someone's believing that things are thus and so in terms of the fact that her experience merely seems to reveal to her that things are thus and so, the explanation depicts the belief as a result of rationality leading its possessor astray, or at best equipping her with a true belief by a fortunate accident. But when we explain someone's believing that things are thus and so in terms of her perceiving that things are thus and so, we are displaying the belief as a result of this kind of operation of rationality in its ideal form.

5. It is important that the connection between conceptual capacities and rationality is a stipulation. It is not that there is a universally shared idea of conceptual capacities, which determines a subject matter about whose properties people disagree. The notion of the conceptual can be used in a variety of ways, for a variety of purposes.

---

4. Clearly I am not using the term "entitlement" as Tyler Burge does in "Perceptual Entitlement". Burge does not locate entitlement in the context of a notion of self-determining rationality. Indeed he discourages the traditional divide between rational and non-rational animals, which he accuses of leading to "hyper-intellectualization" (pp. 503–4). Astonishingly, Burge writes (p. 504, n. 1) as if his "introduction" of "entitlement" used his way, in papers from 1993 and 1995, gave him some kind of patent on the term, so that he can complain that different uses are "indiscriminate". My use is not indiscriminate, and the word, ordinary English as it is, is anyone's property. It can be used with complete naturalness in any "normative" epistemology. I shall consider the accusation of "hyper-intellectualization" in n. 11 below.

It is also important that the notion of responsiveness to reasons as such leaves room for responding to reasons, though not to reasons as such, on the other side of the divide between rational animals and animals that are not rational. And responding to reasons implies awareness of what is responded to.[5]

If someone wants to say an animal with fleeing in its repertoire is thereby shown to have the concept of danger, I need not object. This is to use the concept of a concept otherwise than in accord with my stipulation. But that is all right, provided that we keep track of the divergence, and do not mistake it for a substantive dispute about a supposedly common subject matter.

On this way of talking, a concept of danger is in play in any awareness, or (to accommodate the possibility of mistakes) seeming awareness, of danger. And using the concept of a concept like this affords a way of insisting on a good point: that to be able to be aware of danger, an animal need not be rational, in the sense that figures in the traditional divide between rational animals and others. Obviously this generalizes to other objects of animal awareness.

This is fine by my lights. As I said, the point is a good one. It definitely contradicts the idea that if an animal's fleeing is not a response to a reason as such, the animal's differential responsiveness to danger can be no more than a responsive disposition, in a sense that is not restricted to the discriminating capacities of sentient beings. On this view, the differential responsiveness to danger manifested in an animal's capacity for fleeing would not license crediting the animal with being able to be aware of danger, any more than, say, iron's differential responsiveness to moisture in its surroundings—a disposition to rust if there is moisture and not to rust if there is not—licenses supposing bits of iron can be aware of the presence of moisture.[6] I think this

5. The general point here is that stressing the distinction between rational and non-rational animals is consistent with insisting on a substantial continuity across the divide. In "Perceptual Entitlement" Burge seems oblivious to this possibility. This underlies, among other things, an uncomprehending treatment of Wilfrid Sellars and philosophers influenced by him, at pp. 526–30.

6. Consider Robert Brandom's account of observational knowledge (see chapter 4 of *Making It Explicit*). Brandom's account implies that if we start with capacities for observational knowledge and subtract conceptual capacities, in a demanding sense that can be explained in terms of a connection with rationality, the remainder is nothing but reliable differential responsive dispositions—dispositions of a kind possessed not only by animals but also by inanimate objects such as thermometers or, even more simply, collections of iron filings.

should be rejected out of hand. It flies in the face of common sense about how the behaviour of living animals is to be understood.

But to preserve common sense about animal awareness, we do not need to detach conceptual capacities from responsiveness to reasons as such. My stipulation does not require debunking the idea of awareness that is not conceptual. The restriction effected by my stipulation applies only to awareness that figures in the operations of rationality in the demanding sense. And there is no need to suppose the capacity to figure in the operations of rationality is an element in the very idea of awareness.[7]

6. For a substantive objection to my proposed conception of our perceptual experience, as opposed to the merely terminological divergence I have just been discussing, we need to consider a position that accepts the stipulative identification of conceptual capacities in terms of their potential role in reasoning, but disputes my claim that conceptual capacities, so understood, are operative in our perceptual experience.

Many people have taken this line. A commonly felt incredulity takes this form: if one supposes, as I do, that the content of our experience is conceptual, in a sense in which the conceptual is connected with rationality, one cannot do justice to the *sensory* way in which perceptual experience discloses reality to us.

For instance, Michael Ayers, in arguing that the content of sense experience, including ours, is non-conceptual, stresses *"the way things are presented in experience*, the sensory mode of presentation . . .".* He identifies the claim

---

7. Michael Ayers, in "Sense Experience, Concepts, and Content—Objections to Davidson and McDowell", says (p. 239) that I am equivocal about perceptual awareness on the part of non-rational animals. (He spells out this claim at p. 261. There he says my thinking tends in the direction of a Cartesian view of "animals", though—the other side of my supposedly equivocal stance—my exposition is "larded with disclaimers".) This reflects his finding it obvious that what perceptual awareness is for rational animals cannot be different in kind from what it is for non-rational animals. The result is that when I deny that non-rational animals have, in the way of perceptual awareness, what we have, he cannot hear that except as implying that they do not have perceptual awareness at all. This is an example of the bad effects of bringing one's own sense of what is obvious to reading someone else. It can make for being unable to hear what someone is saying. And it is especially bad practice when, as in this case, the target of the reading is precisely questioning the sense of what is obvious that controls the reading. Ayers's suggestion that my thinking tends towards a Cartesian denial of consciousness to non-rational animals is groundless.

that this is non-conceptual with the claim—which he represents as sheer common sense—"that the way the world is presented in experience is not quasi-linguistic".[8] His thought, then, is that if our experience were conceptual, it would present the world in a quasi-linguistic way, and that is inconsistent with the obvious fact that experience presents the world in a sensory way.

But what I recommended was a conception of our experience as actualization of conceptual capacities *in sensory consciousness*. To adopt that conception of our experience is to accept, indeed to insist, that our experience presents the world in a sensory way. Ayers is disallowing the very possibility of supposing, as I do, that a conceptual mode of presentation might itself be a sensory mode of presentation.

Ayers equates the claim that our experience has conceptual content with the claim that it presents the world in a quasi-linguistic way. That might seem to justify excluding the possibility that a conceptual mode of presentation might be a sensory mode of presentation. But in so far as the equation seems to justify the exclusion, it is tendentious. What is right about the equation is this: it is plausible that the ability to step back from considerations and raise the question whether they constitute reasons for action or belief, which I have invoked as a necessary context for conceptual capacities in the sense of my stipulation, is coeval with command of a language. So only speakers can have conceptual capacities in the sense of my stipulation. But this does not justify claiming that my conception of our experience represents the experienceable world as a text, or, in Arthur Collins's image, that I am committed to a picture in which our experience comes as it were with subtitles—as if the conceptual way in which, according to me, our experience purports to disclose the world to us would be an extra feature of it, additional to its sensory character.[9]

Collins's image helps to make vivid a specific form often taken by the claim that conceptual content cannot accommodate the sensory way experience presents things. There is no plausible elaboration of the image in which subtitles could capture, say, all the differences of shade that normal colour experience finds in the visible world. But this is no problem for my proposal, because the image of subtitles does not fit my proposal. Our visual

---

8. "Sense Experience, Concepts, and Content", p. 249.

9. See Arthur W. Collins, "Beastly Experience", p. 379. For the idea of experienceable reality as a text, see Ayers, "Sense Experience, Concepts, and Content", p. 251, n. 23.

experience can present a shade of colour that is as determinate as our ability to discriminate shades can make it. A determinate shade is present in a sensory way to the subject of such an experience. But its sensory presence to her is an operation of a capacity that belongs to her responsiveness to reasons as such, and hence is conceptual in the sense of my stipulation. This is reflected in the fact that to enjoy the experience is to have a rational entitlement to a belief that the thing has just that shade. In the ideal case, it is an entitlement that amounts to the subject's being in a position to know, by way of an operation of her rationality in the demanding sense, that the thing has just that shade.[10]

In disallowing my proposal that actualizations of conceptual capacities can present things in a sensory way, Ayers assumes a sharp separation between the sensory and the intellectual, as I shall put it to avoid that tendentious implication.

But such a separation is not uncontentiously correct. If a dualism of intellect and senses is merely assumed, it is question-begging to exploit it against me. And what justification can there be for the dualism? It is taken for granted in the empiricist tradition, but in this dialectical context that

---

10. In *Mind and World* (pp. 56–60), I connected these fine-grained conceptual capacities with the ability to capture a shade of colour (say) by using a demonstrative expression that depends for its significance on an experience in which something is seen as having that shade of colour. I wrote of expressions like "that shade". ("Coloured thus" would have been better, for reasons that come out in my response to Christopher Peacocke in "Reply to Commentators", at pp. 414–7.) Ayers, "Sense Experience, Concepts, and Content", p. 260, argues that on this account, the shade would have to be presented in experience independently of a conceptual capacity whose content could receive linguistic expression in that way; so it would have to be presented in experience non-conceptually. But there is no basis for this. Certainly the shade must be presented in experience anyway, for its presence to be able to help determine the significance of the demonstrative expression. But that is consistent with its presence in experience being an operation of a conceptual capacity—one that, thanks to the shade's presence in experience (that is, thanks to this operation of the conceptual capacity it is), can be captured by the demonstrative expression. Ayers's impression to the contrary depends on mishandling the connection between conceptual capacities and language. (In effect, he is allowing the subtitles picture to confuse him.) He proceeds as if I had to suppose the content in question acquires a conceptual form only when language is actually used, in that demonstrative form, to express it. The intelligibility of the demonstrative form would require that the content was already there—hence, on this view, before the content acquired conceptual form. But it is enough for the content to be conceptual that it *can* be given that linguistic expression. It does not become conceptual only when actually given that linguistic expression.

would be an unimpressive basis for defending it. So much the worse for the empiricist tradition, we might say. Resting content with a dualism of the sensory and the intellectual betrays a failure of imagination about the possibilities for finding the rational intellect integrally involved in the phenomena of human life.[11] We should argue in the other direction. Actualizations of conceptual capacities, capacities that belong to their subject's rationality, can present things in a sensory way, and that gives the lie to the dualism.

7. Donald Davidson notoriously claimed that "nothing can count as a reason for holding a belief except another belief".[12] I objected that this does not accommodate the role of experience in making beliefs rationally intelligible. Experiences are not beliefs. But I suggested we can preserve an insight from Davidson's slogan, by saying nothing can count as a reason for a belief except something with conceptual form.[13]

Ayers objects that there is nothing worth preserving from Davidson's slogan. All kinds of things can be reasons for belief. A photograph can be a reason for a belief about the assassination of John F. Kennedy. A perceived zebra can be a reason for a belief about what zebras look like. And so on.[14]

Of course that is right, about a familiar way of using the notion of a reason. But this is a cheap victory, which leaves the spirit of Davidson's slogan untouched.

In the cases the slogan fits (which do not include perceptually based beliefs), Davidson's claim is obviously not that one bases a belief on *one's*

---

11. Burge thinks stressing the self-determining rationality of rational animals leads to "hyper-intellectualization" in epistemology (op. cit., pp. 503–4). But insisting that rational animals are special leads to the excess of intellectualism he rightly deplores only in conjunction with a dualistic separation of the rational intellect from the senses, or more generally from the cognitively relevant endowments we have by virtue of our animal nature. The accusation does not fit what I am urging. Without the dualism, we need not discount the biologically anchored cognitive "norms" Burge discusses. They are surely relevant to understanding the norms that govern the cognitive conduct of rational animals. But we do not fall into "hyper-intellectualism" if we insist that being subject to the latter norms is characteristic of cognition with a categorially different nature.

12. "A Coherence Theory of Truth and Knowledge", p. 141.

13. See *Mind and World*, pp. 141, 143–4.

14. "Sense Experience, Concepts, and Content", pp. 243–4, 248–9.

believing something else—as if, in Ayers's example, one concluded that Kennedy was shot by someone on the ground from the fact that *one believes* a photograph shows someone shooting at him from the ground. It is *what* one believes, not one's believing it, that is one's reason in the sense Davidson is concerned with. And this is easily extended to make room for the idiom Ayers exploits. In that idiom, one describes as reasons items that belong to the subject matter of beliefs that are reasons in Davidson's sense. That is the sense in which the photograph is a reason for a belief about the assassination.

If we abstract Davidson's slogan away from the effects of his blind spot about the possibility of crediting experience with rational significance, we can understand its point on these lines: the capacities at work when one's rationality is operative must be capacities that belong to one's rationality. How could that be wrong? Certainly one can adduce a photograph as evidence for a belief about the assassination, not just out loud, trying to persuade someone else, but also in deciding what to think. The point of Davidson's slogan is not to deny that, but to claim that the photograph can play that role, a role in an operation of rationality, only by figuring in the content of an actualization of capacities that belong to one's rationality: that is, capacities that are conceptual in the sense of my stipulation. I explained earlier (in §4) how this abstract core of Davidson's thought carries over into what we need to say in order to acknowledge the rational significance of experience, as Davidson does not. Ayers's reminder about what he calls (rightly so far as it goes) "a basic kind of reason-giving" (p. 243) does not address these considerations. It leaves them completely unscathed.

8. Let me go back now to the connection with the theme of creativity.

To introduce the notion of rationality I wanted to work with, I contrasted fleeing as the immediate outcome of a natural impulse with fleeing as the result of deciding that a circumstance that is tending to elicit an impulse to flee constitutes a sufficient reason to do so. In the second case, fleeing is not merely voluntary but determined by the agent herself. Generalized, this contrast yields something on these lines: what is special about rational animals is that they are capable of *self-determination*, in thought and action. A rational animal has the capacity to be in control of its life, to live in such a way that its life is something of its own making. If a life is led with the freedom that rationality makes possible, there is some point in comparing it to a work of art that the subject is engaged in creating.

Of course what rationality confers is only the *capacity* to live a life that is one's own in the sense I am gesturing at. To what extent the capacity is exercised, and in which regions of life, depends on all kinds of factors. The conditions under which the potential for freedom can be realized are an important topic for philosophy.

Now what I have proposed is that capacities that belong to this special potentiality of rational animals, capacities for self-determination in thought, are essentially involved in the acquisition by rational animals of perceptually based beliefs.

We need to be careful about how the idea of a capacity to be in charge of one's life fits in this context. Once one has determined such things as the direction of one's gaze, it is not under one's control how one's experience purports to reveal things to be. Moreover, coming to believe something on the basis of experience is not in general happily conceived as deciding what to think. It is true that there are cases in which, with more or less effort, one can refuse to accept that things are as they, say, look to be. If one is familiar with the Müller-Lyer illusion, one inhibits the tendency to judge that one of the two lines is longer than the other, even though, however familiar one is with the illusion, one line goes on looking longer. But perceptual experience can bring facts into plain view. And when that is the appropriate thing to say, it would be absurd to talk of deciding what to think, as if one exercised an option. One does not choose to accept that things are the way one's experience plainly reveals that they are.

We might put this by saying there is a sense in which perceptual experience can compel belief. But because capacities for rational self-determination are at work in one's being subject to this compulsion, it does not detract from one's being in rational control of one's life. Compare the sense in which one can be compelled to accept the conclusion of a cogent argument whose premises one is unshakeably committed to. One does not sacrifice one's freedom if one acquiesces in the authority of what one recognizes as compelling reasons. Recognizing reasons as compelling is itself an exercise of one's capacities for rational self-determination. If one offers no resistance when one's beliefs take the form reason requires them to take, one is not handing over that region of one's life to an alien force. One is not abdicating from the responsibility to be in rational control of one's thinking.[15]

9. Ayers objects to the idea that empiricism cannot credit perceptual experience with a content that goes beyond sensations. He invokes a position with "a respectable empiricist ancestry" (he cites Hobbes), according to which "what is 'given' in a sensation of a green light flashing . . . is just that, a green light flashing". The sensory states enjoyed by a perceiver themselves already have intentional content, and the sense in which perceptual beliefs are grounded in sensation is that they derive their intentional content from the intentional content of the sensory states they are based on. "That, on this view, is what believing one's senses is. No inference is involved, and there is no intermediary. We just accept what the senses conjointly give."[16]

I think this is just the shape an acceptable empiricism must have. It is precisely to make room for a view with this shape that I urge the conception of our experience that Ayers resists. It is precisely to provide for the thought that perceptual experience can directly open us to the world that I claim we must see experience as an actualization of conceptual capacities, capacities that belong to our special character as rational animals.

As I have explained, this is not to deny that non-rational animals become informed or misinformed through their senses, about features of reality that matter to them. It is just to insist on a difference between that and coming to know things through perception as we do, in an operation of rationality in the strong sense, responsiveness to reasons as such.

15. Richard Rorty suggests that conceiving thought as answerable to its subject matter represents the world as a secular counterpart of an authoritarian deity. See, e.g., "Solidarity or Objectivity?" and "The Very Idea of Human Answerability to the World: John McDowell's Version of Empiricism". This is meant to show that regarding objectivity as a constitutive ideal of thought flouts the obligation to think for oneself, which is part of the content of the obligation to live one's own life. I think the considerations I am sketching here show that this position of Rorty's depends on misinterpreting the obligation to think for oneself. The obligation to think for oneself cannot require one to emancipate one's thinking from being controlled by good reasons. And when one's experience reveals to one how things are, one is in possession of an excellent reason to think things are that way. Rorty is right to recoil from various extremist forms of realism, but he is wrong to let that lead him into an undiscriminating attack on all forms of the idea that objectivity is a constitutive goal of thought.

16. All the quotations in this paragraph are from "Sense Experience, Concepts, and Content", p. 241.

Non-rational animals become informed or misinformed through the unmediated functioning of their senses. It would be a failure of ear if one found it appropriate to describe them as *believing their senses* or *accepting what their senses give*. Such talk fits belief-formation by subjects who can *refuse* to believe their senses—belief-formation intelligible as rationality, in the sense of responsiveness to reasons as such, at work.

As I have urged, seeing our acquisition of perceptual beliefs as rationality at work does not imply that we always come to such beliefs by deciding what to think. Normally we arrive at our perceptually based beliefs without reflection. But what we do without reflection can be described as believing our senses or accepting what our senses give only because it is a manifestation of our rationality in the demanding sense, and hence, as I have explained, an actualization of capacities that belong to our rational understanding, capacities we do not share with non-rational animals.

10. Ayers's resistance to the idea that conceptual capacities are operative in our perceptual experience is largely driven by his hostility to the idealism he takes it to open into.

Now there is justice in the thought that the idea can seem to work only in the context of an idealism. And I think this is central to a supposed ground, not unique to Ayers, for disbelieving that capacities that essentially belong to our potential for self-determination can be in play in what is supposed to be our sensory reception of reality. But here we need a distinction Ayers makes nothing of.

Any idealism with a chance of being credible must aspire to being such that, if thought through, it stands revealed as fully cohering with the realism of common sense.[17] Kant, for instance, has that aspiration for his transcendental idealism. This shows in his claim that it coincides with empirical realism. However, because of the way he treats the forms of our sensibility, he fails to entitle himself to that claim. In his picture, the world as we experience it seems, in respect of its apparent spatial and temporal organization, to be a mere reflection of self-standing features of our subjectivity. So the aim at a coincidence with realism fails.

---

17. In *Notebooks 1914–1916*, p. 85, Wittgenstein writes that "idealism leads to realism if it is strictly thought out". (At *Tractatus Logico-Philosophicus* §5.64, the coincidence with realism is directly credited to solipsism, which figures in the route from idealism to realism in the *Notebooks*.)

Of course particular failures cannot undermine the very idea of an idealism that coincides with common sense. Ayers, however, cannot see anything idealism could be, apart from a position that represents features of the structure of reality (so called, we would have to say) as projections from characteristics of a self-standing subjectivity, as Kant's idealism does in spite of his aspiration for it.

In my *Mind and World*, I argue that the conceptual content of a perceptual experience can be, and if all goes well is, something that is the case, an element in the world. We can see experience as directly taking in part of the world, because the world, understood as everything that is the case, is not outside the sphere of the conceptual. I remark that this can seem to be "a sort of idealism, in the sense in which to call a position 'idealism' is to protest that it does not genuinely acknowledge how reality is independent of our thinking" (p. 26). But I work to dislodge such an appearance.

Now Ayers quotes from the sentence I have just quoted from (op. cit., p. 252). But he ends his quotation before the gloss in which I specify the sort of idealism I want to disown. Evidently he thinks the gloss is redundant; as he sees things, idealism just *is* a position that insufficiently acknowledges the independence of reality.

This has consequences. When I reject the accusation that I represent the world as a projection from our subjectivity, Ayers thinks I must be denying that "the form of judgement structures the world as experienced and known" (pp. 254–5). He thinks I must conceive the world as standing to our thought and talk in a large-scale counterpart to the relation in which, say, a zebra might stand to our thought and talk about it. A zebra can be described, but that is no reason to suppose the zebra itself has a form it shares with a description, or with the thought a description expresses. Just so, Ayers thinks I think, with the world. (Anything else would be idealism, and I have declared that I am against that.) And then, if what I say about the world is "no more than a way of putting the platitude that the world and things in it are describable" (p. 253), Ayers cannot see how I can disallow a parallel move about experience. No doubt what experience gives us can be expressed in propositional or conceptual form, but that is no reason to suppose experience itself has conceptual form, any more than zebras do, and hence any more than the world does, on the conception he thinks he finds in me.

Here Ayers has been led into a misreading by his assumption that any notion of the world as itself conceptually structured must imply what I explicitly disavow, that the world is a mere reflection of a self-standing subjectivity. In the passage he is considering, I discuss the remark "The world is everything that is the case", the first sentence in Wittgenstein's *Tractatus*. I urge that we should not take it to express "a grand ontological or metaphysical vision", to use Ayers's words (p. 252). My point is that we can understand the remark as spelling out, truistically, the content of an unimpeachable way to use the notion of the world. My point is not, as Ayers supposes, that we should somehow not mean it when we say the world is everything that is the case. And if we do say that and mean it, we conceive the world, not in the way Ayers thinks I must conceive it, as a totality of the describable things— zebras and so forth—that there are (as we say) in it, but as, precisely, everything that can be truly thought or said: not everything we would *think about* if we thought truly, but everything we would *think*.

This is an idealism in an obvious sense. On this conception, the world itself is indeed structured by the form of judgment. I do not describe this thought as an idealism in my book, where I consider only idealisms of the sort I specify in the gloss Ayers omits, positions that insufficiently acknowledge the independence of reality. But the label is a good fit.

As I said, Ayers thinks the specification of a sort is redundant. He assumes that one cannot equate the form of the world and the form of thought without representing reality as a shadow of something self-standingly subjective. But this depends on assuming that in any such position the form of thought must be taken to be explicable first, before we even consider thought's bearing on reality, and only subsequently said to coincide with the form of the world. In such a view the form is supposed to be in place as informing thought, which is surely subjective, before one argues that it informs reality as well. And then the claim that it informs reality does look like a projection of something that was first in place as subjective on to what is supposed to be objective. But if we say the world is everything that can be truly thought to be the case, we imply no such thing. The image of a projection from a self-standing subjectivity gets no purchase if we insist, as we should, that thought and the world must be understood together. The form of thought is already just as such the form of the world. It is a form that is subjective and objective together, not primarily subjective and thereby supposedly objective—an order of priority that would unmask its claim to be objective as spurious in just the way Ayers envisages.

Here we have, at least programmatically, an idealism that does not diverge from common-sense realism. Given its claim to match common sense, it is appropriate that the slogan that expresses this idealism—"The world is everything that is the case"—should be truistic, as I said, not an expression of some contentious metaphysics.[18]

It may be tempting to protest that if the idealism I am envisaging is supposed to coincide with common sense, we may as well stick with common sense. But as soon as we are alert to the way rational animals are marked out as special by their potential for self-determination, we need to acknowledge that our rationality enters into the possibility of describing ourselves as accepting what our senses give us. As I said, such locutions do not fit just any creature whose senses inform it of things. And idealism is to the point in explaining how such locutions work—how our senses provide something for us to accept, in such a way that, in the ideal case, we directly take in part of the objective world.

This in turn contributes to making it unmysterious that capacities to which it is essential that they can be exercised in self-determination can be capacities for thought at all, with the objective purport that implies. But that topic has not been on my agenda for this essay, and I shall take it no further here.

18. Ayers misreads what he calls "McDowell's quietist patter" (p. 253). He thinks the point of the "quietist patter" is to enable me not to mean it when I say the world is conceptually structured. ("We are not to suppose that talk of 'facts' means that the world . . . is literally propositional in form . . .": p. 254.) But I do mean it; the point of the "quietist patter" is not to take back the claim that the world is conceptually structured, but to insist that it does not express something metaphysically contentious. Ayers's blindness to the possibility of an idealism that is, if properly understood, uncontentious—his conviction that any idealism cannot but depreciate the independence of reality—leads him, at p. 255, to claim that it is "bad metaphysics" to suppose the world as we experience it breaks up into facts. He thinks this is the top of a slippery slope, at the bottom of which lies the idea that reality, so called, is a projection from thought. (See also pp. 248–9.) He insists, here, on the contrasting thought that "the world, on the scale at which we experience it, is to an extent broken up into unitary material objects, and that is *how* we experience it". It is worth noting that this does not sit well with his approval, at p. 241, of the idea that "we just accept what the senses conjointly give". What it makes sense to say we accept is surely putative revelations by the senses of how things are. We do not accept unitary material objects; we accept, say, that we are confronted by them.

PART III

Reading Hegel

The Apperceptive I and the
Empirical Self: Towards a
Heterodox Reading of
"Lordship and Bondage"
in Hegel's *Phenomenology*

1. Hegel's *Phenomenology* traces an education of consciousness, as a result of which it is to attain the standpoint of absolute knowing. For consciousness (as such) its object is other than itself. The goal is for this otherness to be *aufgehoben*—cancelled as the simple otherness it at first appears to be, though preserved at a higher level, as a "moment" in a more comprehensive conception. Inquiry will then in principle be able to avoid a certain sort of philosophical anxiety. We shall no longer need to be troubled by the spectre of a gulf between subject and object, which is the pretext for a transcendental scepticism.

2. At the standpoint of absolute knowing, the progress of knowledge is to become intelligible as the free self-development of "the Notion".[1] Hegel sees this conception as indebted to Kant, in a way he makes explicit when he writes, in the *Science of Logic* (p. 584): "It is one of the profoundest and truest insights to be found in the *Critique of Pure Reason* that the *unity* which constitutes the nature of the *Notion* is recognized as the *original synthetic* unity of *apperception*, as the unity of the *I think*, or of self-consciousness."[2] This is

---

1. This section and the next two use material from Essay 4 above. The inspiration for arriving at Hegel from the Kantian material I shall exploit comes from Pippin, *Hegel's Idealism*. The reading of Kant comes from working through him with James Conant and John Haugeland.

2. Pippin, *Hegel's Idealism*, p. 18, cites this passage as central to his reading of Hegel's idealism.

obviously an allusion to the Transcendental Deduction. There—especially in the second-edition recasting—Kant comes close to Hegel's conception of absolute knowing.

I shall begin by spending some time on this Kantian background. That will place the apperceptive I, whose unity is the unity of the *I think*, in the picture.

Intuitions are immediately of objects. In the so-called Metaphysical Deduction, Kant says (A79/B104–5): "The same function which gives unity to the various representations *in a judgment* also gives unity to the mere synthesis of various representations *in an intuition*; and this unity, in its most general expression, we entitle the pure concept of the understanding." The objective purport of intuitions is to be understood, then, in terms of their exemplifying logical unities that are characteristic of judging. And in the Transcendental Deduction, Kant says judging is bringing given cognitions *(Erkenntnisse)* to the objective unity of apperception (B141). Given that conception of judging, the identification of the unity of judgment with the unity of intuition explains why he says: "The transcendental unity of apperception is that unity through which all the manifold given in an intuition is united [into] a concept of the object. It is therefore entitled objective . . . ."[3] By "concept of the object" here, Kant must mean something like "conceptually informed awareness of the object". That intuitions are of objects, he is urging, is to be understood in terms of their possessing the kind of unity that results when, in judging, one brings cognitions to the unity of apperception.

So Kant places spontaneous apperceptive activity at the centre of his picture of the objective purport of sensory consciousness. The free activity of bringing cognitions to the unity of apperception is a precursor, in Kant, to what figures in Hegel as the free self-development of "the Notion"—a setting within which the idea of thought's directedness at objects no longer includes anything that could appear as a gulf between subject and object.[4]

3. Kant's idea is that categorial unity—conformity to the requirements of the understanding—accounts for the possibility of subjective states that are

---

3. B139. I substitute "into" for Kemp Smith's "in" (Kant wrote "in einen Begriff", not "in einem Begriff"). See Richard E. Aquila, *Matter in Mind*, p. 136.

4. Kant describes the understanding—which is "the faculty of apperception" (B134n.)—in terms of spontaneity, e.g. at A50/B74. And spontaneity is the theme of the opening section of the B Deduction.

cases of consciousness of objects. The Deduction is intended to vindicate the objective validity of the categories. But the structure of Kant's conception poses a threat to this aim, a threat to which he is especially sensitive in the second-edition version (which I shall call "the B Deduction"). A condition for objects to be thinkable (one might suppose) is not thereby a condition for them to be able to be given to our senses. Surely (one might go on) conditions for objects to be able to be given to our senses are for Kant a separate topic, dealt with independently in the Transcendental Aesthetic. So for all any Deduction can show, objects could be present to our senses, conforming to the requirements considered in the Aesthetic, without meeting the requirements of the understanding.[5] And now the requirements of the understanding look like mere subjective imposition on our part, needed for us to get objects into our thoughts, but perhaps nothing to do with objects themselves.

In the B Deduction Kant aims to avert this threat, by arguing that the conditions for objects to be able to be given to our senses are not, after all, separate from the conditions he connects with apperceptive spontaneity. In the second half of the B Deduction, he works out consequences of the fact that space and time, as "formal intuitions" (B160n.), are themselves cases of the combination of a manifold into a single intuition. By the basic principle that governs the Deduction, it follows that the spatio-temporal form required by our sensibility is not, after all, intelligible independently of appealing to apperceptive spontaneity.[6] As Hegel appreciatively puts the point in "Glauben und Wissen": "Here [in the Transcendental Deduction], the original synthetic unity of apperception is recognized also as the principle of the figurative synthesis, i.e., of the forms of intuition; space and time are themselves conceived as synthetic unities, and spontaneity, the absolute synthetic activity of the productive imagination, is conceived as the principle of the very sensibility that was previously characterized only as

---

5. See A89–91/B122–3 (in the preamble to the Transcendental Deduction, common to both editions). Kant is here explaining why the task of a Transcendental Deduction (showing "how *subjective conditions of thought* can have *objective validity*") is so difficult.

6. Kant puts the basic principle like this (in the opening section of the B Deduction, which is devoted to elaborating the thought): "But the combination *(conjunctio)* of a manifold in general can never come to us through the senses, and cannot, therefore, be already contained in the pure form of sensible intuition. For it is an act of spontaneity of the faculty of representation . . ." (B129–30).

receptivity."[7] The Aesthetic does not, after all, lay down independent conditions for objects to be available to our senses, in a way that leaves it still open whether they are conformable to the activity of apperceptive spontaneity. So Kant takes himself to be entitled to claim that the categories apply to "whatever objects may *present themselves to our senses*" (B159). There is, after all, no threat that objects might be present to our senses but not meet the requirements of the understanding.

If we describe them as requirements of the understanding, we attribute categorial requirements to a faculty of the cognitive subject, and thus depict them as subjective conditions. But by extending the scope of apperception's unifying activity into what had seemed the independent terrain of the Aesthetic, Kant aims to undermine a picture in which objects satisfy independent requirements for them to be able to be sensibly present to us, and we then impose on them conditions demanded by the understanding. Thereby he aims to show that the requirements of the understanding, though as so described they have to be counted as subjective conditions, are simultaneously and equally conditions on objects themselves.[8] In this conception, with its equipoise between subjective and objective, between thought and its subject matter, we have something it is plausible to see as an inspiration for Hegel's conception of absolute knowing.

4. However, Kant's way of making out that the requirements of the understanding are equally conditions on objects themselves depends essentially on its being acceptable to gloss "objects themselves" with "objects as they are given to our senses". And in Kant's thinking this gloss embodies its own subjective imposition, at a different point from the one where the threat arose.

In the second half of the B Deduction, Kant contrives to represent the combination of manifolds into the "formal intuitions", space and time, as

---

7. *Faith and Knowledge*, pp. 69–70.

8. See B138: "The synthetic unity of consciousness is . . . an objective condition of all knowledge. It is not merely a condition that I myself require in knowing an object, but is a condition under which every intuition must stand in order to become *an object for me*." ("For me" spoils this formulation, in a way that should begin to become intelligible when I discuss how Kant's conception is still, by Hegel's lights, a merely subjective idealism: §4 below.) For the general idea of conditions that are subjective and objective together (not primarily subjective and thereby allegedly objective), see A158/B197: ". . . the conditions of the *possibility of experience* in general are likewise conditions of the *possibility of the objects of experience* . . . ."

the work of apperceptive spontaneity. But he leaves it a separate fact about us, a reflection of the specific character of our sensibility, that what are so unified, in our case, are manifolds that are specifically spatial and temporal. The Aesthetic encourages us to entertain the thought that there could be differently formed sensibilities, which would be associated with different "formal intuitions". That makes it irresistible to contemplate a different gloss on "objects themselves": things in themselves, as that idea figures in the Aesthetic—things such that it is beyond our ken whether they themselves are spatially or temporally ordered.[9]

Kant tries to demonstrate objective validity for the categories by arguing that they are applicable to things as they are given to *our* sensibility. He is clear that according to his argument it is "only *our* sensible and empirical intuition" that can confer *Sinn* and *Bedeutung* on the pure concepts of the understanding (B149). But in view of his doctrine that our sensibility is the way it is independently of the character of things in themselves, and independently of our capacity for apperceptive unification, to which it furnishes materials, that means there is an unassimilated subjectivity, a subjectivity with no balancing objectivity, within what purported to be the objective side of a proto-Hegelian equipoise. The most Kant can claim to establish in the Deduction is that there is no extra subjective imposition in demanding that objects of our experience conform to the requirements of the understanding, over and above the subjective imposition involved in requiring that our world be spatially and temporally ordered. But this latter is, as Kant conceives it, a subjective imposition. There is a mere reflection of a fact about us at the foundation of Kant's construction. And corresponding to this unassimilated subjectivity at the putatively objective pole of the attempted equipoise, there is an unassimilated objectivity, the perhaps non-spatial and non-temporal thing in itself, left outside the equipoise altogether, and looking as if it would have to be the genuine article.[10]

A genuine equipoise between subjective and objective would require discarding Kant's distinction of things as they are available to our senses from

9. For the localization to the Aesthetic, see Jean Hyppolite, *Genesis and Structure of Hegel's Phenomenology of Spirit*, p. 144. The noumenon of the Analytic is different, and the related notion in the Dialectic is different again.

10. See ¶238 of Hegel, *Phenomenology of Spirit*. (In what follows, I shall modify Miller's translation, or substitute my own, in which I shall allow myself to count words like the untranslatable "*aufheben*" as English.)

things as they may be in themselves.[11] It would require not leaving the spatial and temporal character of our sensibility outside the scope of intellectual freedom. Here we can begin to see a point in insisting that there is nothing outside the free unfolding of "the Notion". Absolute knowing is a whole-hearted counterpart to the activity of apperceptive spontaneity as Kant conceives it in the Transcendental Deduction, where, just because the specific character of our sensibility is left outside its scope, the intended equipoise between subjective and objective is not genuinely achieved.

Hegelian whole-heartedness brings everything within the scope of free subjective activity. If one takes such a description out of context, it can seem that the move abandons the realism of common sense—that it obliterates anything genuinely recognizable as objective reality, in favour of projections from unconstrained movements of the mind.[12] But the context gives the lie to this. It is Kant's half-heartedness that spoils his attempt at an equipoise between subjective and objective.[13] Expanding the scope of intellectual freedom does not tip the scale to the side of the subjective, as if the objective (so-called, we would have to say) can only be a projection of subjective activity, taken to be independently intelligible. That is just what happens in Kant's unsuccessful attempt at the equipoise. Because there is unassimilated subjectivity at the base of Kant's construction, it amounts to no more than a subjective idealism. That is a Hegelian accusation often thought to be outrageous, but we are now in a position to find justice in it. The point of expanding the scope of intellectual freedom is to achieve a genuine balance between subjective and objective, in which neither is prior to the other. Achieving a genuine balance would allow subjectivity to be

11. It does not help with the problem I am posing for Kant to inveigh against "two-world" readings of Kant. Let it be acknowledged, by all means, that he identifies "things as objects of experience" with "those same things as things in themselves" (Bxxvii). But this does not alter the fact that according to him the spatial and temporal organization of things as objects of our experience reflects a fact about us rather than characterizing the things themselves. And he himself stresses that his attempted vindication of the objective validity of the categories essentially turns on that feature of things as objects of experience.

12. For an understanding of "post-Kantian absolute idealism" on these lines, see Michael Friedman, "Exorcising the Philosophical Tradition: Comments on John McDowell's *Mind and World*", especially at 439–44.

13. Hence the unhappy addition of "for me" at B138, cited above; and hence also his willingness to accept the Copernican image (Bxvi–xviii), which certainly suggests a priority of subjective over objective.

conceived as engaging with what is genuinely objective. To hold that the very idea of objectivity can be understood only as part of such a structure is exactly not to abandon the independently real in favour of projections from subjectivity.[14]

5. Clearly there is more to be said.[15] But perhaps that is enough to let us begin to understand why, in the remark I began with, Hegel praises Kant for equating the unity of "the Notion" with the unity of apperception. When Hegel says "With self-consciousness we have entered the homeland of truth" (¶167), we can put his point in Kantian terms, like this: we have begun to see how to understand knowledge in terms of the unifying powers of apperceptive spontaneity.[16]

But this can make what Hegel does in the "Self-Consciousness" chapter of the *Phenomenology* mysterious. How is someone's baulking at a struggle to the death and submitting to enslavement by someone else related to the

14. These remarks bear on Henry Allison's characterization of transcendental idealism as insisting on a distinction between "conditions of the possibility of knowledge of things" and "conditions of the possibility of the things themselves" (*Kant's Transcendental Idealism: An Interpretation and Defense*, p. 13). Transcendental realism rejects the distinction by seeing conditions of the possibility of knowledge as merely derivative from autonomous conditions of the possibility of things. Allison maintains that the only other way to reject the distinction is to embrace a subjectivistic phenomenalism—which one might describe, as in my text, as an abandonment of the independently real in favour of projections from subjectivity. That would be a symmetrical counterpart to transcendental realism, taking subjective conditions to be autonomous as such where transcendental realism takes objective conditions to be autonomous as such. What goes missing here is the Hegelian alternative, which is inspired by how Kant wants to think of the requirements of the understanding. Hegel rejects Allison's distinction on the ground that the relevant conditions are inseparably both conditions on thought and conditions on objects, not primarily either the one or the other.

15. For one thing, a proper treatment of Hegel's relation to Kant would need to take account of Fichte's intervening contribution. For another, something would need to be said about how what in Kant is the activity of the understanding becomes, in Hegel, the self-fulfilment of reason, in the face of Kant's sharp distinction between understanding and reason. For yet another, something would need to be said about how Hegel sees his idealism as related to Kant's practical philosophy, which I have not mentioned at all. (These are all no doubt connected.)

16. We need to arrive at the significance of apperception through the experience of mere consciousness, rather than just starting with it (like Kant and Fichte), because just starting with it leads only to the subjective idealism of ¶238. See Hans-Georg Gadamer, "Hegel's Dialectic of Self-Consciousness", pp. 54–5.

Aufhebung of otherness between consciousness and its object, the balance between subjective and objective that Kant aimed at but failed to achieve?[17] Much commentary seems unconcerned with such questions. In "Lordship and Bondage", for instance, commentators often take Hegel to be arguing that there can be self-conscious individuals only in mutually recognitive communities. To me the text there does not seem to say what these commentators would like it to, that recognition by an unrespected inferior cannot validate a superior's self-certainty—so that self-consciousness can find a truth corresponding to its certainty only in a community of equals. At any rate I find it hard to read that thought into Hegel's play with the mismatch between the master's self-certainty and the servile consciousness as the truth of that certainty (¶192). But anyway, even if that is the point, how does it advance us towards Reason's certainty of being all reality, the *Aufhebung* of otherness between subjective and objective that is the culmination of this chapter (¶230)?

In what follows, I shall go through the first two sections of the chapter, working towards a reading that would not be vulnerable to this puzzlement. At least to begin with, I shall stay so close to the text as to risk merely duplicating its obscurities; I hope things will become clearer as I go along.

I do not mean to suggest that this, or any other, section of the *Phenomenology* traces the route into Hegelian thinking from a Kantian starting-point that I began with. I am not trying to find in "Lordship and Bondage" a Hegelian improvement on Kant's treatment of the forms of our sensibility. The point of starting with the Kantian material was only to provide a frame for the significance that Hegel credits to self-consciousness at the beginning of the "Self-Consciousness" chapter.

6. We begin with self-consciousness on the scene as the result of the final movement in the experience of (mere, as it were) consciousness, whose object is conceived as simply other than it. That object—empirically knowable reality—does not just disappear with the advent of self-consciousness. If it

17. See, e.g., Pippin, *Hegel's Idealism*, p. 143: "Suddenly we are talking about desire, life, struggles to the death, masters and slaves." Pippin tries to read the chapter's first two sections (the third is, as he remarks, easier to accommodate) so as to fit his overall conception of the *Phenomenology*'s point, but his details (for instance, desire as emerging out of the idea of a lack that drives the pursuit of knowledge) strike me as far removed from what actually happens in the text.

did, we would have only "the motionless tautology of: I am I". Without otherness in the picture, self-consciousness could not be in the picture either. The otherness of the object of consciousness must be *aufgehoben*, not simply obliterated. So self-consciousness "has a doubled object", or an object with two moments. The first moment is "the whole expanse of the sensible world", what previously figured as the independent object of consciousness. The second moment is self-consciousness itself. These two moments show up as mutually opposed, the first as "*for* self-consciousness marked with the *character of the negative*",[18] and the second "only, at first, in opposition to the first". Hegel says: "Self-consciousness presents itself here as the movement wherein this opposition is *aufgehoben* and the identity of itself with itself gets to be [explicit] for it." (All citations in this paragraph are from ¶167.)

So far so good, we might say, given that we are trying to find in this text a progress towards absolute knowing. Supposing we can make sense of the so far only schematic idea of overcoming an opposition between those two moments in the object of self-consciousness, the result should be a picture in which the otherness of the empirically accessible world is prevented from threatening to constitute a gulf, by being embraced within the object of self-consciousness, which is seen as having an internal complexity, while as the object of self-consciousness it is not other than the conscious self. In one sense apperception has only itself for object. But we are to work towards seeing how it can have "the whole expanse of the sensible world" as its object, in another sense that is unthreatening just because of how it is integrated with the first.

We might be tempted to derive a less schematic understanding of the movement here attributed to self-consciousness from Hegel's invocation of desire. But I think the text should discourage this hope. Hegel offers "Self-consciousness is desire *überhaupt*" (¶167) as a paraphrase, not here further elaborated, of one of his schematic descriptions of the required movement. The explanatory relation seems to be the wrong way around for that hope of concreteness. We understand what Hegel means by introducing desire only to the extent that we understand those schematic descriptions of the movement of self-consciousness. "Desire *überhaupt*" functions as a figure for the general idea of negating otherness by appropriating or consuming, incorporating into oneself, what at first figures as merely other. That is,

18. Self-consciousness is the shape in which consciousness is now present, and for consciousness the essential thing about its object is that it is not—is other than—itself.

schematically, what self-consciousness has to do to the first moment in its doubled object. There is no suggestion here of anything as specific as a mode of consciousness that has objects in view only in so far as they can be seen as conducive or obstructive to its purposes.[19]

7. Hegel says that the first of those two moments in the object of self-consciousness has, for us or in itself, returned into itself and become life (¶168). Here he is harking back to the closing phase in the experience of consciousness (see ¶162), where what had appeared as the independent object of consciousness turned out to be the self-developing movement of "the absolute Notion".[20] That was what brought self-consciousness on to the scene. As it often does in Hegel, life there served as a figure or model for his conception of "the Notion", which generates differentiation within itself rather than being externally related to a subject matter that is simply other than it. But here, in the opening section of the "Self-Consciousness" chapter, life becomes more than a figure. It becomes, so to speak, itself.

Hegel now gives an exposition of life as the genus dissolving all differences, having its actuality in the living individual separating itself out from that negative universality (¶¶169–72). This is the second pole in "the antithesis of self-consciousness and life", into which "this Notion [life] sunders itself" (¶168). At this stage life is not *for itself* (¶¶168, 172); it is *for* the consciousness, now self-consciousness, that is the first pole in the antithesis of self-consciousness and life.

All I want from this obscure material at this stage is the structure. Life as the difference-dissolving genus, actual in the shape of a living individual, is the guise in which the first moment in the doubled object of self-consciousness now appears—the moment in respect of which self-consciousness continues to be consciousness, and "the whole expanse of the sensible world is preserved for it" (¶167). At this stage this object, or moment in a doubled object, is not for itself, not a subject, but in view only as an object for a subject, for self-consciousness as consciousness.

19. Cf., e.g., Pippin, *Hegel's Idealism*, p. 149. Pippin says that "this chapter . . . does not begin a case for the primacy of practical reason" (p. 288, n. 11). I am not sure about this claim, when we come to the slave's emancipation through work. But Pippin is talking about the role of desire in the chapter, and I think he is right that that feature of it does not point us to practical reason. However, Pippin's denial is muted by his taking "desire *überhaupt*" too literally.

20. Fortunately, in this essay I do not have to try to explain how this happens.

This belongs with the fact that the unfolding of life Hegel has given so far has been "for us" rather than for the consciousness whose experience we are about to witness. The exposition, as is usual after a mutation of consciousness, recapitulates how this new consciousness appeared on the scene, though from its own point of view it is simply present, having forgotten what constrained it to take its present shape. The previous movement ("Force and the Understanding") reached a position in which the otherness of the object of consciousness was in principle *aufgehoben*. The object of consciousness turned out to be the freely self-developing "Notion", in which consciousness was in principle enabled to see nothing other than itself. But this new object, the Notion—which is life—"sunders itself", and, at the beginning of the "Self-Consciousness" chapter, consciousness finds itself immediately present as self-consciousness but, because of the lack of mediation, still confronted with unassimilated otherness. That much is typical of the transitions in the *Phenomenology*. The point for now is that the unassimilated otherness is here in the form of life.

8. Now we start to observe the experience of this consciousness as self-consciousness, the subject for which life has so far appeared as object. Hegel describes the experiencing subject as "this other life, for which the genus as such is" (¶173). It is another life, because it was life that sundered itself into the antithesis between self-consciousness—now referred to as "this other life"—and life as Hegel has just expounded it, life as object for the consciousness that self-consciousness is (¶168).

The subject life, he says, is "for itself genus". That fits with its being life, and picks up the conception of the genus as dissolving differences. This life is self-consciousness, which "has itself as pure I for object" (¶173), and "is certain of itself only by the *Aufheben* of this other that presents itself to it as independent life" (¶174). It is aware of itself as needing to dissolve the difference between itself and "this other", the first of the two moments in its doubled object. This is what we had already (in ¶167) as the movement of self-consciousness—overcoming the antithesis between the two moments of its object. Here we have the added specificity that the moment that first appears as opposed to self-consciousness, the moment whose antithesis with self-consciousness is to be overcome, has been elaborated as life.

The simplest way to effect this required overcoming of otherness would be by reducing to nothingness (*vernichten*) the independent other.

Self-consciousness is, as we already know, desire *überhaupt* (¶167). But desire in particular (so to speak) cannot reduce otherness to nothingness by its activity of appropriation and consumption. It needs independent objects to be what it appropriates and consumes. In the experience of desire specifically (as opposed to desire *überhaupt*), self-consciousness learns that reducing to nothingness is not what it needs to do to its other. As was promised in ¶168, it thereby "makes the experience of the self-standingness [*Selbständigkeit*: independence]" of its object—that is, of the first of the two moments of its doubled object.

But to find a truth corresponding to its self-certainty, it still needs the otherness of that object to be *aufgehoben*. What it has learned is that it is no good attempting a unilateral annihilation of the other; the other must preserve its independence. The object must present itself as negative of its own accord, rather than being marked with the character of the negative by something other than itself, namely the self-consciousness that is trying to overcome the otherness of (one moment in) its object. This requirement of independent negativity reveals the object—the other moment in the doubled object—as itself consciousness after all, not, as it hitherto appeared, something that is only an object for consciousness. It is in the nature of consciousness to maintain its independence even while, in distinguishing itself from its object, it presents itself as negative.

And in fact this object is not just consciousness but self-consciousness. We know anyway, from the end of the "Consciousness" section, that if it is consciousness it is self-consciousness. ("Consciousness of an other, of an object as such, is indeed itself necessarily *self-consciousness*": ¶164.) But here Hegel reveals this object as self-consciousness by noting that in the sphere of life independent negativity takes the form of "the universal independent nature in which negation is present as absolute negation", and that "is the genus as such, or self-consciousness" (¶175). This is just how self-consciousness conceived itself at the beginning of the experience he has just described (¶¶173–4). It has now turned out that its object, or the first moment in its doubled object, needs to be conceived in just the same way. After the initial exposition of it, life, as one of the two moments in the object of self-consciousness, was not for itself but only for consciousness (¶172). But now it has emerged that that moment in the doubled object "is itself for itself genus, universal fluidity in the peculiarity of its separateness; it is a living self-consciousness" (¶176).

9. It is in summing up this result that Hegel says: *"Self-consciousness achieves its satisfaction only in another self-consciousness"* (¶175).[21] I think this is usually taken to claim that there can be a self-conscious individual, say a self-conscious human being, only if there are at least two, each recognizing the other as another of what it is one of. And I do not dispute that much in what follows can be made out to fit this conception of multiple individuals mutually recognizing one another. But this raises in an urgent form the puzzlement I started from, about the role of Hegel's moves here in the progress towards absolute knowing. Or—another way of making the same point—there is a problem about how to fit this remark, so taken, into the flow of the text I have been working through.

The otherness that needs to be *aufgehoben* by the movement of self-consciousness appeared in the first instance as the otherness of "the whole expanse of the sensible world" (¶167), one moment in the doubled object of self-consciousness, whose movement is to overcome the antithesis between that moment and the other, namely itself. It was that moment in the doubled object, "the whole expanse of the sensible world", that returned into itself and became life (¶168), and then revealed itself as consciousness and finally as self-consciousness. This is the "another self-consciousness" of our passage. It should surely be in some sense the same object, or moment in a doubled object, that we began with, only now more hygienically—less immediately—understood. But if "another self-consciousness" here is a literally other mind, say a different human being, what has happened to "the whole expanse of the sensible world"? How does replacing that first moment in the doubled object of self-consciousness with someone else's self-consciousness belong with the unfolding of that moment that Hegel seemed to be offering in the text up to this point? And how does it help towards disarming a threat that might be posed by the otherness of the object of consciousness?

These questions are forestalled, and the progression I have been working through begins to fall into place, if we take it that when Hegel talks of "another self-consciousness" here, he is saying how things are, not for us or in

---

21. "Achieves its satisfaction" rather than, more plainly, "finds its truth" because we are still working with the conception of self-consciousness as desire *überhaupt*, though in the experience of ¶175 it learned not to conceive itself as appropriating its object in anything like a literal sense. See §6 above.

themselves, but for a consciousness still in the midst of the movement of self-consciousness, the overcoming of the antithesis between those two moments. This consciousness is one for which *Aufhebung* of otherness is still an unfinished task (as indeed it is at all stages short of absolute knowing). So "another", in "another self-consciousness", reflects how things seem to consciousness at this stage of its education, not how things actually are.[22]

The otherness that confronts my self-consciousness, at the beginning of the chapter, is the otherness of the world as the scene of conscious life—in fact my life, though it will take a while before that specification is straightforwardly available. When "the whole expanse of the sensible world" returns into itself and becomes life, that makes available another way of pointing to that otherness, by speaking of an antithesis between my self-consciousness and the individual conscious life whose scene is my world. It is that life, or the individual living it, that is progressively revealed as itself consciousness and then self-consciousness. What it actually is is my self-consciousness, not someone else's.[23] When that becomes clear, empirical consciousness will be integrated with apperceptive consciousness, and the otherness of the world that confronts my empirical consciousness will be purged of its threat to open a gulf between subjective and objective. But by the stage we have reached—the end of the first section of the "Self-Consciousness" chapter—that is not yet clear. As Hegel will say early in the next section, self-consciousness must *"aufheben* this its other-being" (¶180).

This suggestion—that Hegel is not here talking about multiple human beings—may seem to ignore the very end of the first section, where Hegel says that with its final development, "the Notion of spirit is already present for us" (¶177). But that remark does not, as is often supposed, salute the appearance before us of a concept of communal being. Hegel makes it clear

22. No doubt the remark also works if taken straightforwardly, without that understood frame. I think this is quite common in the *Phenomenology*. What I am disputing is only that the straightforward reading captures what Hegel has argued for in his approach to the remark.

23. Self-consciousness starts this movement in its experience with "itself as *pure I* for object" (¶173). Hegel announces there that in its subsequent experience "this abstract object will enrich itself and undergo the unfolding we have seen in life". It is going to turn out to *be* what was there unfolded.

that by "spirit" here he means an object that "is just as much I as object".[24] That is exactly what becomes present for us when the problematic moment of the doubled object of self-consciousness is revealed as itself self-consciousness, itself I. And that is so whoever the I thus revealed as an object is—it does not need to be someone other than the subject of the experience we are observing.

I am not denying that the spiritual will not be fully in view for us until communal being is in the picture. But Hegel here locates "I that is we and we that is I" in "what still lies ahead for consciousness", "the experience of what spirit is". That seems to amount to saying the interplay of singular and plural will come into view only later. It is not supposed to be the result of the experience we have so far witnessed.

10. What I am proposing may become clearer if I say a little, at last, about what may by now be obvious, how this reading of the chapter's opening section carries over into "Lordship and Bondage". I shall be sketchier here, partly because there is no time for more, but partly because I hope the ground has been sufficiently laid for it to be plausible that the details can in principle be made to fall into place.

Hegel introduces the struggle to the death like this (¶187): "The *presentation* of itself, however, as the pure abstraction of self-consciousness consists in showing itself as pure negation of its objective mode, or in showing it to be connected to no determinate *existence*, not to be connected to the universal singularity of existence as such, not to be connected to life." This fits the suggestion I am making, that only one biological individual is really in play. The description of the struggle to the death works as an allegorical depiction of an attempt, on the part of a single self-consciousness, to affirm its independence, by disavowing any dependence on "its objective mode", which is the life that has come to stand in for the otherness of the world whose scene that life is. So far, the life that is the "objective mode" has revealed itself as the life of a consciousness, indeed a self-consciousness. In fact it is the very same self-consciousness that here tries to disavow it. It is that self-consciousness not *qua* attempting to affirm its independence but

---

24. Compare what he says in the Preface about "grasping and expressing the true not [just] as *substance*, but no less as *subject*" (¶17). Compare also ¶790, where he says (ironically), of Observing Reason's culminating identification of the soul with a thing, that "according to its concept it is the most richly spiritual". The concept of spirit as it figures here is the concept of something that is equally object and subject.

qua living through "the whole expanse of the sensible world". But the subject that is undergoing this experience is not yet aware that those are two
different specifications of what is in fact itself. Unassimilated otherness now
takes the form of an alienation from what is in fact its own consciousness as
living through its world, its own empirical consciousness. Hegel makes this
alienation vivid with the image of one living individual confronted by another.[25] And he makes the attempt to disavow dependence on what is in
fact one's own life vivid with the image of trying to end the life of the other
that confronts one.

There is a textual curiosity in this vicinity. Immediately after the passage I
just quoted as introducing the struggle to the death, Hegel says (still in
¶187)): "This presentation is the *doubled* doing [compare ¶182]: doing of the
other and doing of oneself. In so far as it is doing of the *other*, each goes after
the death of the other." This is quite mysterious at the level of the image of
two individuals trying to kill each other.[26] How can pursuing the death of
the other be the doing of the *other*? But if the other is really the subject itself, *qua* "sunk in the being of life" (¶186), the idea makes a certain sense. If
one is to affirm one's independence as a self-consciousness by showing that
one is indifferent to mere life, it is actually oneself *qua* alive—what figures
here as the other—that must subject itself to the risk of death. "However",
as Hegel goes on to say, "therein the second [aspect of the doubled doing],
the doing through oneself, is also present; for the former doing implies the
staking of one's own life". This works both within the image—one cannot
seek the death of another without staking one's own life—and as antici-
pating what self-consciousness trying to affirm its independence learns in
this phase of its experience: that the life it is attempting to disown is something whose continuation is necessary to its continuing independence, so
that its own life is at risk when it goes after the death of the supposed other.
This is actually because the supposedly other life just is its own life, but that
is not how the lesson immediately strikes the consciousness whose experience we are observing.

On this account, the struggle to the death gives allegorical expression to
the need to acknowledge that self-consciousness cannot be independent of

25. It is part of the image that, for the consciousness whose experience we are considering, the other views it in the same way. But this symmetry need not carry over into
what the image is an image for.

26. I have not seen this obvious point noted by commentators.

what, in the frame of mind its experience is here dislodging it from, it would like to think of as mere life, only inessentially related to it. "In this experience, it becomes [clear] to self-consciousness that life is as essential to it as pure self-consciousness" (¶189).

This takes us smoothly to lordship and bondage. Hegel's presentation here makes good sense if understood as a continuation of the allegory. Enslaving another individual who backs down in a struggle to the death stands in for an attempt on the part of self-consciousness—the apperceptive I—to acknowledge the indispensability to it of, but refuse to identify itself with, the subject of a life lived through and conditioned by "the whole expanse of the sensible world"—which is in fact itself, *qua* empirical subject, though self-consciousness at this stage cannot see how to combine acknowledging that with continuing to affirm its independence. This self-consciousness conceives its "objective mode" as a distinct consciousness, bound up with and dependent on external objects. It tries to preserve its own independence of external objects by delegating dealings with them to a consciousness that it attempts to appropriate or see as its own in some sense, while holding back from identifying itself with it.

We might be reminded here of how Kant sees apperceptive self-awareness as contentless. For him, content for self-knowledge can be supplied only by (inner) intuition, which is distinct from apperception (see B157–9). This certainly makes it hard to identify the I of apperception with the self that figures in substantive knowledge of the course of one's experiential life.

This attempt to affirm that one's real self is independent of one's empirical self, though the empirical self is in a way one's own, is vividly captured in the way the master interposes the slave between himself and the objects of consciousness, thereby putatively achieving independence with respect to them (see ¶190). The project fails because in thus consigning its "objective mode" to mere dependence, this masterly self-consciousness, attempting to affirm its own independence, ensures that it can find no objective truth answering to its self-certainty (see ¶192).

At the beginning of the last section of the "Self-Consciousness" chapter, a new shape of consciousness has appeared on the scene: "consciousness that *thinks*, or is free self-consciousness" (¶197). This new shape of consciousness emerges not out of the master consciousness's failure to affirm its independence, but out of an achievement on the part of the servile consciousness. The servile consciousness manages to emerge from the dependence to which the master consciousness relegates it—to "posit *itself* as a negative in the element of abiding" (¶196), in activity whose significance is informed by the prospect of death. The details of this development are too complex and difficult to go into now. But even without trying to be specific, it seems clear that at least it makes for no extra difficulty of interpretation if we suppose, as I have suggested, that it is only within an allegorical presentation that the master consciousness and the servile consciousness are embodied in two separate individuals. The real topic is two aspects of the consciousness of a single individual, though at a stage at which that is not clear to the individual in question. The immediate appearance of thinking consciousness marks a temporary integration of the two aspects, in which a consciousness bound up with the world it lives through, a consciousness that was previously seen as merely dependent on that world, achieves a kind of independence in its formative activity, which becomes the freedom of thought ("movement in Notions", ¶197). We might put this by saying an empirical consciousness *becomes* an apperceptive consciousness.

The achievement of integration by thinking consciousness, as it immediately makes its appearance, is short-lived. Self-consciousness can have individuality only as the individuality of a living being, bound up with its specific immersion in the world. Thinking consciousness is a descendant of the servile consciousness, not the master consciousness, of "Lordship and Bondage". But the shift to thinking itself makes it harder to keep hold of the importance of immersion in life, because with the introduction of "movement in Notions", a new temptation arises to separate the ideal, conceptual aspect of one's relation to reality from a material residue that is then naturally conceived as the merely animal aspect of one's engagement with one's life-world. Stoicism attempts to locate itself exclusively in the separated ideal, withdrawing from immersion in life, and thus loses determinate content for its thinking. Scepticism oscillates between the separated ideal and what is left for immersion in life to be once the ideal is skimmed off (the "animal life" of ¶205). The unhappy consciousness sees that it must have both aspects, but cannot see how to bring them together. Seeing that it must have both aspects is an advance over the consciousness that undergoes the experience narrated in "Lordship and Bondage". Hegel registers the advance when he says, in introducing the unhappy consciousness, that "the duplication that formerly divided itself into two individuals, the master and the slave, is here lodged in one" (¶206). This remark might seem difficult for me. But as before, I can say that the point about division into two individuals is that that is how things looked to the consciousness in question, not that that is how things really were.

11. I have urged that "Lordship and Bondage" describes a failure and then a temporary success at integrating, within a single individual, a consciousness aiming to affirm itself as spontaneously apperceptive and a consciousness that is conceived as immersed in life in the world. This immersion in life is at first conceived mainly as a matter of theoretical cognition, in line with the experience of mere consciousness. But with the temporary success, which turns on finding oneself in one's formative activity, immersion in life becomes centrally a practical matter.

A complete case for such a reading would of course require not only much more about how the passage itself works, but also an assessment of how it fits into the movement of the whole book. But I hope I have said enough to suggest that a proposal on these lines might be worthy of consideration.[27]

27. I have seen a few precedents for this proposal. Joseph C. Flay, *Hegel's Quest for Certainty*, p. 86, says that "master" and "slave" refer not to separate individuals but to different aspects of consciousness. George Armstrong Kelly, in his "Notes on Hegel's 'Lordship and Bondage' ", offers an intra-personal reading as a supplement to the more typical interpersonal readings. And Robert M. Wallace, in an unpublished book manuscript, says that "a self-consciousness . . . can, in principle, be its own 'other' ". But none of these authors has what seems to me to be the essential connection between the master/slave dialectic and the project of overcoming otherness.

Towards a Reading of Hegel on Action in the "Reason" Chapter of the *Phenomenology*

1. Human individuality is not just biological, not exhausted by the singleness of a particular human animal. A fully-fledged human individual is a *free agent*. A free human agent is not simply a human being who moves in determinate ways. And it is not enough to add that the movements are exercises of bodily control; that is something ordinary animals also have. Freedom is responsiveness to reasons. It is not a natural endowment, not something we are born with, or acquire in the sort of biological maturation by which an ordinary animal comes to be able to control movements of its body and thereby to effect alterations in its environment. Rational agency is a normative status. Understanding it requires a social context.

That may be vague enough for nearly everyone to agree that it is Hegelian. (Of course not everyone would agree that it is correct.) But Robert Pippin's reading of Hegel gives a distinctive twist to a position with this shape. In Pippin's reading, "being a free agent—an actual or successful agent—is said to depend on being recognized as one by others whose free bestowal of this recognition depends in turn on their being recognized as such free bestowers".[1] Again: "A priest, a knight, a statesman, a citizen, are not . . . natural kinds. One exists as [a member of] such a kind by being treated as one, according to the rules of [some] community. And the radicality of Hegel's suggestion is that we treat being a concrete subject of a life, a free being, the same way."[2]

Pippin emphasizes how unconventional this is: "It sounds quite counterintuitive to suggest that one counts as a practically responsible subject by

---

1. "Recognition and Reconciliation: Actualized Agency in Hegel's Jena *Phenomenology*", p. 128.

2. "Recognition and Reconciliation", p. 133.

being taken to be one (clearly a cart before the horse problem), but that is Hegel's position."[3] He notes a natural sceptical response: "Can't I be free whether or not anyone else notices, acknowledges me, assists me, expresses solidarity with me, etc.?"[4]

I think the sceptical thrust of this question is well placed. And I do not believe that is an objection to Hegel. Of course Hegel is not above being counter-intuitive, but we should not find him so unless we have to. And I think Pippin mislocates the undeniably Hegelian connection between free individuality and recognition.

2. A model Pippin offers, for the kind of status free agenthood is, is being a speaker of a natural language.[5] I think it is an excellent model. (And not just a model; I shall come back to this.)

Much of what Pippin says, on Hegel's behalf, about freedom is true, on a certain assumption, about being a speaker of, say, English. That there is such a status is a historical result, and the status has a normative shape that is maintained and, in Robert Brandom's metaphor, groomed by the continuing practice of a community. The idea of the status is inseparable from the idea of participation in a communal practice. In that sense the status is essentially social.

This is not uncontroversial; that is why I said "on a certain assumption". Donald Davidson, for instance, argues that there is nothing essentially communal about the ability to make oneself understood by, say, doing what we call "speaking English". According to Davidson, the idea we express by means of that specification of a thing one can do is a mere construction out of possibilities of mutual understanding between individuals who are (unsurprisingly, given their histories) such that their expressions of this or that thought would sound much the same. What we call "the English language" is a concatenation of "I"–"thou" relations, not a practice that is essentially the property of a "we".[6]

If being a speaker of English is to be a model for a Hegelian conception of being a free human individual, Davidson must be wrong about the idea of a

---

3. "Hegels praktischer Realismus: rationales Handeln als Sittlichkeit", p. 302. I quote, here and later, from the text of which the published article is a translation.

4. "What is the Question for which Hegel's Theory of Recognition is the Answer?", p. 156.

5. "What is the Question . . . ?", p. 162.

6. See, e.g., "A Nice Derangement of Epitaphs".

natural language. But I need not discuss this here. For my purposes in elaborating and exploiting Pippin's model, I can simply presuppose that Davidson is wrong.[7]

The model is not just a model, because it is by being initiated into one's first language that one comes to have a conception of reasons at all. It is not that prelinguistic human beings are already responsive to reasons (in a strong sense: to reasons *as* the reasons they are),[8] and that when they learn to speak they acquire a means to give expression to exercises of that supposedly antecedent capacity.

The topography of the space of reasons is encapsulated in the content of concepts. And one does not acquire first one concept, then a second, and so forth. There must be several concepts if there are any. In Wittgenstein's image: "Light dawns gradually over the whole" (*On Certainty* §141).

When light has dawned, one is no longer dependent on one's teachers for knowing what to do in the practice they have been initiating one into. One has become a self-moving practitioner, able to make one's own way around in the space of reasons, which includes being able to be critical of one's inherited conception of its layout.[9]

Now suppose light has dawned for one, in the specific way that consists in becoming a speaker of English. If there are other speakers of English around, they will recognize one as a speaker of English. That is not an empirical claim—as if speakers of English just happen to be good at identifying others of their kind (like gay people, as some folk wisdom has it). Being a speaker of a language is not contingently connected with the ability to recognize one's fellow-speakers. It *includes* that ability. It makes no sense to suppose someone might be a speaker of English though people who recognize one another as speakers of English do not recognize her as one, or she does not recognize them as fellow-speakers. This is an *a priori* link between the status and the idea of recognition.

---

7. For some discussion, see my "Gadamer and Davidson on Understanding and Relativism".

8. An ordinary animal might flee in response to apparent danger. Danger is, in one obvious sense, a reason for fleeing, but the fleeing of an ordinary animal is not a response to it *as* the reason it is. That would require being able to consider whether to flee, given a danger one takes oneself to face. This is what I mean by speaking of responsiveness to reasons in a strong sense.

9. We should not picture this as happening at an instant; light dawns gradually.

But consider a counterpart of Pippin's sceptical question: "Can't I be a speaker of English whether or not anyone else notices, acknowledges me, etc.?" We needed that proviso: if there are other speakers of English around. Suppose there are not. Suppose everyone around me dies just as light is dawning for me, so there is no one to recognize me as a self-moving speaker of English. It would be wildly implausible to think it follows that I do not have that status. Suppose years later English-speakers from the Antipodes arrive on the scene of the disaster that I alone, of my local community, survived, and they recognize me to be expressing thoughts in English. It would be wildly implausible to think I had to wait for their recognition of me to acquire that capacity. (Suppose I tape-recorded my thoughts while I was alone.)

The scenario is far-fetched, but it is perfectly to the point when we are considering the thesis that one is a speaker of English by being taken to be one. (Compare Pippin's claim, on Hegel's behalf, that "one is a practically responsible subject by being taken to be one".) The answer to the sceptical question is "Yes". We can respect a constitutive connection between the status and a *possibility* of its being acknowledged, without needing to accept that it is *conferred* by acknowledgment—that one has it by being taken to have it.

Similarly with the status for which being a speaker of English is a model, the status of being a free individual. As I said, it is not just a model. Becoming a speaker of English is one way to become free, in the sense of being responsive to reasons as such.

3. Someone can manifest rationality only in responding to considerations that she takes to be reasons. But nothing can count as a conception of the layout of the space of reasons unless the considerations that the subject takes to be reasons are, at least on the whole, genuinely reasons. (What "genuinely" can mean here will become an issue in a moment.) If we try to envisage too much error, the attempt undermines itself, by making it impossible to suppose the subject is sufficiently in touch with reasons to be able to be wrong about them.

Still, people can be wrong about reasons. Freedom can be more or less fully realized, and its degree depends on the extent to which the supposed reasons in the light of which someone acts are genuinely reasons.[10] When they are not, the weight of explanation falls through the supposed reasons, and comes to rest on whatever accounts for the subject's taking them to be

10. This is a thought of Pippin's. See "What is the Question . . . ?", p. 169, n. 10.

reasons—say, social subservience or the hold of dogma. And if the ultimate explanation of an action is at that level, the action is not perfectly free, not a full expression of the subject's self. So the "rational agency" conception of freedom needs a way to make sense of the force of reasons as something one can be right or wrong about.

Now the role of actual acknowledgment in Pippin's reading of Hegel is sustained by a philosophical necessity that he thinks this requirement imposes. To understand this, we need to consider how Kant's conception of ethics seemed to him to be compulsory, and we need to consider a Hegelian variant on Kant's view of how the bindingness of ethical reasons needs to be understood.

A broadly Humean outlook may be framed as a scepticism about the very idea of reason. But alternatively the materials of such an outlook—natural tendencies and inclinations—may be used in a purported explication of what it is to be right about reasons. Such an approach is also sometimes credited to Aristotle.[11] Now Hegel would join Kant in rejecting any such naturalistic reconstruction of reason. Kant and Hegel would agree that one cannot build an authentic notion of being right about reasons out of propensities that are simply given.

Hegel would join Kant also in rejecting a pre-critically rationalistic intuitionism: a position that conceives the space of reasons as a peculiar tract of reality, constituted independently of anything human, into whose layout we are capable of insight by virtue of a more or less mysterious faculty that we naturally, or perhaps supernaturally, have.

Kant sees no alternative except what has come to be called "Kantian constructivism". If the normative force of reasons is, as against naturalism, a subject matter for what Kant would recognize as exercises of reason, but, as against intuitionism, not an independent reality, a topic for discernment, the only possibility left, in Kant's view, is that we determine it ourselves, by legislating for ourselves in an exercise of pure practical reason.

Hegel thinks this cannot work. The purity of Kant's legislating reason consists in its having only formal considerations to guide it. Hegel thinks it follows that Kant cannot provide for substantive content. He concludes

---

11. I would question whether this is a correct view of Aristotle, but we need not go into that here. I mention this reading of Aristotle only to make room for a way Pippin sometimes puts things.

that we must take the normative force of reasons to impinge on us not as possessors of pure practical reason, but as participants in a concrete, historically situated form of life.

But Pippin's Hegel retains the Kantian idea that the only alternative to naturalism and intuitionism is that the normative force of reasons is instituted by self-legislation. And Pippin's Hegel, like Pippin's Kant, takes this talk of *institution* very seriously. Pippin resists the suggestion that the point of the self-legislation image is just to give vivid expression to this thought: one is genuinely subject to some normative authority only in so far as one can acknowledge its legitimacy. Pippin insists on a reading of the self-legislation image according to which acknowledgment is not just recognition of the legitimacy of norms—leaving their source to be otherwise understood—but *creates* their legitimacy.

So in Pippin's reading, Hegel's departure from Kant is a move from one constructivism to another. Pippin's Hegel replaces a position in which norms are legislated by pure practical reason with one in which norms are constructively determined in the recognitive practices of historically actual communities. And he applies this not just to ethical norms, but to normativity in general. Pippin's Hegel embraces "a radical anti-realism or constructivism about norms".[12] He thinks this is the only position left open to him: "there is just nothing left to 'counting as a norm' other than being taken to be one, effectively circulating as one in a society."[13]

The application to normativity in general includes the thesis I have questioned, that the normative status of free agenthood is conferred by recognition. So Pippin's Hegel thinks that thesis is forced on him: "Without a possible Aristotelian appeal to the realization of natural capacities in order to establish when one is really acting in a practically rational way (realizing one's natural potential), and without an appeal to a formal criterion of genuinely rational self-determination, this turns out to be the only criterion left: one is an agent in being recognized as, responded to as, an agent; one can be so recognized if the justifying norms appealed to in the practice of treating each other as agents can actually *function* within that community *as* justifying, can be offered and accepted (recognized) as justifying."[14]

---

12. "What is the Question . . . ?", p. 163.
13. "What is the Question . . . ?", p.163.
14. "What is the Question . . . ?", p. 163. On the mention of Aristotle, see n. 11 above.

4. But this argument by elimination of alternatives is unconvincing. It presupposes that we should model all uses of the idea of a topic for investigation—something that calls for discovery as opposed to construction—on a certain conception of how the idea works in, say, astronomy. That is what makes it seem that realism about norms could only be pre-critical rationalism. But we should query the model rather than let it shape how we picture our dealings with norms.

The idea of participation in a communal form of life is needed for a satisfactory understanding of responsiveness to reasons. But why exactly? Not because it allows us to see rationality as a communally conferred status, like being entitled to vote. We should not be frightened away from holding that initiation into the right sort of communal practice makes a *metaphysical* difference. In this respect achieving free agenthood is quite unlike reaching voting age. Responsiveness to reasons, the very idea of which is inseparable from the idea of communal practices, marks out a fully-fledged human individual as no longer a merely biological particular, but a being of a metaphysically new kind—like Rousseau's citizen, in a conception that is surely an ancestor of Hegel's thinking.

To belong to this metaphysical kind is to be able to find one's way around in the space of reasons. That imagery expresses a realism about reasons, but not the pre-critical rationalism Pippin rightly regards as a non-starter for Hegel. Pre-critical rationalism is unacceptable because it attributes unmediated independence to the space of reasons, as against the communal practices that, to stay with the realist imagery, open our eyes to its layout. (Such a picture of our relation to a subject matter is already wrong about astronomy, though it is intelligibly more tempting in that sort of context. I shall return to this at the end of this essay.) Pippin's Hegel recoils into an equally one-sided attribution of independence to the practices, refusing to countenance any sense in which reasons have the independence, as against the practices, that the realist imagery requires. The right response is a characteristically Hegelian balance, with independence and dependence on both sides. That yields a realism of a different kind.

If affirming realism about some inquiry means crediting its subject matter with unmediated independence as against the practices that constitute the inquiry, then realism is certainly wrong about norms. That is the point of rejecting pre-critical rationalism. But realism in that sense is equally wrong about the subject matter of the natural sciences. If we allow the label "realism" to fit wherever there is a subject matter that enjoys some independence with respect to our practices of inquiry, then realism becomes available about norms no less than about the subject matter of the natural sciences. Pippin's idea that normativity needs a special treatment, an anti-realism or constructivism, is not Hegelian.

I conclude that the argument that Pippin thinks limits Hegel to a communal constructivism about normativity in general, and about free individuality in particular, is not cogent. I urged that we should not attribute a counter-intuitive thesis to Hegel unless we must. Similarly, we should not read him as convinced by a bad argument unless it is unavoidable. Moreover, those considerations about dependence and independence indicate that the argument Pippin takes Hegel to be moved by is not just unconvincing, but out of tune with the characteristic shape of Hegel's thinking.

5. In Pippin's reading, the "Reason" chapter of the *Phenomenology* contains an expression of the conception of agency whose attribution to Hegel I am questioning. If this reading is right, that trumps the Principle-of-Charity considerations that are most of what I have said so far against the attribution.[15] The Principle of Charity says we should not attribute bad philosophy to someone unless we must. But the attribution is unavoidable if a text requires it, and Pippin thinks the "Reason" chapter requires attributing that conception of agency to Hegel. (Of course Pippin does not think the philosophy is bad.) However, Pippin's reading of the "Reason" chapter is questionable.

Pippin writes: "In the last two sections of Chapter Five in the Jena *Phenomenology*, Hegel proposes to show various ways in which what the deed means to me, inwardly, as I intend it and given the reasons I take to justify it, can easily come to be experienced by such a subject as in some tension with the way the 'actual' deed plays out and with the real or external social world. This tension involves the way the deed might be construed by others or contested by them."[16] This comes to a head, on Pippin's account, in the section on "die Sache selbst", whose moral Pippin summarizes like this: "What I take the act to be, its point, purpose and implication, now has none of the privileged authority we intuitively attribute to the agent. In such an account I do not exercise any kind of proprietary ownership of the deed, cannot unilaterally determine 'what was done'. This is, as it were, up for negotiation within

---

15. Not all; the point about dependence and independence is not a Principle-of-Charity consideration.

16. "Hegels praktischer Realismus", p. 305.

some concrete social community, the participants of which must determine what sort of deed *'that'* would be in our practices, how our rules apply."[17]

To begin with a general objection: I am sceptical whether this can be made out to cohere with Hegel's account of what drives the transitions from one shape of consciousness to another in the *Phenomenology*. A transition is compelled by "experience" of failure to meet a criterion. In the Introduction, Hegel explains that the criterion at any stage is internal to consciousness. "It is in it [consciousness] one thing *for* another, or it has the determinateness of the moment of knowledge altogether in it; at the same time, to it this other is not only *for it*, but also outside this relationship or *in itself*; the moment of truth."[18] What compels a transition is a mismatch *within* consciousness, between what the object is *to* it and what the object is *for* it, given the materials it has, at the stage it has reached, for a conception of the object. (This may become clearer from some examples, which I shall give when I sketch a reading of V.B.) "Experience" in the *Phenomenology* is what a shape of consciousness undergoes in becoming aware of tensions *within* its self-conception, not *between* its self-conception and external reality. No doubt it would be more natural to apply "experience" ("Erfahrung") to awareness of how things play out in practice. But that is not how the Introduction tells us the concept of experience is going to function.

6. In V.B. the target for consciousness is "the actualization of rational self-consciousness through itself".[19] This emerges out of V.A, where the aim was an "observationally" warranted identification of rational self-consciousness with (an) actuality. The thought that the outer is the expression of the inner should, in principle, enable consciousness to understand itself as not other than what, thanks to that thought, it would recognize as its own embodied self, actual precisely in being embodied. But when consciousness is restricted to "observation", the best it can make of that thought is physiognomy and phrenology. This failure teaches consciousness that its identity with an actuality needs to be understood in terms of its self-conception as an agent, rather than established by "observation", and that yields the new target of V.B.

17. "Recognition and Reconciliation", p. 137; "Hegels praktischer Realismus", p. 311.

18. ¶84. I cite by the paragraph numbers given in Miller's translation, since (with a small amount of work) a passage so identified can be found in any text. But I have not followed Miller's rendering.

19. Hegel's title for the section.

The actuality in question should still be one's own embodied self. So we can be more specific about the target of V.B: it is an understanding of certain bodily goings-on as oneself acting.

What happens, in three different ways, in V.B is that an attempt at such a conception on the part of consciousness—what *itself acting* is *for* it—turns out, in its "experience", not to be a conception of itself acting. *To* it its object is itself in action, but when it thinks through what its object is *for* it, it sees that that falls short of being what it was supposed to be.

First, consciousness tries to build what itself acting is *for* it out of an idea of the satisfaction of appetite.[20] What emerges in its "experience"—in its thinking through this attempted conception of its target—is that in this conception it has not, after all, "thrown itself from dead theory into life" (¶363), as the transition from V.A to V.B required. What was meant to be itself acting is, *for* it, "empty and alien necessity" (ibid.). The idea of a happening motivated by the drive towards the kind of pleasure that consists in satisfaction of appetite is not an idea of something with the significance of an exercise of agency. One might put the point here by saying that consciousness, which has long been self-consciously rational, realizes in its experience that this first attempt at a self-conception as an agent takes it back to a merely animal mode of being, somewhat as in the scepticism section of IV.B (¶205).

Consciousness learns from this failure that if it is to survive this "loss of itself in necessity" (¶366), the materials for its conception of the target must include the idea of a necessity that is its own. This is the necessity of "the law of the heart"—a self-generated demand on what happens in the relevant region of actuality, namely, still, what is in fact one's own body. The hope is that an idea of something necessitated by the law of the heart will be an idea of something with the significance of intentional action. The hope is dashed because the actuality to which the law of the heart is addressed is conceived as subject to an independent necessity (¶369). What consciousness hoped would be an idea of conformity to a necessity of one's own turns out to be an idea of something under the sway of that independent necessity (¶372). Deranged by this failure to achieve a conception in which the law of the heart is efficacious, consciousness blames its failure on its having aspired to a conception of *individual* self-actualization (¶377).

---

20. *Epithumia* as in Plato and Aristotle: a kind of motivating force that is by definition aimed at pleasure.

That leads into the third stage. "Virtue" is a de-individualized descendant of the law of the heart. "The way of the world" is a descendant of the alien necessity that thwarted the attempt to see the law of the heart as efficacious, in the failure consciousness blamed on its aiming at *individual* self-actualization. The hope now is that the idea of a victory for virtue in a contest between these parties will be an idea of happenings, in what previously figured as the domain of the alien necessity, with something like the significance of intentional actions. The hope is that such happenings will be intelligible as, in some sense, intentional in that they conform to the descendant of the law of the heart—though because the law has been de-individualized, they cannot be conceived as conforming to the intentions of someone in particular. (There are echoes of the renunciation of individuality in the final phase of IV.B.) This hope is dashed because the imagined contest is only a sham fight (¶386). Success in this project is failure. What it would be for virtue's legislation to be efficacious is that an embodied human individual engages in determinate behaviour. So in what consciousness wanted to conceive as a victory over individuality, individuality prevails.

Consciousness learns from this that it was mistaken in supposing individuality was what stood in the way of its achieving a conception of happenings with the significance of intentional actions. The result is a conception of individual self-actualization as free exercise of one's bodily powers (¶393). That is the shape in which consciousness finds itself (having, as usual, forgotten the route by which it arrived at this position) at the beginning of V.C.

Before I turn to V.C, let me emphasize a divergence from Pippin's reading of V.B. On the reading I have sketched, consciousness in V.B is working towards being so much as entitled to the idea that something's happening in objective reality can be itself acting. Pippin's reading is in terms of tensions between a subject's conception of its deeds and how things play out. But that implies that consciousness has, already, the idea that, in my reading, it is still working towards, the idea of its deeds: the idea of itself getting things done. I think this means that Pippin misses some intriguing philosophy, in the way Hegel shows consciousness progressing towards that idea.

7. I shall consider only the first movement of V.C, and I shall be just as sketchy about it, perhaps even sketchier.

V.C starts with consciousness secure, for the moment, in a conception of its self-actualization as the free exercise of its bodily powers. It is aware of the determinateness of its powers. But that does not figure for it as a limitation on its freedom; it is only a specificity in the space of possibilities that constitutes its being an agent at all ("the simple colour of the element in which it moves"; ¶399).

To begin with, consciousness conceives acting as a self-contained unity that embraces circumstances, end, means, and work or achievement (¶401). But the place of achievement in this unity is hard to preserve. It can easily come to seem that achievements are thrown out by acting consciousness into a realm of actuality that confronts it. In response, consciousness tries to keep a version of that self-contained unity, in what it hopes will still be a conception of itself acting, while not allowing that what happens in the realm of actuality that it takes to confront it is relevant to the content of the conception. This is the so-called honest consciousness (¶412).

The lesson consciousness now learns in its "experience" is that it cannot get away with affirming that its doing is nobody's business but its own. If the idea of doing something is to have application, something needs to happen objectively—that is, for others, in the sense of being publicly available. This has the obviousness that characterizes Wittgenstein's "reminders". It is not part of a controversial conception of agency as up for negotiation in a communal practice.

Communal practice certainly starts to matter in this section. One might say it makes its absence felt. The trouble this shape of consciousness gets into is a loss of the comfortable conception it began with, of itself acting by freely exercising its determinate bodily powers, its original nature. At the beginning of the section, the determinateness of the original nature merely fixed the space within which acting consciousness exercises its freedom. But the work, the achievement, "has received into itself the whole nature of the individuality" (¶405). So the extrusion of the work into an alien actuality takes on a look describable like this: "the work is thrown out into a state of *existing* in which the *determinateness* of the original nature turns itself in the deed against other determinate natures, encroaches on them as these others do on it, and loses itself as a vanishing moment in this universal movement" (ibid.). This is a picture of a meaningless clash of attempts at self-realization. It is intolerable as a picture of what it is to act in a world in which others act too. And that is suggestive of how this section contributes to the final lesson of V: that one cannot make satisfactory sense of the target conception, a conception of oneself getting things done, except in the context of "the ethical life of a people" (¶441).[21]

The lesson this section thus puts consciousness on the path to learning is that agenthood, like citizenship in Rousseau, is not intelligible except in the context of the idea of a communal life. As I argued earlier (§4), this does not imply that agenthood in general, and particular instances of that status such as having done this or that, are conferred by acknowledgment from others.

One cannot unilaterally, independently of participation in a communal practice, give bits of one's behaviour the kind of meaning actions have. The significance of actions consists in their being practical employments of conceptual capacities, and the idea of conceptual capacities makes sense only in the context of a shared practice. But that is not to say actions are what they are by being taken to be what they are by other participants in the practice.

The point here is not peculiar to the practical employments of conceptual capacities that actions are. If one cannot make a putative conceptual grasp on something—whether an action one is engaging in or a state of affairs one confronts—convincing to people with whom one can otherwise reach agreement, that should raise a doubt about the putative conceptual grasp, given that the idea of conceptual capacities makes sense only in the context of a communal practice. Perhaps the others will come around; it may take time for the merits of new uses of concepts to be recognized. Perhaps, though, one is only under the illusion of a conceptual grasp. If things are as one thinks one takes them to be, employing—one thinks—a concept that belongs to a certain communal practice, the practice had better provide for at least a potential consensus that things are that way. But that is not to say that things being that way is *constituted* by such potential consensus. In fact it is not clear why there should seem to be a need for anything that things being a certain way is constituted by—except, of course, things being that way.

8. In Pippin's reading, Hegel's treatment of action in the "Reason" chapter opposes a "conventional modern understanding of agency", which "makes a . . . distorting error by clumsily separating the inner intention from the outer manifestation of the 'inner,' and so by explaining the action by reference to the isolated separate intention as prior cause".[22]

21. To make this more than suggestive would require much more detail than I can go into here.

22. "Hegels praktischer Realismus", p. 305.

Pippin's Hegel corrects this over-emphasis on the independence of the inner aspect of action, the intention, by a balancing assertion that the inner depends on a socially constituted outer. Pippin thinks this leads to some counter-intuitiveness, though he claims there is no conflict with Hegel's affirmation of the "right of subjectivity" in the *Philosophy of Right*.[23] He writes: "Of course it seems a bit paradoxical to claim that we can only know what we intended to do after we have actually acted and in a way dependent on the reactions of others, but there is little doubt that Hegel holds something like such a position. Consider: 'Ethical Self-consciousness now learns *from its deed* the developed nature of what it actually did' " (the quotation is from *PhG*, ¶469).[24] If you have written a bad poem, Pippin's Hegel says the poem you have written "is a perfect expression of what your intention *turned out to be*".[25]

By framing the material as he does, Pippin implies that the education of consciousness needs to overcome a reluctance to relinquish the independence of the inner, reflecting that "conventional modern understanding". But since V.A, consciousness has been trying to see itself as not other than its own outer actuality, by exploiting the thought that the outer is the expression of the inner. The problem is not to overcome a resistance on the part of consciousness to the idea that the inner and the outer are interdependent. The problem is to enable it to see how it can have that idea—as it wants to—in the face of intelligible difficulties. And there is no reason to suppose the difficulties depend on a prior inclination to exaggerate the independence of the inner.

As for what Pippin takes to be Hegel's commitment to "an unusual retrospective determination of intention, even for the agent",[26] I think this is a misreading.

Hegel is scornful of the temptation to evade answerability for bad performances by retreating into a private sphere where everything is supposedly all right. Someone who has written an unimpressive poem must not be allowed to claim that he had a good poem in his mind, and merely failed to get it out into the open. The inner poem is mythical; the only relevant poem

---

23. Pippin argues most extensively in unpublished work. But see the parenthetical paragraph (missing its final parenthesis) at "Hegels praktischer Realismus", pp. 306–7.

24. "Recognition and Reconciliation", p. 136; "Hegels praktischer Realismus", p. 308.

25. "Hegels praktischer Realismus", p. 312.

26. "Recognition and Reconciliation", p. 137; "Hegels praktischer Realismus", p. 311.

is the one he has written. But we can insist on that without needing to abuse the concept of intention by saying his intention turns out to *have been* the intention to write that poem. It is true that he has intentionally written that poem—he has intentionally strung just those words together in just that order. But in realizing his intention he *gave* it that specificity; he did not find out what it was all along.

I do not believe Hegel holds the paradoxical position Pippin says there is little doubt that he holds. In the very paragraph that Pippin cites from (*PhG*, ¶469), Hegel goes on to say this: "Actuality . . . does not show itself to consciousness as it is in and for itself—it does not show the son the father in the one who offends him and whom he slays, or the mother in the queen whom he takes as his wife." The allusions to the Oedipus story make it clear that his topic in the remark Pippin quotes is learning the nature of one's *Tat* as opposed to one's *Handlung*—to use Hegel's terms for a distinction he makes much of in the *Philosophy of Right*. Given a specification of what one has done in the sense of one's *Tat*, it is the "right of subjectivity" to deny that one did that intentionally. It is routine, not paradoxical, that one learns what one has done, in that sense, from how things turn out. This is not learning what one's intention was.[27]

9. The social constructivism Pippin attributes to Hegel can seem to imply relativism. Pippin interprets the developmental character of the *Phenomenology* as, at least in part, a response to this threat. The *Phenomenology*'s progression is supposed to reassure us that our view of what is a reason for what is not just one view among others but, on the whole at least, correct, in the only sense "correct" can bear in the constructivist context. The idea is that our stance is displayed as the outcome of a development that is progressive, in that each succeeding stage corrects "the partiality of some prior attempt at self-imposed normative authority".[28] Pippin conceives this as a developmental successor to, for instance, a transcendental vindication.

27. In unpublished work, Pippin also cites, to document this "paradoxical" commitment on Hegel's part, *PhG*, ¶401: "an individual cannot know what he is until he has made himself a reality through action." But the topic here is the "original nature". Hegel's point is not that there is "an unusual retrospective determination of intention", but that one comes to know one's bodily powers only in the exercise of them. This is not counterintuitive or paradoxical.

28. "Hegel's Practical Philosophy: The Realization of Freedom", p. 188.

I want to end by objecting to this understanding of the developmental character of the *Phenomenology*. To begin with, most of the *Phenomenology*'s progression has nothing to do with diminishingly partial attempts at self-imposed normative authority. That would imply that the stages are successive ways of trying to make a go of human life. But nothing like that is in question until the shapes of spirit (see ¶441). And, secondly, even there, any shifts that come into view in the content of conceptions of reasons (say in conceptions of what one owes to one's kin) are, I believe, incidental to Hegel's point.

The point is to equip the consciousness that is the recipient of the education recapitulated in the *Phenomenology* with a satisfactory conception of what it is to be an autonomous inhabitant of the space of reasons *at all*. Consciousness learned at the end of V that such freedom must be understood in the context of "the ethical life of a people" (ibid.). But one is not autonomous if one is unreflectively immersed in a communal form of life. And one does not become autonomous by merely opposing what pass for norms in the society one is brought up in. (Followed generally, that is a recipe for the collapse of the social setting required for anyone to have a chance of autonomy at all.) What is needed is awareness that one is in touch with reasons only by virtue of one's formation in a *Sittlichkeit*, combined with a critical attitude to the conception of reasons one finds oneself with.[29]

What Hegel depicts as happening, when Greek *Sittlichkeit* becomes untenable, is not that some specific constellation of putative norms loses its grip. The shift he is concerned with is from a mode of life whose normative shape is simply *there* as the context, unquestioningly taken for granted, in which one acts, say as a man or as a woman, to a way of being in which acting in conformity to one of the norms that used to shape such a life is something for one to commit oneself to, or not, as the particular individual one is. That is, initially, a loss of situatedness in a *Sittlichkeit*, since to begin with there is nothing for situatedness in a *Sittlichkeit* to be apart from the unreflective immersion that lapses with the onset of individuality. What needs to happen next, through the vicissitudes—certainly historically

---

29. This indicates a basis for thinking about the question how "the ethical life of a people" ought to be organized. It must have whatever features are necessary for it to enable the formation of subjects who are free in that way. This is the frame in which we should approach Hegel's thinking about "rational" modern institutions.

situated—that *Geist* goes through, is a laborious recapturing of *Sittlichkeit*, but without giving up the individuality whose coming on the scene figures at first as a loss of *Sittlichkeit*. The result is a certain conception, in a sense formal rather than involving any specific content, of one's relation to norms *überhaupt*. No doubt the content of putatively authoritative norms changes with the shifts *Geist* goes through, but, as I said, I do not believe that is Hegel's concern.

The *Geist* chapter culminates, then, in a consciousness that is once again situated in a *Sittlichkeit*, but is now critically or reflectively oriented towards the *Sittlichkeit* in which it is situated. I want to make a couple of remarks about this invocation of a reflective or critical attitude.

First, there is a strand in the Introduction in which Hegel rejects the idea that the *Phenomenology*'s progress can be controlled by an aspiration to take nothing for granted. Any attempt to direct critical reflection at some shape of consciousness would have to rest on assumptions currently not in question. And such a procedure would not be an expression of the radical scepticism that the *Phenomenology* aims to bring to completion. But that stands in no conflict with what I have said about the culmination of the *Geist* chapter: that when *Geist* achieves full self-consciousness, the content of its consciousness includes an obligation to adopt a critical stance. A critical stance was not sufficient to guide the progress of consciousness, but that does not exclude its being part of the result of the progress.

Second, the invocation of a critical attitude is not the routine move it might seem to be. Its point here belongs with the point Hegel makes by talking, in the Preface, about the project of overcoming rigidly determined thoughts or bringing them into a state of fluidity (*PhG*, ¶33). He gives vivid expression to the thought with the image of the True as a Bacchanalian revel (*PhG*, ¶47). The sober sense of this is that no putative conceptual grasp is ever sacrosanct, fit to be placed once and for all in an archive of achieved wisdom. If one rejects a proposed conceptual innovation for no better reason than that it flouts established ways of thinking, one has violated the obligation to reflectiveness.

When one's consciousness has achieved the combination of individuality and *Sittlichkeit* with which the *Geist* chapter culminates, one is able, and obliged, to *think for oneself*—ideally, no doubt, in discussion with others—about whether putative reasons really are reasons.

When we think about how to conduct our lives, there is nothing on which to found confidence that we are getting things right, apart from the persuasiveness of the considerations we find compelling. We can step out-side the discussion, and focus on the sheer fact that we are capable of being moved by reasons. And Hegel helps us to understand that aspect of our self-conception. But that leaves us still needing to think things out for our-selves.

If we find that responsibility alarming, Pippin's picture offers a kind of comfort. We can tell ourselves that since we are constructing norms for our-selves, the results of our activity are ultimately up to us, and the develop-mental story assures us we are better placed than our predecessors to do the constructing well.

I think the very fact that it offers this comfort makes the picture suspect. It embodies an avoidance of the real difficulty of understanding oneself as a modern subject. That that topic is central to Hegel's philosophy is a thought of Pippin's own, but I think Pippin's Hegel mishandles the topic.

On Pippin's construal, as I said, the developmental character of the *Phenomenology* is aimed at freeing a supposedly compulsory constructivism from relativistic implications. But as I explained earlier (§4), the constructivism looks compulsory only because of a bad picture of what realism about norms would be: a picture according to which being open to a reality not of our making would be letting it imprint itself immediately on us. We can be encouraged into a picture of "observational" knowledge on those lines by its seeming to liberate us from the burden of responsibility for get-ting things right. But that is a dubious motivation, and the picture is a bad one already in what might seem its proper home. If we reject it, we make room for a conception according to which norms are no less suitable as a candidate for a realistic attitude than, say, the layout of the heavens.

So as Pippin understands it, the developmental character of the *Phenomenology* responds to an anxiety—a fear of relativism—that is felt only under the influence of bad philosophy. If one sees through the bad philosophy, as I think Hegel does, one is invulnerable to that anxiety.

And Pippin's reading of Hegel does not properly deal with a different anx-iety that, as modern individuals, we are (in a way) *right* to feel, or at least to be aware that we risk feeling: the anxiety of responsibility. In reflecting about how to think and act, we cannot take on trust the deliverances of any received authority. We are entirely on our own. Full awareness of that fact and its significance is the result of the *Phenomenology*'s progression.

Reason gives us resources for reflecting about how to think and act. And one starting-point can be less vulnerable than another to illusions of rational cogency, deriving from the continuing grip of traditions that ought to be discarded. But even if we are convinced that our starting-point is as good as it could possibly be in such respects, that is not an external ground for confidence in the results of our reasoning. There is *nothing* outside our reasoning on which we could found confidence in its results.

Hegel's aim is to equip us—the possessors of the consciousness that has been educated by his work into full self-consciousness—with an open-eyed awareness that that is how things are for us. A conviction of groundlessness can easily induce panic. If we allow ourselves to feel that panic, we fall into characteristic philosophical attempts to alleviate it. The vision Hegel aims to convey is a clear-sighted awareness of groundlessness, bringing with it the understanding that *all* such attempts at grounding are misguided. Hegel aims to liberate us from the felt need to have philosophy fill what, when we feel the need, presents itself as an alarming void: the supposed need that expresses itself in an empiricistic foundationalism, or in a rationalistic postulation of insight into the independently constituted intelligible structure of reality, or in a transcendental grounding for a conceptual scheme. Or—to bring the point home to Pippin—in a developmental story conceived as a successor and counterpart to a transcendental grounding. There is no ground, and it was wrong to suppose there was any need for one.

On Pippin's Postscript

1. In my "Responses", I devoted three pages to Robert Pippin's "Leaving Nature Behind, or Two Cheers for 'Subjectivism' ". Pippin reprinted that paper in his *The Persistence of Subjectivity*,[1] with a fifteen-page postscript, in which he connects a response to my response with some of the broader themes of the book. This is a response to Pippin's response to my response, and I suppose I should worry about diminishing returns. But there is room for clarification of some issues.

2. In my *Mind and World*, I recommended a conception of perceptual experience as actualization of conceptual capacities in sensory consciousness, on the ground that such a conception opens a path between a mythical Given and a coherentism that does not give the world a satisfactory position in the credentials of empirical belief.

This conception of experience, which is at least roughly Kantian, is not widely recognized as a possibility. I identified a line of thought that accounts for that. Sensibility, the capacity for sensory consciousness, is clearly in some sense a natural endowment. But talk of conceptual capacities belongs in what Wilfrid Sellars calls "the logical space of reasons" ("Empiricism and the Philosophy of Mind", §36). Sellars distinguishes placing things in the space of reasons from placing things in nature, on a conception we can easily find compelling: nature as the domain of the kind of intelligibility uncovered by the natural sciences.[2] If the space of reasons is alien to the space of nature, the idea that conceptual capacities could inform sensibility seems incoherent.

---

1. My page references will be to the reprinted version.
2. That familiar label for a kind of intellectual pursuit makes it evident how this conception of nature can easily seem to be beyond dispute.

I dissolved this seeming difficulty by invoking the familiar but easily forgotten notion of second nature. What is natural need not be equated with what is explicable by the natural sciences. Second nature is nature too. Having our sensory consciousness shaped by conceptual capacities belongs to our second nature. We can still insist that the idea of actualizations of conceptual capacities does not belong in the logical space in which the natural sciences function.

3. In "Leaving Nature Behind", Pippin argued that I should not have dragged nature in at all. I objected that he was casting nature as a direct participant in my attempt to show how the world can figure in the warrant for empirical thinking.[3] My reminder about second nature, I protested, was only meant to liberate my conception of experience from that seeming incoherence. What does the transcendental work is the conception of experience, not the appeal to nature.

In his postscript, Pippin acknowledges this. But he complains that the appeal to second nature does not help with a broader Kantian worry, a "worry about naturalism and its general threat to the possibility of a space of reasons" (p. 209).

I want to make two points about this.

First, the supposed problem I address by invoking second nature is not simply separate from that broader worry. We can align Sellars's space of reasons with Kant's realm of freedom. Kant and Sellars think phenomena involving responsiveness to reasons are *sui generis*, as compared with what can be comprehended by the natural sciences. Pippin's broader worry is this: if reason is *sui generis* in that sense, how can it be efficacious? How can free responsiveness to reasons make a difference to what happens in the world, where it is tempting to suppose natural forces have universal sway? It is just a specific application of that question to ask: how can capacities of the spontaneous understanding be actualized in operations of sensibility, which ought as such to be phenomena in nature? If second nature is helpful in connection with the specific worry, as Pippin in effect concedes, that ought to carry over to the general worry.

Second, Pippin writes as if dealing with the general worry would require an argument that natural science *cannot* accommodate responsiveness to

---

3. And, in a different context, in dealing with supposed difficulties about the idea of responsiveness to reasons for acting.

reasons. He is right that my appeal to second nature does not provide such an argument. But he is wrong to imply that it would need to.

As Pippin reads it, my appeal to second nature provides no more than a frame for ways of talking by which people think they can bring responsiveness to reasons within the reach of natural science.[4] But that misses the dialectical point of the appeal.[5]

In the Kantian view, our thought and action are not outcomes of natural forces. Pippin's worry about this comes from a natural-scientific naturalism with pretensions to universal scope. Now who has the burden of argument in a clash between these two outlooks? If a naturalism of the sort that figures in Pippin's worry had a default status, the burden would rest on the other side. There would need to be positive arguments that freedom exempts our thought and action from being naturalistically intelligible. But why not suppose that is the default position, to be accepted unless positively shown to be untenable?

It can seem that this must be wrong, because a modern world view implies reluctance to accept anything unnatural or supernatural.[6] But if second nature is nature too, parts of our lives can be outside the scope of scientific understanding, even though, as parts of our lives, they belong to nature. So the principle that we should not accept the non-natural beyond necessity yields no ground for placing a burden of argument on defenders of a substantial freedom. We need not seek to show that programmes for bringing thought and action within the scope of natural science *cannot* be executed. The point is that they have nothing in their favour but a bare faith in the universal competence of such disciplines, falsely representing itself as dictated by a modern respect for science.

In "Leaving Nature Behind", considering such programmes, Pippin says (p. 204): "surely the right response . . . is 'I won't hold my breath' and not a rush to enchant nature." "I won't hold my breath" is exactly right. Its dismissive tone does not go well with his complaining, in the postscript, that

---

4. For instance, "neural-net, training up, self-monitoring, self-correcting software jargon" (p. 210).

5. This is something I tried to convey at p. 303, n. 5 of "Responses", in rejecting Pippin's picture of bald naturalists "nodding in agreement" ("Leaving Nature Behind", p. 197) at what I say about second nature.

6. I have put this so as to leave room for the thought that on some questions accepting a role for the supernatural is unavoidable. We can consider the present issue without prejudging whether it is possible to incorporate religion into a genuinely modern world view.

my appeal to second nature is not a positive defence of the possibility of a genuine autonomy. And when I wrote of reenchanting nature, it was only to insist that there is nothing obligatory about equating nature with the domain of natural-scientific intelligibility. That is exactly why we can ignore those naturalizing programmes, rather than holding our breath in anticipation, or fear, of their success.

4. The second cluster of topics in Pippin's postscript centres on the Transcendental Deduction in Kant's first *Critique*, especially the second-edition version. In his *Hegel's Idealism*, Pippin sketched a reading that made sense of some approving things Hegel says about the B Deduction in "Glauben und Wissen". I found Pippin's treatment inspiring, and I have tried to build on it.[7]

Hegel applauds Kant's effort, in the B Deduction's second half, to undo an impression one might get from the seemingly self-contained character of the Transcendental Aesthetic: that the conditions on our experience that reflect the forms of our sensibility—the conditions that require the objects of our experience to be spatially and temporally ordered—are self-standing, in force independently of the conditions that reflect the requirements of the understanding. Accurately capturing Kant's insistence that that is not how he wants to be read, Hegel writes (*Faith and Knowledge*, pp. 69–70): "Here [that is, in the second half of the B Deduction] the original synthetic unity of apperception is recognized also as the principle of the figurative synthesis, i.e. of the forms of intuition; space and time are themselves conceived as synthetic unities, and spontaneity, the absolute synthetic activity of the productive imagination, is conceived as the principle of the very sensibility that was previously characterized only as receptivity."

As Pippin registers, I think that in spite of this promising move Kant's picture is not finally satisfactory. And now questions arise. Would a position that improved on Kant in the ways I envisage still be Kantian in any recognizable sense? And would it be Hegelian?

---

7. Relevant essays of mine include Essays 4 and 5 above, and "Hegel and the Myth of the Given". My attempt to point things in the direction of Hegel in these essays reflects the inspiration I found in Pippin's writings. The reading of the B Deduction, which I am still trying to get straight, comes from grappling with that text, and the first Critique in general, in many conversations with James Conant and John Haugeland.

5. I have two separate dissatisfactions with what Kant does.

The first is that at least in some places (e.g., B129–30), Kant writes as if all combination into unities with objective purport is a result of intellectual *activity*. He applies this in particular to the unity of intuitions. Against this I urge that enjoying intuitions should be seen as passive.

The second is that even while he denies that the requirements of our sensibility are independent of apperceptive spontaneity, Kant leaves it looking like a peculiarity of human cognitive equipment, not something that would be a feature of any experience whatever, that the world presents itself to us as spatially and temporally ordered. I urge that this undermines his claim that his transcendental idealism coincides with a common-sense empirical realism. In Kant's picture our world seems, in its apparent spatial and temporal organization, to reflect a mere quirk of human sensibility. The effect is that what he wants to see as our empirical knowledge is not recognizable as knowledge, in so far as it relates to the spatial and temporal structure the world appears to us to have.

6. Pippin mischaracterizes what I propose on the first score. He writes (p. 212): "McDowell . . . wants to 'correct' Kant's tendency, once he gets rolling in this blurring-the-boundary project [the project Hegel applauds], to understand even the formal (nonderived) aspects of our immediate contact with the world as *manifestations of apperceptive spontaneity . . . .*" There are two things wrong here.

First, this runs my first dissatisfaction together with the second. It will become clearer as I go along why this matters.

Second, I do not object to Kant's understanding intuitions as manifestations of apperceptive spontaneity. Pippin goes on to formulate my proposed improvement to Kant like this (p. 213): "The possibility of . . . perceptual objective purport *only* requires us to be in the possession of certain conceptual capacities. It is not the case that we are actively judging by means of these capacities or that we are spontaneously at work in any way in intuiting the world." This is at best misleading. I think Kant should hold not just that we need to *possess* conceptual capacities for our experience to have objective purport, but—in this respect not diverging from Kant himself, unreformed—that those capacities are *operative* in experience. My Kant holds, as Pippin says, that in intuiting we are not actively judging or spontaneously at work. But capacities to whose character it is essential that we can use them in active judging, capacities that belong to our spontaneity, are actualized in intuitions (not just required somehow in the background, as Pippin's wording implies). For my corrected Kant, no less than for Kant himself, intuitions are manifestations of apperceptive spontaneity.

7. In Pippin's reading, the Deduction addresses a worry that the categorial features of our thinking are "merely our way of categorizing" things (p. 212)—a worry that other ways of being minded might yield a world view superior to ours in categorial respects. Pippin thinks the Deduction aims to reassure us that the forms our understanding requires are a good fit for something else, "the sensible presence of the world in our immediate, receptive contact with it" (ibid.). Pippin's Kant argues (not just in the Deduction but "all the way through the argument of the Analogies" [p. 214]) that this "something else" could not fail to fit "the requirements of our mindedness" (p. 212). And Pippin complains that in my supposed improvement I just help myself, not to that claim, but to the less impressive claim that the sensible presence of the world to us just does fit those requirements—"as if [the deliverances of sensibility] just 'happen' to come that way, fortunately for us, given our own unavoidable requirements" (p. 213).

I think this involves a fundamental misrepresentation of the task Kant sets himself. And that skews Pippin's understanding of my proposal.

Kant's concern is not that in framing our world view in the forms required by our understanding, we may *get reality wrong* in categorial respects—that other forms of thought might do better than ours at capturing the categorial shape of reality. Such a worry would *presuppose* that our understanding enables us to direct thought at reality. Kant's concern is with that presupposition. He aims to vindicate our entitlement to suppose that instantiations of the forms required by our understanding are thereby equipped with objective purport.

In a sort of preamble to his discussion of the Kant-Hegel cluster of issues, Pippin says, rightly, that Kant's concern is with "the very possibility of any representation of an object" (p. 211). But the worry he takes the Deduction to address arises only if one *assumes* that our categories equip us with a possibility of representing objects. The worry is merely whether, in exploiting that possibility, we *misrepresent* objects in categorial respects. So the remark in the preamble seems no more than lip service to a thought Pippin has not taken to heart.

Kant's question is this: given that our intellectual engagement with reality requires the availability of objects to the senses, how can we know *a priori*, concerning forms required by the pure understanding, that they provide for objective purport in instantiations of them?

In the first half of the B Deduction, Kant elaborates a conception of intuitions as instantiations of forms required by the pure understanding in sensory receptivity, abstractly conceived—not specified as formed the way our sensibility is formed. This is potentially a move towards showing that those forms provide for objective purport. If he can entitle himself to suppose that the categorial form of intuitions enters into their making objects immediately present to subjects, that will display those forms as essential to what can be conceived as the ground-level case of objective purport.

In introducing this idea of intuitions as categorial shapings of sensory receptivity, my corrected Kant stresses "receptivity". He insists that in intuitions forms required by the understanding come into play without activity on the part of subjects. Pippin sees this as theft rather than honest toil, in a response to the worry his Kant addresses. But the real Kant's question is still pressing for my corrected Kant, in just the way it is pressing for Kant himself, unreformed. (This is why the Deduction needs its second half.) The question takes this form: how can we know *a priori* that this idea of intuitions is an idea of items that have objective purport by virtue of instantiating forms required by the pure understanding?

The question is urgent because the Transcendental Aesthetic can seem to have provided sensibility-related conditions on our experience, satisfiable independently of the understanding-related conditions that are Kant's concern in the Deduction. If the sensibility-related conditions were independent, the Aesthetic would have yielded a self-standing account of a possibility for objects to be given to our senses. But if that were so, the requirement of categorial unity in intuitions would be extra to something sufficient for our sensory states to relate to objects. Categorial unity would pull no weight in showing how our intuitions relate to objects. It would secure merely that the objects given in the sensory states that our intuitions are are thinkable.

It is true that, since we cannot know objects except through our powers of thought, sensory states in which objects were present to our senses without being thinkable would be nothing to us (compare B132). But even so, if there could be such states, the requirement of thinkability would be additional to that by virtue of which objects are present to the senses in our sensory states, including those that are not nothing to us, intuitions. Only states in which objects are given to us in thinkable form can provide us with subject matter for exercises of our powers of thought. But that is a mere tautology. It cannot help towards showing that conformity to the requirement of thinkability has anything to do with the capacity of states of our sensory consciousness to relate to objects at all.

This is why, at the start of the second half of the B Deduction, Kant undertakes to show, "from the mode in which . . . empirical intuition is given in sensibility, that its unity is no other than that which the category . . . prescribes to the manifold of a given intuition in general" (B145). Pippin quotes this passage (p. 214), but I think he misreads it. Kant is not setting out to reassure us that our categories are a good fit for objects as they are present to our senses. He is setting out to ward off the threat that a possibility of objects being present to our senses is provided for by conformity to the requirements of our sensibility, independently of any condition involving thinkability.

In the second half of the Deduction, Kant does just that. He argues that the unity of the mode in which empirical intuition is given in our sensibility, the unity involved in the requirement of ordering in space and time, is not other than the categorial unity that is part of the conception of intuitions elaborated in the first half. The requirements of our sensibility are not satisfiable independently of the requirement of categorial structure. And now he can claim, in effect, that the idea of an object's presenting itself to our senses coincides with the idea of our enjoying an intuition, something with categorial structure. He can say, of "whatever objects may *present themselves to our senses*" (B159), that it is in intuitions, with their categorial unity, that they are given to us. There is, after all, no possibility of objects being present to our senses otherwise than in intuitions. It was that seeming possibility that threatened to leave the categorial structure of intuitions an idle wheel in an account of how it is that our intuitions are of objects.

Kant executes this task in the Transcendental Deduction, not, as in Pippin's reading, in an argument extending through the Analogies.[8] In warding off the threat, he talks abstractly of "the category". Specific instances of our categories figure only in illustrations. The point is to show how the very idea of categorial unity connects with the possibility of objective purport, not to reassure us that our categories in particular enable our thinking to fit the world.

I do not believe Kant ever concerns himself with the worry Pippin's Kant addresses, the worry that reality might be better categorized otherwise than

---

8. Of course that is not to deny that there is a larger task that needs both the Deduction and the Analytic of Principles for its fulfilment.

as our understanding constrains us to categorize it. At B145 he calls the requirement of categorial unity "a peculiarity of our understanding". But it is
clear from the context that he means a peculiarity of our understanding *qua*
discursive, finite, dependent on sensibility, not *qua* specifically human. So
far as I can see, he conceives the pure forms of our thought as forms of
thought *überhaupt*, forms instantiated in any discursive engagement with
reality.

It is different with the forms of our sensibility. They are supposed to be
distinctively ours, not necessarily shared by all discursive knowers.[9] So
when the categories are schematized in terms of our sensibility, they are
likewise, for Kant, distinctively ours. But there is no opening here into the
worry Pippin reads Kant as addressing, about the requirements of our
mindedness as opposed to that of conceivable others. That is a worry
Pippin's Kant thinks he can alleviate without questioning the idea that the
spatial and temporal form of the world as we experience it is a reflection of
a sensibility that is distinctively ours.

8. Let me now return to the points I made in §6.

The divergence I considered in §7 explains why Pippin runs my two dissatisfactions together, and why he misunderstands my first correction to
Kant. In Pippin's reading, "blurring the boundary" between sensibility and
understanding is Kant's strategy for reassuring us that sensibility's contribu-
tions to experience could not fail to fit the forms required by our understanding. Pippin tries to place me in a landscape shaped by that conception
of Kant's aim. This is the context in which he takes me to deny that intuitions are manifestations of apperceptive spontaneity, and to conceive them
instead as occurrences that happen to be structured so that our understanding can get a grip on them.

But my Kant does not envisage deliverances of sensibility, independent of
understanding, possessing structures that allow thought to relate to them.
Intuitions exemplify the forms required by understanding, not through fortunate happenstance, but because apperceptive spontaneity is operative in
them—though (this is my proposed reform) not by way of activity on our
part. Intuitions are not a "something else" whose fit with the forms required
by our understanding could reassure us that thinking within those forms
gets things right. Kant's aim is to show, by elaborating their role in the con-

---

9. This brings us into the area of the second of my two dissatisfactions.

stitution of intuitions, what those forms have to do with possession of objective purport at all, right or wrong.

9. I turn now to my second dissatisfaction.

"Blurring the boundary" does not dislodge Kant from the doctrine that space and time are transcendentally ideal. In the Deduction's second half, he argues that the requirements that reflect the forms of our sensibility are not satisfiable independently of the requirements that derive from the understanding. But he leaves the specifics of the sensibility-related requirements, the spatial and temporal organization they demand in any world we can experience, apparently in force only for us, not common to any discursive take on reality. The effect is that the whole package is a merely subjective idealism, as Hegel notoriously said. The object of what Kant wants to see as our empirical knowledge is, in pervasive respects, a mere reflection of features of our subjectivity.

I suggested we can fix this by reconceiving how the requirements of spatial and temporal organization relate to empirical thinking. In Kant's picture those requirements impinge from outside on apperceptive spontaneity. But we should see them, rather, as a "moment" within a Hegelian descendant of the operations of apperceptive spontaneity: the self-realization of the Concept, say. The self-realization of the Concept is the unfolding of thought, and as such subjective. But it is equally the self-revelation of reality, and as such objective. In this conception, empirically accessible reality is not seen as even in part a reflection of self-standing features of our subjectivity.

Pippin protests that this is not the thinking of a reformed Kant. And at some level that is obviously right. Kant could not lightly abandon the transcendental ideality of space and time.

Even so, it is worth stressing how awkwardly this sits with other things Kant cares about. It should be a truism that things are knowable by us only thanks to their conforming to whatever conditions there are for its being possible for us to know them.[10] And a truism about the possibility of knowledge should not raise doubts about the status as knowledge of some of what it is meant to apply to. Kant shows his responsiveness to such considerations when he represents transcendental idealism as protecting a common-sense empirical realism. But given the way he treats the sensibility-related conditions, the so-called knowledge they are conditions on is not recognizable as knowledge.

10. Compare a remark of Pippin's at p. 214.

Pippin's protest goes beyond the point that the transcendental ideality of space and time is dear to Kant's heart. He urges that "to remain Kant (the one who thinks he needs a Deduction)" (p. 214), Kant cannot give up the limitation of our so-called empirical knowledge to a so-called world that reflects how our sensibility is formed. This is correct too, but not, I think, as Pippin means it.

Pippin's idea is that if it is to be possible for Kant to argue that our categories fit objects as they present themselves to our senses, the formal structure of presence to our senses must be external to the operations of apperceptive spontaneity. Only so are there two things between which Kant can argue that there is a fit. Pippin's Kant cannot give up seeing the requirement of spatial and temporal ordering as external to the operations of apperceptive spontaneity, because that externality is essential to the way he averts the threat that our forms of thought may be a worse fit for reality than others.

But as I have urged, this misrepresents what the Deduction is for. It is true that thinking a Deduction is needed requires that externality. But this is not because the externality is needed for an argument to reassure us that our thinking gets things right in categorial respects, but because the externality is a condition for so much as seeming to be faced with the different question that is Kant's concern. To repeat, Kant's question is this: how can we know *a priori* that the forms required by the pure understanding enter into providing for the possibility of objective purport? The question is urgent because Kant thinks our intellectual engagement with reality requires objects to be given to our senses. If we reconceive Kant's sensibility-related requirements as a "moment" within the self-realization of the Concept, we can no longer take the forms of thought, the forms instantiated in the self-realization of the Concept, to be pure, in the sense of being independent of the availability of objects to our senses. Kant's question arises only because he conceives the forms of thought as belonging to an understanding that is pure in that sense. After the move I recommend, Kant's question lapses.

What my second reform implies, then, is not that the Deduction needs to be recast, but that we are liberated from the apparent need to do what it sets out to do.

That is to concede what Pippin says in his protest (though not as he means it) in quite a strong form. The result of my second reform is no longer Kantian in any but the thinnest sense. But that is no threat to anything I think. My proposal—whose shape I took from Pippin himself—was that we can understand at least some aspects of Hegelian thinking in terms of a radicalization of Kant. The radicalization need not be accessible to someone who would still be recognizably Kant. It is enough if there is a way to arrive at a plausibly Hegelian stance by reflecting on the upshot of the Deduction. It is no problem for this that, as I am suggesting, this reflection undermines the very need for a Transcendental Deduction—provided such a result emerges intelligibly from considering what is promising and what is unsatisfactory in Kant's effort.

10. Pippin's Hegel pursues a counterpart to the project of Pippin's Kant: to "establish that we could not be other-minded than we are (and so that our form of mindedness counts as the form of objecthood)" (p. 215). Pippin thinks Hegel addresses a worry that our form of mindedness is merely ours, so that alternative forms of mindedness may do better at getting reality right. We cannot exclude that by helping ourselves to the claim "that the deliverances of sensibility must exhibit the kind of unity that would allow their thinkability" (p. 215). The problem with Kant's approach "cannot be fixed by McDowell's correction" (p. 214). Instead Pippin's Hegel argues that our form of mindedness conforms to requirements on any mindedness, and hence is not inferior to possible alternatives. He does this "not deductively but developmentally, by appeal to a retrospective account of attempts at rendering self-conscious the necessary, unavoidable elements of any form of shared mindedness" (p. 215).

But this picture of Hegel starts from what I have urged is a falsification of Kant. Kant's aim in the Deduction is not to reassure us that objects fit our mindedness, in the face of a worry that they might better fit some other. His aim is to show how forms required by a pure understanding can be *a priori* guaranteed to be forms of mindedness—of thought about reality, right or wrong—at all. So the project Pippin credits to Hegel does not have a Kantian precedent. The argument Pippin envisages is not a different way of doing something Kant was already trying to do.

And Pippin misrepresents my proposed reform of Kant. No doubt we cannot fix Kant by helping ourselves to deliverances of sensibility that fit the forms of our understanding. That is Pippin's distorted representation of my first correction to Kant. (Here it matters that there are two separate corrections.) But Kant makes our supposed empirical knowledge unrecognizable as knowledge, and that *can* be fixed by my second correction, as I explained in §9. There I put the resulting picture in at least roughly Hegelian terms: the sensibility-related conditions on empirical knowledge are a "moment" in the self-realization of the Concept.

Pippin's Hegel does not consider how to improve on Kant's treatment of the forms of our sensibility. Instead he undertakes to establish that our mindedness has progressed to having a form that a shared mindedness must have. But a Hegel who engaged in such a project with a view to doing something he thinks Kant tries but fails to do would not be as good a reader of Kant as I think Hegel was. He would not understand what Kant's problem about the forms of thought was.

In §7, I expressed a disbelief that Kant has a worry about whether our categories are merely ours. I do not believe Hegel has a matching worry about our form of mindedness. Pippin writes of "Hegel's very different approach to the problem of a concept's objectivity" (p. 211), as if that specified a problem that is simply there for anyone. But what problem is it supposed to be? *Kant* has a problem about the objective purport of conceptual activity, because he thinks its forms are determined by an understanding that is pure, in the sense of being independent of the availability of objects to our senses. Kant's question is how, given that, the forms of conceptual activity can enter into the possibility of objective purport. If we reconceive sensory receptivity as a "moment" in the self-realization of the Concept, the result is a picture within which that problem does not arise. This is indeed a different approach to Kant's problem. But it is not an answer in different terms to Kant's question. It reconsiders the conceptions that pose Kant's problem, with the result that the problem disappears.

If the forms of thought have their source in the pure understanding, but objects are given to us only through the senses, it is a substantive task to argue that the forms of thought are the forms of reality. Kant's effort at executing what is in effect that task cannot succeed, because his idealism, based as it is on the transcendental ideality of space and time, degenerates into a merely subjective idealism.

To reconceive the way our sensibility is formed as a "moment" in the self-realization of the Concept is to provide a picture of thought that is not confronted with that substantive task. That the forms of thought are the forms of reality can now stand revealed as a platitude. (At least until someone thinks of some other reason to find it problematic.) There is no way to conceive reality except in terms of what is the case, and there is no intelligible idea of what is the case except one that coincides with the idea of what can be truly thought to be the case.

I mean what can be truly thought to be the case, period; there is no need to make a fuss about adding "by us". As I have insisted, Kant's problem is not that the forms we employ may be merely ours. And the Hegelian conception that dissolves Kant's problem does not inherit such a worry from Kant.

It may seem absurd to suggest that the identity-in-difference of thought and reality is a platitude. But it takes work to enable it to present itself as the platitude it is, in the face of our propensity to mishandle immediacy. Pippin implies that in, say, the *Phenomenology* Hegel depicts successive forms of mindedness, ancestral to ours, coming to grief by their own lights, with a view to demonstrating that with us, mindedness has progressed to a form mindedness must have to be satisfactory to itself, which gives that form a better claim than alternatives to coincide with the form of reality. But what Hegel does there is, rather, to show successive attempts at a picture of mindedness *überhaupt*—whose form anyway coincides with the form of reality—coming to grief because they include unmediated immediacy. At each stage until the last, the trouble is temporarily fixed by mediating the troublesome immediacy, reconceiving it as a "moment" in the self-realization of the Concept. But at the next stage an intelligible impulse to acknowledge an immediacy, a brute externality, arises in a new form, and we need more "experience" of the deleterious effects, and more mediation, until at the ideal endpoint the identity of thought with reality is no longer vulnerable to seeming problematic in that way.

I am not suggesting that the dissolution of Kant's problem about conceptual objectivity exhausts Hegel's thinking; not even that it exhausts his thinking about the relation between thought and reality.

For one thing, Kant's problem reflects only one way in which unmediated immediacy can make the relation seem problematic.

For another, I have sketched the Hegelian response with an abstractness that matches Kant's in the Deduction. In the Deduction, as I said, Kant talks about "the category" rather than specific categories. My Hegel has so far talked with similar abstractness about the forms of thought. But of course Hegel is interested in the question what the forms of thought are. And it is familiar that he thinks he can do better than Kant in responding to that question.[11] I am not playing down the centrality to Hegel's thinking of his logic.

---

11. He accuses Kant of uncritically accepting his list of the forms of thought from current logic.

But Hegel's logic is not a counterpart to the Transcendental Deduction. It would be more nearly right to say it does for Hegel what the so-called Metaphysical Deduction does for Kant[12]—though it does not serve to determine a list of items whose objective validity is to be shown in a counterpart to the Transcendental Deduction. Hegel needs no counterpart to the Transcendental Deduction. In the new environment, "pure" in "pure forms of thought" no longer means what it means in Kant, and it is that conception of the purity of the forms of thought that poses the apparent problem Kant responds to in the Deduction. Hegel does not need to work at making a place for transcendental logic. In the new environment, an investigation of the pure forms of thought already belongs, just as such, to a logic that is transcendental in something like Kant's sense.

11. Pippin says I hold that objects simply occupy a position of authority over our thinking (p. 215, n. 11). But "simply" makes this a travesty. To entitle ourselves to conceive our thinking as answerable to objects, in my view, we need to get clear how forms of thought enter into the constitution of intuitions. And the characterization of intuitions cannot do its transcendental work apart from the role of those forms in intellectual activity. Pippin's contrary impression belongs with his idea that my reformed Kant does not conceive intuitions as manifestations of apperceptive spontaneity.

In "Leaving Nature Behind", Pippin wrote (p. 195, n. 18): "McDowell's claim is that there would be nothing for a 'context of justification' [the topic of 'Hegelian talk of social bases of normativity'] to be *about* if we could not account for [the objective purport of perceptual states] independently of it." In my response, I protested that "independently of it" is exactly wrong. Conceptual capacities, and therefore a "context of justification", are essentially involved in my account of the objective purport of perceptual states. And conceptual capacities are intelligible only in the context of a social practice.

12. At least as Hegel understands Kant. But the accusation that Kant has nothing but current logic to justify his list of categories is arguably unfair. The Analytic of Principles equips Kant with a much more impressive case for saying that just these are the forms thought must take. There is no reason to think the determination of the list of categories is supposed to be completely executed in the Metaphysical Deduction. In Kant's view, current logic is no more than a clue to what the forms of thought are, as is indicated by the proper title of the section that contains the so-called Metaphysical Deduction.

In his postscript, Pippin brushes this aside. He writes (p. 215): "As far as I can see, McDowell's appeal to sociality is only a gesture toward the unavoidability of socialization into a community (some community or other), a matter of acquiring a shared form of mindedness." His suggestion is that "Hegelian talk of social bases of normativity" would require the authority of objects to be over subjects who have acquired not just some shared form of mindedness or other, but one that exemplifies "genuine answerability to each other (where 'genuine' has something to do with real mutuality of recognition among free, rational beings)" (p. 216).

I agree that such mutuality of recognition would be needed, in Hegel's view, for a complete realization of freedom. And perhaps we should find that ideal implicit in the very idea of social practices. Perhaps a nisus towards real mutuality of recognition is part of, for instance, the combination of authority and dependence that is an element in being a speaker of a natural language.

But this does not imply that thought's answerability to objects requires a realization of the ideal. Are we to suppose that members of downtrodden minorities, say, or those who oppress them, cannot have their empirical thinking rationally controlled by objects they perceive? No doubt restrictions on freedom to act can have effects on freedom of thought. But it would be absurd to claim that there is no thinking, and hence no involvement of capacities for thought in perceptual experience, unless there is full mutuality of recognition.

I doubt that Hegel would make any such claim. I would resist reading it into the fact that thought makes its appearance, in the *Phenomenology*, at the end of the dialectic of "Lordship and Bondage". What Hegel gives there is not a sociologico-historical account of the origin of thought—as if slave-owners and slaves were incapable of conceptual activity. It is a treatment, in allegorical terms, of one of those defective pictures of mindedness that I described in §10. Thought emerges with the overcoming of an attempt by self-consciousness to affirm its independence over against what is in fact itself, in the guise of a consciousness dependent for its content on its dealings with the empirical world.[13]

And anyway, if Hegel did think thought can be beholden to its subject matter only in the context of complete mutuality of recognition, the right response would surely be "So much the worse for Hegel".

13. For some discussion, see Essay 8 above.

12. The final issue in Pippin's postscript is self-legislation. In my response to "Leaving Nature Behind", I agreed that the image of legislating for oneself is fundamental to German idealism. But I urged that it makes no sense to conceive subjecting oneself to norms as an action undertaken in a normative void. In a remark Pippin quotes, I wrote ("Responses", p. 276): "Our freedom, which figures in the image as our legislative power, must include a moment of receptivity." What the image comes to is that we are subject to norms only in so far as we can freely acknowledge their authority, so that being subject to them is not being under the control of an alien force. But apart from special cases, their authority is not brought into being by acknowledgment.

I did not particularly intend to suggest that Pippin was committed to making too much of the image. He registers, as I noted, that "we cannot . . . legislate arbitrarily" ("Leaving Nature Behind", p. 198, n. 22).[14] I only wanted to warn against exploiting the self-legislation theme in order to represent me as opposed to the subjectivism of German idealism. Apperceptive spontaneity, and hence subjectivity, are central to my account of how thought relates to reality. The subjectivism I attack is not that of German idealism. For that subjectivism, as I understand it, I give three cheers, whereas Pippin can muster only two for what he makes of it.

But in his postscript Pippin comes enthusiastically to the defence of an extreme form of the self-legislation idea, with no concessions to "the fans of receptivity" (p. 219). He adds (n. 22): "Or at least friends of a receptivity that can, on its own, do some serious transcendental heavy lifting." We have been here before: one way of putting something I said in §11, and had already said in my response to "Leaving Nature Behind", is that I am not a friend of receptivity in this sense. Pippin's target is a straw man.

His star exhibit for the defence is Kant's conception of practical reason. Kant holds that reason has no insight into the pursuit-worthiness of substantive ends. For Kant the requirements of practical reason are purely formal, and he sets out that view in strong expressions of the self-legislation idea. The authority of the moral law consists in its being what we legislate for ourselves when we exercise our pure practical reason.

---

14. I did not even quite accuse Brandom of being committed to the claim that we can bring norms into existence out of a normative void, as Pippin says I did (p. 208). I said only that Brandom's story about the social institution of norms risks falling foul of the fact that such an idea makes no sense.

But taking this to be bad news for "the fans of receptivity", in any sense that includes me, would betray a failure to appreciate how abstract the requirement of a moment of receptivity is. Even in Kant's version of the self-legislation theme, we cannot legislate just anyhow and thereby make ourselves subject to something authoritative. There are constraints, and that is a moment of receptivity in our legislative power, even in this extreme version in which the constraints are purely formal.

Pippin concedes that Hegel's rejection of Kantian formalism yields a conception of the ethical more like what I recommended for responsiveness to reasons in general: a conception according to which "it can be said that some sort of second-nature *Bildung* has made it possible to see a reason 'in the world' that exists as such a reason even if unacknowledged by many" (p. 220). But he thinks this is not much of a concession, given what he takes to be Hegel's view of the normative import of these reasons, and what he takes to be the point of my insistence on receptivity.

The issues here are quite general, but I shall sketch a reaction by going back to the authority of objects over thought. Observed facts present us with *entitlements*, to make claims about how things are, and *requirements*, to refrain from denying those claims.[15] The content of the norms underlying these statuses is summarily captured in the metaphor of responsibility to observable objects. Allegiance to these norms should be as good a context as any for the self-legislation idea.

As I said in §11, Pippin is wrong to represent me as holding that objects *simply* occupy a position of authority over thought. But I think Pippin's alternative is wrong too. Pippin says (p. 215, n. 11): "They only have the authority bestowed on them, and Hegel is out to show why that granting is necessarily social." And he points to his discussion of the self-legislation theme as a context for this remark.

I can approach what I find dubious about this by considering what Pippin makes of a remark he quotes from me (p. 220, n. 24): "forms of life . . . are both products of drawn-out historical evolution and dependent for their continuation on whole-hearted participation by mature individuals, those who have acquired the faculty of spontaneity."[16] Pippin's idea is that this is all right if we insist that what drives the historical evolution of forms of life is self-legislating spontaneity.

15. We cannot be obliged to make them.
16. This is from my "Responses", p. 297.

Now in one sense that is innocuous. Social practices evolve, at least to some extent, as a result of free acts. And the image of legislating for oneself is an image of freedom, so those free acts are, just as such, acts of self-legislation.

But in another sense the claim lacks all plausibility, and this is the sense required for Pippin's talk of the authority of objects as socially bestowed. It is surely a Hegelian point that the shifts in practices effected by those free acts need not have figured in anyone's intention. Practices evolve in ways that nobody envisages or plans. When that happens, there are binding rules that have not been legislatively instituted. I have granted that they may be in force as a result of free acts. But the intentional content of the acts did not include making those rules binding.

However, anything we could reasonably call "bestowing authority" would have to be intentional under that description. And if we ask who did this supposed bestowing of authority on objects, there is no sensible answer. It is not that someone did it, but we do not know who, because the bestowing is lost in the mists of prehistory. No one did it. This cannot be undermined by speculations, however plausible, about behaviour engaged in by our ancestors with the cumulative, but surely unintended, effect that moves they or their descendants made took on the character of empirical claims, responsible to observable objects.

That objects are authoritative over thought—certainly over its expression—is a feature of a social practice that has evolved into being as it is. The authority is genuine, because we can freely acknowledge it. But the idea of bestowing it on objects does not apply to anything we do, or anything any of our predecessors did.

PART IV

Sellarsian Themes

The Constitutive Ideal
of Rationality:
Davidson and Sellars

The nomological irreducibility of the mental does not derive merely from the seamless nature of the world of thought, preference, and intention, for such interdependence is common to physical theory, and is compatible with there being a single right way of interpreting a man's attitudes without relativization to a scheme of translation. Nor is the irreducibility due simply to the possibility of many equally eligible schemes, for this is compatible with an arbitrary choice of one scheme relative to which assignments of mental traits are made. The point is rather that when we use the concepts of belief, desire, and the rest, we must stand prepared, as the evidence accumulates, to adjust our theory in the light of considerations of overall cogency: the constitutive ideal of rationality partly controls each phase in the evolution of what must be an evolving theory. An arbitrary choice of translation scheme would preclude such opportunistic tempering of theory; put differently, a right arbitrary choice of a translation manual would be of a manual acceptable in the light of all possible evidence, and this is a choice we cannot make. We must conclude, I think, that nomological slack between the mental and the physical is essential as long as we conceive of man as a rational animal.[1]

Richard Rorty has recently[2] aimed to represent the ideas expressed in this familiar passage as an aberration, something that could be removed while leaving the basic thrust of Davidson's philosophy undamaged and indeed purified. I have some reservations about some of the detail of the passage, but I think, against Rorty, that its basic claim—that an ideal of rationality is constitutive of the very idea of the mental, and that that ensures a special

1. Donald Davidson, "Mental Events", pp. 222–3.
2. For instance, in "McDowell, Davidson, and Spontaneity".

irreducibility of concepts of the mental to concepts of the natural sciences and their kin in everyday thought and speech—is central to an authentically Davidsonian philosophy. To begin on urging that Rorty's suspicions are misplaced, I am going to juxtapose the Davidsonian irreducibility claim with a parallel claim made by another great twentieth-century North American philosopher, and another of Rorty's heroes, Wilfrid Sellars—a claim expressed by Sellars in passages that, it seems to me, Rorty bowdlerizes, in a way that fits with his distaste for this and similar passages in Davidson.

The point Davidson makes in this passage relates to the constitutive role of rationality in our thought and talk of the mental in general. In the second part of this essay, I want to consider an aspect of how the point applies to the semantical in particular—the characteristics of our linguistic repertoires that enable us to give expression to our mental states, as we might say in order to bring out the connection between the semantical and the explicit topic of that passage from "Mental Events". Here too I shall exploit Sellars, this time not as thinking in parallel with Davidson, but as subject to a blind spot concerning a feature of Tarskian semantics about which Davidson is completely clear. The blind spot persists, I think, into Rorty's attempt to appropriate Davidson for his own purposes, and it vitiates Rorty's reading of Davidsonian semantics.

1. First, then, an echo of the Davidsonian irreducibility thesis in Sellars. Where Davidson says that our thought and talk of the mental is governed by a constitutive ideal of rationality, and that this ensures that its concepts cannot be reduced to concepts that figure in ways of thinking and talking that are not so governed, Sellars says that our thought and talk of the epistemic needs to be understood as functioning in the logical space of reasons, and that this ensures that concepts of the epistemic cannot be understood in terms of concepts that do not so function.[3] It seems irresistible to suppose that the logical space of reasons, in Sellars, plays a role that corresponds to the role of the constitutive ideal of rationality, in Davidson.

When Sellars's thought is put, as I have just put it and as Sellars sometimes does, in terms of the epistemic, it can seem that it relates exclusively to knowledge, so that Sellars's irreducibility claim has a different topic from Davidson's. This appearance enables Rorty to thin down Sellars's thought

---

3. See "Empiricism and the Philosophy of Mind", §36.

into the idea that the acceptability of knowledge claims—the supposed exclusive target of Sellars's remarks about the logical space of reasons—is a matter of "victory in argument".[4] Thus Rorty can suggest that the point is to discourage the idea that knowing is a factual feature of a person, irreducible, in a way that risks looking mysterious, to what can be truly said about her in naturalistic terms, let alone that mindedness is such a feature, by registering that victory in argument cannot be had without actually arguing; who wins an argument is not, for instance, predictable by exploiting a theory in some special science.

I think this is a misreading. Sellars exploits attributions of knowledge only as a particularly clear case for the point he wants to make. In fact, he uses "epistemic" as a term of art, covering far more than what the word's etymology would suggest. For instance, he counts something's looking red as an epistemic fact about the thing, as opposed to a natural fact.[5] ("Natural" is his way of gesturing towards the concepts to which concepts of the epistemic cannot be reduced, as we are to appreciate by seeing that concepts of the epistemic function in the logical space of reasons.) And at one point he writes, strikingly, of "the epistemic character, the intentionality" of expressions such as "thinking of a celestial city".[6] Here it is even clearer that the word "epistemic" comes loose from its etymology. I think this example shows that the epistemic, for Sellars, covers states or episodes that involve the actualization of conceptual capacities and as such have intentionality or objective purport, whether or not they amount to cases of knowledge. This makes the irreducibility thesis that Sellars underwrites by invoking the logical space of reasons a pretty exact match for the irreducibility thesis that Davidson underwrites by invoking the constitutive ideal of rationality. A thesis that applies to thinking of a celestial city cannot be captured by Rorty's appeal to victory in argument. Sellars's thought is a version of the irreducibility claim that Rorty wishes Davidson had not embraced.

There is a precedent for Sellars's using "epistemic" in this at first sight strange way, so that it matches the way Davidson uses "mental" in "Mental Events". The precedent I mean is Kant's first *Critique*. From the language of that work, one might think knowledge is its primary concern. But in fact

4. *Philosophy and the Mirror of Nature*, p. 156.
5. "Empiricism and the Philosophy of Mind", §17.
6. "Empiricism and the Philosophy of Mind", §7.

Kant's concern is not knowledge so much as the directedness of thought at objects, the intentionality or objective purport, that is a prerequisite for anything to be even a candidate to be a case of knowledge. Heidegger says: "*The Critique of Pure Reason* has nothing to do with a 'theory of knowledge'".[7] That is surely excessive, but in its over-the-top way it points towards a claim that would be correct, and one that could also be correctly made about Sellars's "Empiricism and the Philosophy of Mind".

Of course the presence in Sellars of a thesis to the effect that the intentional or the conceptual has a special irreducibility, matching the special irreducibility Davidson attributes to the mental, does not by itself address Rorty's wish that there were no such thing in Davidson. If I am right that the same thought is in Sellars, Rorty will simply include Sellars in the wish that it were not so. We need to consider the grounds for the wish.

So why does Rorty deplore the irreducibility thesis? The answer is: he fears that it merely encourages philosophy in a certain traditional vein— philosophy of a sort that he is surely right to think Davidson, like Rorty himself, wants to display as superfluous, rather than something that responsible intellectuals have an obligation to go in for. Davidson urges that concepts of the mental are irreducible to concepts of the natural sciences in a special way, to be traced not simply to the fact that talk and thought of the mental hang together holistically—as perhaps talk and thought of, say, the biological do also—but to the need to invoke rationality in characterizing this as a particular and special instance of holistic interconnection. The point turns not on holism as such but on a special holism, in which the elements hang together in a way that can be captured only by invoking an ideal of rationality. Rorty's fear is that when Davidson thus singles out concepts of the mental as subject to a special irreducibility, that encourages a familiar sort of philosophical mind-boggling at how peculiar the mental is, and a familiar sort of philosophical project in which we take ourselves to have to tell supra-empirical stories to reestablish connections to ordinary reality for minds, conceived thus as peculiar and concomitantly as separated from ordinary reality. Within this sort of project, it will seem that we need to choose among the standard options for dealing with "the mind-body problem" and "the problem of knowledge", thus engaging in the kind of traditional philosophical activity whose unsatisfactoriness Rorty is so

---

7. *Kant and the Problem of Metaphysics*, p. 11. Heidegger's word is "Erkenntnistheorie", which might have been translated "epistemology"; see Taft's note, p. 188.

good at bringing out. Rorty cannot see how the thesis of a special irreducibility can do anything but undermine a purpose he and Davidson share, to dissolve the appearance that we are intellectually obliged to go in for that sort of activity. The shared purpose is, for instance, that we should entitle ourselves to "tell the sceptic to get lost", rather than look for a way to answer him.[8]

I think this is exactly wrong. The idea of a special irreducibility, which I am representing as common to Davidson and Sellars, is precisely a condition of properly understanding how it comes to seem that the mental poses that kind of problem for philosophy, and thereby a condition of achieving the very goal that Rorty thinks the idea threatens: seeing through the potentially gripping illusion that we need to acknowledge and deal with problems of that kind.

The separation of logical spaces or constitutive ideals that underwrites the irreducibility thesis reflects a distinction between two ways of finding things intelligible. Both involve placing things in a pattern. But in one case the pattern is constituted by regularities according to which phenomena of the relevant kind unfold; in the other it is the pattern of a life led by an agent who can shape her action and thought in the light of an ideal of rationality. In the modern era a distinction on these lines acquired a deep cultural significance, with the first kind of understanding, as contrasted with the second, coming to be seen as the business of natural science—a pursuit that achieved intellectual maturity in part precisely by virtue of having the kind of understanding that is its proper goal increasingly sharply separated from the kind exemplified by seeing a phenomenon as an agent's attempt to live up to an ideal, so that, for instance, it no longer counted as science to read nature as a meaningful text. While this kind of significance was attaching itself to the distinction between the two sorts of understanding, there will have been an increasingly sharp sense of a specialness on the part of concepts whose functioning is bound up with finding things intelligible in the second way, the way that involves conceiving of human beings as rational animals (to echo the passage I quoted from "Mental Events"). This is the sense of specialness that Davidson and Sellars formulate in the theses that disturb Rorty, and so far it is, I think, an innocuous recapitulation of something that was essential to the maturing of modern natural science.

8. Compare Davidson's "Afterthoughts".

However, at a primitive stage in the intellectual and cultural development I am talking about, it would be natural that there should be an attempt to accommodate this specialness, as yet only vaguely sensed, by trying to conceive the subject matter of thought and speech about the mental as a special region of what was, at the stage I mean to be considering, only beginning to come clear as the proper subject matter of the natural sciences—the disciplines whose business is in fact the other kind of understanding. This is a recipe for making sense of Cartesian philosophy of mind, at least on the more or less Rylean reading under which Descartes figures in the standard contemporary picture of how philosophy of mind developed. On this reading, Descartes confusedly wanted the relations that organize the mental to be just special cases of the sorts of relations that organize the proper subject matter of the natural sciences—relations that are displayed when phenomena are captured by descriptions suited for subsuming them under laws. But the specialness of the mental, to which on this reading Descartes was responding without a proper comprehension of its basis, requires those relations, supposedly suitable for natural-scientific treatment, to do duty for the relations that constitute the space of reasons. That is why Cartesian thinking takes a form to which Ryle's term of criticism "para-mechanical" is appropriate. Cartesian immaterialism is intelligible within the framework I am describing; no part of material nature could be special enough to serve the essentially confused purposes of this way of thinking. If one tries to make connections of the sort that figure in descriptions of law-governed processes do duty for relations of justification or warrant, one will naturally lapse into an appeal to magic, masquerading as the science of a weird subject matter; what one intends to postulate as simply mechanisms, though of a special kind, will degenerate into what Ryle lampoons as para-mechanisms.

On this account, the Cartesian Real Distinction, which is the point of origin of the supposed "mind-body problem", reflects a confused attempt to make a distinction within the subject matter for natural science—a distinction that inevitably degenerates into pseudo-science on one of its sides—out of the differentiation of batteries of concepts that is common to Davidson and Sellars, which is in fact not that kind of distinction at all. The puzzlements of traditional epistemology have the same source. Understanding the illusory obligations of traditional philosophy, which includes appreciating how the illusion can be gripping, requires that we understand the temptation to fall into this confusion. Hence it exactly requires that we not discard the distinction of batteries of concepts that bothers Rorty, but rather that we understand it correctly, seeing through the temptation to misconceive it in the Cartesian way.

I said that I have reservations about some of the detail of the passage I quoted from "Mental Events", and I shall end this first part of my essay by connecting one of them with the way I have been formulating its basic claim. I have been expressing the point of invoking the constitutive ideal of rationality by talking in terms of a distinctive way of finding things intelligible: seeing them as part of the life of an agent concerned to live up to an ideal of rationality. I have not connected the point, as Davidson does, with Quine's thesis of the indeterminacy of translation. Some of the resonances of that way of pointing to what underwrites the irreducibility strike me as unfortunate. In particular, if the appeal to indeterminacy imports Quine's thesis that there is no fact of the matter concerning correct interpretation, it risks leaving the impression that the claim is that the mental is non-factual, or at least less factual than what it is contrasted with; as if we were to suppose that on the one hand there is finding out how things are, and on the other hand there is making sense of people. I think making sense of people is a case of finding out how things are—a case that is special, in ways that Davidson has shown us how to understand without letting it seduce us into philosophy in the Cartesian vein, but a case for all that. Denying that, as we certainly seem to if we accept that there is no fact of the matter, is merely an extreme move in the kind of philosophy that lets its agenda be set by Cartesian conceptions; that is, precisely the kind of philosophy from which Davidson's thought, properly seen, promises to help us liberate ourselves.

2. I have been considering the Davidsonian thesis that making sense of people, in general, is governed by the constitutive ideal of rationality. I now want to consider an issue that arises when we apply the thesis to making sense of what people say, in particular.

According to Rorty, the results of interpreting linguistic behaviour as Davidson conceives that activity, formulated in theories of truth in the style of Tarski, are "descriptive", and as such not just to be distinguished from, but not even combinable in a unified discourse with, any way of talking in which "true" expresses a norm for inquiry and claim-making. In particular, truth in a sense that can be glossed in terms of disquotability, which is that whose conditions of application to the sentences of this or that language Tarski showed how to pin down in the kind of theory Davidson adapts to his purposes (provided that we can find a suitable logical form in, or impose a suitable logical form on, the sentences of the language), must, according to Rorty, be held separate from truth as a norm for inquiry.[9]

I think this makes no sense of the obvious connection between, on the one hand, the familiar T-sentences of Tarskian theories and, on the other, such truisms as this: what makes it *correct* among speakers of English to make a claim with, say, the words "Snow is white" (to stay with a well-worn example) is that snow is indeed white. I stress "correct": truth in the sense of disquotability—what Tarskian theories of truth are theories of—is unproblematically normative for the practice of using the sentences mentioned on the left-hand sides of T-sentences in order to make assertions. It does not take much inquiry to entitle oneself to make the particular assertion that I have picked as an example, but the point obviously carries over: truth in the sense of disquotability is a norm for inquiry, just because it is a norm for the claim-making that inquiry aims at. The force of this norm is part of the demandingness of the constitutive ideal of rationality. Rorty's attempt to separate Tarskian theory from such a norm cannot be sustained.

I surmise that this aspect of how Rorty reads Davidson traces back to a doctrine of Sellars about the very idea of the semantical. In discussing this, I shall no longer be drawing a parallel between Sellars and Davidson, but rather setting Sellars in a contrast with Davidson that is to Sellars's disadvantage. The relevant Sellarsian doctrine is that there are no semantical or meaning-involving *relations* between, as he puts it, elements in the linguistic order or the conceptual order, on the one side, and elements in the real order, on the other. Sellars holds, indeed, that this "non-relational character of 'meaning' and 'aboutness'" is "the key to a correct understanding of the place of mind in nature".[10]

How can Sellars hold that meaning and aboutness are, flatly, non-relational? Consider a statement of what some expression stands for, say " 'Londres' stands for London". It certainly looks as if that affirms a relation, between a name and a city. But according to Sellars, if such a statement is indeed of semantical import, the expression that figures on its right-hand side is not used, or at any rate not used in the ordinary way, namely to mention a city—as it would need to be for the statement to affirm a relation between the mentioned expression and the city. Rather, the expression serves to *exhibit* its own propriety-governed use. If we were to *state* the relevant

9. See "Pragmatism, Davidson and Truth".
10. *Science and Metaphysics*, p. ix.

proprieties, we would be saying that there *ought to be* certain relations between, on the one hand, utterances of the expression, considered as elements in the real order, and, on the other hand, other elements in the real order, most notably in this case a city. A relatedness to extra-linguistic reality is normatively required of ordinary utterances of the expression that figures on the right-hand side of a statement of meaning. By virtue of the non-ordinary use to which the expression is put there, the substance of that required relatedness to extra-linguistic reality is reflected into what the statement says about the expression mentioned on its left-hand side, even though it relates that expression only to another expression. That is how Sellars thinks a statement that affirms a relation only within the linguistic order can nevertheless capture the contribution made by the expression mentioned on its left-hand side to the intentional character, the directedness at the extra-linguistic order, of linguistic acts in which the expression figures.

Sellars's conviction that we must thus explain away the appearance that semantics deals with relations reflects, I believe, a failure to see the point of Tarskian semantics. He sometimes discusses Tarskian semantics, but he never, so far as I know, engages with the genuine article.

Sometimes he suggests that the very idea of word-world relations as they figure in Tarskian semantics is "Augustinian", in the sense that fits the opening sections of Wittgenstein's *Philosophical Investigations*.[11] But that is simply wrong. It is perfectly congenial to Tarskian semantics to say that the notions of such word-world relations as denotation and satisfaction are intelligible only in terms of how employments of such notions contribute towards specifying the possibilities for "making moves in the language-game" by uttering whole sentences in which the relevant words occur. These relations between words and elements in the extra-linguistic order should not be conceived as independently available building-blocks out of which we could construct an account of how language enables us to express thoughts at all. Davidson has made this perfectly clear, for instance in "In Defence of Convention T".

In other places Sellars suggests that proponents of relational semantics conceive the word-world relations that they take semantical statements to affirm in terms of "ideal semantical uniformities".[12] This is an allusion to

11. See "Empiricism and the Philosophy of Mind", §30. Compare Robert Brandom's contemptuous remarks about "a supposed word-world relation of reference", at pp. 323–5 of *Making It Explicit*.

12. See *Science and Metaphysics*, pp. 86–7, 112.

those propriety-governed genuine relations, between linguistic acts considered as elements in the real order and other elements in the real order, that figure in his picture as partly constitutive of the non-relational content of statements of meaning. Here Sellars is reading Tarskian semantics in the light of his own understanding of the possibilities. Statements of those "ideal semantical uniformities"—which are not themselves semantical statements—are the closest his view can come to the idea of semantical statements that themselves affirm relations to elements in the real order. So the best Sellars can do in the way of understanding this idea is to suppose that proponents of relational semantics mistakenly think those statements of "ideal semantical uniformities"—which do deal with relations, relations that there ought to be, with elements in the extra-linguistic order among their relata—*are* semantical statements. He assumes that his opponents are working within a dimly grasped version of his picture, and misconstrue the significance of its elements.

But that is not the point of the idea that statements of, for instance, the form ". . . stands for —" relate words to objects. Sellars simply does not engage with a proper understanding of that idea, which is on the following lines. First, the expression that figures on the right-hand side of such a statement is used in an ordinary way, not in the peculiar way that figures in Sellars's account of semantical statements; so we can see the statement as itself affirming a relation between the expression mentioned on the left-hand side and whatever element in the real order can be mentioned by a standard use of the expression on the right—for instance a city, in my earlier example. But second, the idea of the relation thus expressed by "stands for" is—to borrow a Sellarsian phrase—itself fraught with "ought", in a way that reflects what ensures that this conception of semantics is not "Augustinian".[13] We make sense of the very idea of such relations only in terms of how cases of them enter into determining the conditions under which whole sentences are correctly or incorrectly asserted. Here "correctly" and "incorrectly", applied to performances of making claims, indicate the "oughts" with which relations of, say, denotation are fraught. As I said about the norm constituted by truth as disquotability, these "oughts" ultimately reflect the demands of rationality on inquiry and the claim-making that gives expression to its results.

---

13. For "fraught with 'ought' ", see, e.g., "Truth and 'Correspondence' ", at p. 212.

A descendant of this Sellarsian blind spot for Tarski can account for Rorty's getting himself into the impossible position of needing to deny that disquotability is a norm. Rorty knows that the Tarskian "semantics" Davidson adapts to his purposes is nothing if not relational. Sellars would insist that as such it cannot really be semantics, but the point is not just about the word. The Sellarsian blind spot operates in Rorty's reading of Davidson in the form of a thought on these lines: since the Tarskian theories that Davidson envisages certainly deal with relations between elements of the linguistic order and elements of the extra-linguistic order, they cannot be semantical in Sellars's sense; that is, they cannot deal with meaning or aboutness in any sense that is fraught with "ought". This shows up in Rorty's idea that the Tarskian theories Davidson envisages can have nothing to do with truth as a norm for inquiry. But this line of thought inherits the flaw in Sellars's take on Tarski. It misses the fact that "ought" is already built into the very idea of such word-world relations as those expressible, in neo-Tarskian theory, by ". . . denotes —" (or ". . . stands for —") or ". . . is satisfied by —". That is a way of putting the point of "In Defence of Convention T". There is no basis for Sellars's thought, still present in Rorty's reading of Davidson, that we have to choose between relationality and normative import.

Sellars has a blind spot for Tarski. Is that the end of the story? I shall mention two ways of putting the blind spot in context. I think they are ways of approaching the superiority, and philosophical fruitfulness, of the way of thinking about the semantical that Davidson, exploiting Tarski, has made available to us.

First, it has emerged that there are two different ways in which one might construe the idea that our thought of meaning and aboutness is fraught with "ought". Sellars contemplates only one, and it is less satisfactory than the other, which he does not consider. On the Tarskian-Davidsonian conception the "oughts" in question—the "oughts" that are built into the idea of, say, denotation—are not separable from the idea of correctness in assertion. So they are not seen as prior to the very idea of directedness at the world or objective purport. Sellars, by contrast, envisages "oughts" that relate uses of expressions, as happenings in the real order, to other elements in the real order, in statements of proprieties that can be specified independently of anything semantical; these proprieties can then be seen as determinants, from outside the semantical, of the significance of elements in a language or of the aboutness of unexpressed thoughts. He thinks a language must be constituted by "rule-governed uniformities" that "can, in principle, be exhaustively described without the use of meaning statements".[14] This opens the way to the transcendental sociologism that is elaborated by Robert Brandom in his *Making It Explicit*.

I think once we see that the intuition that meaning and aboutness are "ought"-laden does not require the relevant "oughts" to be pre-semantical, as they are in Sellars's picture, we can see that there is no ground for the idea that linguistic behaviour must be able to be seen as governed by the sort of proprieties Sellars and Brandom envisage, proprieties that can be formulated in non-semantical terms. There is no reason to suppose the directedness of thought and speech at the world must be thus constituted, from outside the semantical, by norms that, though social, are not yet themselves semantical. One might think that if such formulations are not available, that leaves meaning and aboutness irredeemably spooky. But once we see that the relevant "oughts" can be as it were on the semantic surface, we can take in stride that meaningful speech, and thought directed at the world, are unproblematically part of our lives—as Wittgenstein says, "as much part of our natural history as walking, eating, drinking, playing".[15]

The second approach to Sellars's blind spot for Tarski that I want to exploit is through an argument from Sellars's remarkable paper "Being and Being Known". The context is a standing Sellarsian thesis, that the aboutness of unexpressed thought is to be understood on the model of the semanticity of speech. In "Being and Being Known", Sellars frames that thesis in terms of a Thomistic conception of intellectual acts as (second) actualizations of intellectual words. This allows him to express the idea that the intentionality of non-overt intellectual acts—mental acts—is to be *modelled* on the semanticity of overt intellectual acts—acts of speech—by representing the intentionality of non-overt intellectual acts as a *case* of the semanticity of words. The intentionality of a non-overt intellectual act is determined by the semantics of the intellectual words that are actualized in it. And now his blind spot for the possibilities for Tarskian semantics shows up as a blindness to the possibility that the semantics of intellectual words might be captured in Tarskian terms.

This blindness matters for an argument Sellars offers for his doctrine that aboutness is non-relational. The argument works by assuming that the

14. *Naturalism and Ontology*, p. 92.
15. *Philosophical Investigations*, §25.

alternative is to suppose that "intellectual acts differ *not* in their intrinsic character as acts, but by virtue of being directly related to different relata".[16] For my purposes here, I do not need to go into the detail of the argument, which consists in finding drawbacks in two different ways of spelling out such a conception. Independently of detail, Sellars is surely right to find the conception—"the notion that acts of the intellect are intrinsically alike regardless of what they are about" (p. 42)—utterly unprepossessing.

Having arrived at this conclusion, with more detail than I have rehearsed, Sellars writes (p. 43): "But what is the alternative? In general terms it is to hold that acts of the intellect differ intrinsically *qua* acts in a way which systematically corresponds to what they are about, i.e. their subject-matter." This is a version of his standard view of meaning and aboutness. Acts of the intellect, mental acts, differ intrinsically in their semantic properties, which, in the Thomistic image, are the semantic properties of the intellectual words that are actualized in them; and the semantic properties systematically correspond to what the acts are about by way of the reflection, into what semantical statements say, of relations there ought to be whose relata include what the acts are about.

This has the form of an argument to establish Sellars's doctrine that aboutness is non-relational by eliminating any alternative. But the argument is vitiated by the blind spot for Tarski. Sellars's argument assumes that, if someone wants to say intellectual acts differ, not in a way that systematically corresponds to what they are about, but *in* being about what they are about, she will admit to supposing that intellectual acts do not differ intrinsically at all. He assumes that a relational difference between a pair of intellectual acts could only be an extrinsic difference. And a proper appreciation of Tarski gives the lie to this assumption. It is Sellars's own reasonable thought—the basis on which he rejects the only competing possibility he considers—that a difference in intentional directedness between a pair of intellectual acts is an intrinsic difference between them. It is Sellars's own reasonable thought that we can frame a difference in intentional directedness between a pair of intellectual acts as a difference in the semantics of the intellectual words that are actualized in them. If we conceive the semantics of intellectual words in a Tarskian way, as involving relations between elements in the intellectual order and elements in the real order, with the relations fraught with "oughts" ultimately reflecting the demands of the

16. "Being and Being Known", p. 41.

constitutive ideal of rationality, that yields, untouched by Sellars's argument, a conception according to which intellectual acts, mental acts, can differ intrinsically *in* being related—semantically in the extended sense opened up by the Thomistic image—to different things.

We open this possibility by exploiting the conception of the semantical that Davidson, exploiting Tarski, has made available. I want to end by mentioning an implication for the idea of the subjective. Under the label "The Myth of the Subjective", Davidson has attacked a conception of the subjective whose effect is to make our access to the objective, and our understanding of ourselves, problematic in the familiar ways that characterize philosophy in the Cartesian vein.[17] Of course I have no wish to defend the target of that attack. However, it seems to me to be a shame to concede the very idea of the subjective to philosophy in that vein. A Davidsonian understanding of semantics allows us to take it that mental acts are intrinsically characterized by being semantically related—in the extended sense of "semantically"—to elements in the extra-mental order. On that basis we can begin to reclaim an idea of the subjective from the philosophical distortions that enter into the Myth. In the first part of this essay, I urged that the point of invoking the constitutive ideal of rationality, in situating the idea of the mental, is to dismantle Cartesian assumptions. This exploitation of a relational conception of intentionality would go further in that direction.

17. See "The Myth of the Subjective".

Why Is Sellars's Essay Called
"*Empiricism* and the
Philosophy of Mind"?

1. I take my question from Robert Brandom, who remarks in his "Study Guide" (p. 167): "The title of this essay is '*Empiricism* and the Philosophy of Mind,' but Sellars never comes right out and tells us what his attitude toward empiricism is." Brandom goes on to discuss a passage that might seem to indicate a sympathy for empiricism on Sellars's part, but he dismisses any such reading of it. (I shall come back to this.) He concludes: "Indeed, we can see at this point [he has reached §45] that one of the major tasks of the whole essay is to dismantle empiricism" (p. 168).

I am going to argue that this claim is quite wrong.

To do Brandom justice, I should note that when he defends his claim, what he mentions is, specifically, *traditional* empiricism. But he nowhere contemplates a possibility left open by this more detailed (and correct) specification of Sellars's target—the possibility that Sellars might be aiming to rescue a *non-traditional* empiricism from the wreckage of traditional empiricism, so that he can show us how to be good empiricists. I think that is exactly what Sellars aims to do in this essay.

2. Traditional empiricism, explicitly so described, is in Sellars's sights in the pivotal Part VIII of "Empiricism and the Philosophy of Mind".

Traditional empiricism answers the question "Does empirical knowledge have a foundation?", which is the title of Part VIII, with an unqualified "Yes". Traditional empiricism is foundationalist in a sense Sellars spells out like this (§32):

One of the forms taken by the Myth of the Given is the idea that there is, indeed *must be*, a structure of particular matter of fact such that (a) each fact can not only be noninferentially known to be the case, but presupposes no

221

other knowledge either of particular matter of fact, or of general truths; and (b) . . . the noninferential knowledge of facts belonging to this structure constitutes the ultimate court of appeals for all factual claims—particular and general—about the world.

This formulation is in abstract structural terms. It does not mention experience. But from the way Part VIII flows, it is clear that what Sellars is rejecting when he rejects this form of the Myth is what he labels "traditional empiricism" at the part's conclusion (§38). To make the connection, all we need is the obvious point that according to traditional empiricism, *experience* is our way of acquiring the knowledge that is supposed to be foundational in the sense Sellars explains in §32. In traditional empiricism, experience is taken to yield non-inferential knowledge in a way that presupposes no knowledge of anything else.

Sellars takes pains to draw our attention to this supposed freedom from presuppositions, the second sub-clause of clause (a) in his formulation of an unqualified foundationalism. §32 continues like this:

It is important to note that I characterized the knowledge of fact belonging to this stratum as not only noninferential, but as presupposing no knowledge of other matters of fact, whether particular or general. It might be thought that this is a redundancy, that knowledge (not belief or conviction, but knowledge) which logically presupposes knowledge of other facts *must* be inferential. This, however, as I hope to show, is itself an episode in the Myth.

When he rejects traditional empiricism at the end of Part VIII, he is rejecting that sub-clause in particular. The rest of the affirmative answer to the question about foundations can stand. In §38 he says:

If I reject the framework of traditional empiricism, it is not because I want to say that empirical knowledge has *no* foundation. For to put it in this way is to suggest that it is really "empirical knowledge so-called," and to put it in a box with rumors and hoaxes. There is clearly *some* point to the picture of human knowledge as resting on a level of propositions—observation reports—which do not rest on other propositions in the same way as other propositions rest on them. On the other hand, I do wish to insist that the metaphor of "foundation" is misleading in that it keeps us from seeing that if there is a logical dimension in which other empirical propositions rest on observation reports, there is another logical dimension in which the latter rest on the former.

Dependence in this second dimension is the presupposing missed by traditional empiricism. To recognize the second dimension is to accept that what is now—just for this reason—only misleadingly conceived as foundational knowledge presupposes knowledge of other matters of fact, knowledge that would have to belong to the structure that can now only misleadingly be seen as built on those foundations. If we stayed with the metaphor of foundations, we would be implying that the foundations of a building can depend on the building.

This passage characterizes a non-traditional empiricism. To make that explicit, we only need to register that it is *experience* that yields the knowledge expressed in observation reports. Recognizing the second dimension puts us in a position to understand observation reports properly. The knowledge they express is not inferentially grounded on other knowledge of matters of fact, but—in the crucial departure from traditional empiricism—it presupposes other knowledge of matters of fact. It is knowledge on which Sellars continues to hold that other empirical knowledge rests in the first dimension. By introducing an explicit mention of experience, we made it possible to see Part VIII as beginning with a formulation of traditional empiricism, as we needed to do in order to make sense of how Part VIII ends. The same move enables us to see that the position Sellars recommends at the end of Part VIII, as a replacement for traditional empiricism, is a reformed empiricism.

3. That is still somewhat abstract. To fill out this specification of a reformed empiricism, we would need to give a detailed picture of experience, explaining how it can yield non-inferential knowledge, but only in a way that presupposes other knowledge of matters of fact—in contrast with the presupposition-free knowledge-yielding powers that experience is credited with by traditional empiricism.

And that is just what Sellars offers, starting in Part III, "The Logic of 'Looks' ". Experiences, Sellars tells us, contain propositional claims (§16). That is an initially promissory way (as Sellars insists) of crediting experiences with intentional content. He delivers on the promissory note in the first phase of the myth of Jones (Part XV). The topic there is "thoughts"— inner episodes with intentional content—in general. But Sellars reverts to the intentional character of experiences in particular in a retrospective remark at the beginning of the next part, in §60. There he indicates, in effect, that he has finally put the verbal currency he issued in §16 on the gold standard.

In §16 bis, Sellars says it is clear that a complete account of (visual) experience requires "something more", over and above intentional content, namely "what philosophers have in mind when they speak of 'visual impressions' or 'immediate visual experiences'". (It can be questioned whether this *is* clear, or even correct, but since my aim is entirely exegetical I shall not consider that here.) When Sellars introduces this "something more", he remarks that its "logical status . . . is a problem which will be with us for the remainder of this argument". His final treatment of this topic comes at the end of the essay, in the second phase of the myth of Jones (Part XVI). The myth of Jones offers an account of the non-dispositional mental in general. But in "Empiricism and the Philosophy of Mind" it clearly has a more specific purpose as well: to complete the account of *experience*, in particular, that Sellars begins on in Part III. The first phase vindicates his promissory talk of experiences as having intentional content, and the second deals with the "something more" he thinks is needed to accommodate their sensory character.

And already in Part III, when the attribution of intentional content to experiences is still only promissory, and Part VIII is yet to come, Sellars has his eye on ensuring that the capacity to yield non-inferential knowledge that he is beginning to provide for, by attributing intentional content to experiences, is not as traditional empiricism conceives it. In Part III Sellars is already insisting—to put things in the terms he will use in Part VIII—that an experience's having as its intentional content that such-and-such is the case, and hence the possibility that such an experience might yield non-inferential knowledge that such-and-such is the case, presupposes knowledge other than that non-inferential knowledge itself.

Part III is largely devoted to a telling example of this: visual experience of colour. Here it might be especially tempting to suppose experience can yield knowledge in self-standing chunks, without dependence on other knowledge. Experiences that, to speak in the promissory idiom, contain the claim that something in front of one is green are experiences in which it is at least true that it looks to one as if something in front of one is green. Some experiences that are non-committally describable in those terms are experiences in which one *sees*, and so is in a position to know non-inferentially, that something in front of one is green. The ability to enjoy experiences in which it looks to one as if something in front of one is green is part of what it is to have the (visually applicable) *concept* of something's being green. And Sellars argues that having colour concepts "involves the ability to tell what colors things have by looking at them—which, in turn, involves knowing in what circumstances to place an object if one wishes to ascertain its color by looking at it" (§18). The possibility of having experiences in which it looks to one as if something is green, and hence the possibility of acquiring non-inferential knowledge that something is green by having such an experience, depend—not inferentially, but in what is going to come into view as the second dimension—on knowledge about, for instance, the effects of different lighting conditions on colour appearances.

4. Brandom conceives observational knowledge, the knowledge expressed in observation reports, as the upshot of a special kind of *reliable differential responsive disposition*—a kind that is special in that the responses its instances issue in are not *mere* responses, like an electric eye's opening a door when its beam is broken, but claims, moves in an *inferentially* articulated practice. Brandom attributes this picture of observational knowledge to Sellars; he calls it "Sellars's two-ply account of observation".[1]

In favourable circumstances dispositions of this kind issue in expressions of observational knowledge. But a disposition of this kind can be triggered into operation in circumstances in which it would be risky to make the claim that is its primary output. Perhaps the claim would be false; certainly it would not express knowledge. Subjects learn to inhibit inclinations to make claims in such circumstances. For instance subjects learn, in certain lighting conditions, to withhold the claims about colours that, if allowed free rein, their responsive dispositions would induce them to make. In such conditions "looks" statements serve as substitute outlets for the tendencies to make claims that the responsive dispositions embody. "Looks" statements *evince* responsive dispositions (of a specifically visual kind) whose primary output one is inhibiting.

If something appropriately conceivable as *sensory consciousness* figures in our acquisition of observational knowledge, Brandom thinks that is a mere detail about the mechanism by which the relevant responsive dispositions work in our case. There could perfectly well be responsive dispositions that issue in knowledge-expressing claims without mediation by sensory consciousness, at any rate sensory consciousness with a content matching that of the knowledge yielded by the dispositions. Perhaps there are. (This is how it is with the chicken-sexers of epistemological folklore.) And Brandom thinks

---

1. See his essay "The Centrality of Sellars's Two-Ply Account of Observation to the Arguments of 'Empiricism and the Philosophy of Mind' ".

this possibility (or actuality, if that is what it is) lays bare the essential nature of observational knowledge. On this view, experience—a kind of shaping of sensory consciousness—is inessential to the epistemology of observational knowledge, and hence to the epistemology of empirical knowledge in general. If empiricism accords a special epistemological significance to experience, there is no room in this picture for empiricism, traditional or otherwise.

This is not the place to consider the prospects for this radical project of Brandom's, to dispense with experience in an account of empirical knowledge, and hence to leave no room for even a reformed empiricism. But given the question I have set out to address, I do need to consider Brandom's attempt to read the project into Sellars. I think this flies in the face of the plain sense of "Empiricism and the Philosophy of Mind"—the whole essay, but to begin with Part III in particular.

5. In §16, where Sellars introduces the idea that experiences contain claims, he is not beginning to show us how to do without experience in our conception of empirical knowledge. On the contrary, he is beginning to *explain* experience, as a kind of inner episode that can figure in our understanding of empirical knowledge without entangling us in the Myth of the Given. Only beginning, because he needs the myth of Jones, to vindicate the very idea of inner episodes, and in particular the idea of inner episodes with intentional content, before he can claim to have completed the task.

In the doctrine Brandom thinks Sellars is trying to expound in Part III, claims figure only in the guise of overt linguistic performances—the primary outlet of responsive dispositions, what subjects evince an inhibited tendency towards when they say how things look to them. But Sellars uses the notion of claims in an avowedly promissory first shot at attributing intentional content *to experiences*, to be vindicated when Jones introduces concepts of inner episodes with intentional content on the model of overt linguistic performances with their semantical character. Claims figure in Brandom's picture only in the sense in which claims are Jones's *model*. What Sellars needs Jones to model on claims in the primary sense, to finish the task he begins on in Part III, is not on Brandom's scene at all.

Obviously looking forward to the myth of Jones, Sellars says, in §16, that justifying his promissory talk of experiences as containing propositional claims is "one of [his] major aims". When Jones starts work, his fellows already have the subjunctive conditional, hence the ability to speak of dispositions, and they can speak of overt linguistic behaviour with its semantical character. (Sellars adds that to the original "Rylean" resources in §49, before Jones begins.) To fulfil the major aim Sellars acknowledges in §16, he needs to follow Jones in going decisively beyond those pre-Jonesian resources. Only after the first phase of Jones's conceptual innovation does Sellars in effect declare that he has discharged his promissory note (§60). Brandom offers to account for "looks" statements in terms of dispositions, which can be inhibited, to make claims in the primary sense, overt linguistic performances of a certain sort. But this apparatus is all available before Jones's innovation. In implying that his apparatus suffices for Sellars's aims in Part III, Brandom precludes himself from properly registering the promissory character Sellars stresses in his moves there.[2]

In §15, Sellars rejects the idea that a "looks" statement reports a minimal objective fact—objective in being "logically independent of the beliefs, the conceptual framework, of the perceiver", but minimal in being safer than a report of, say, the colour of an object in the perceiver's environment. He is certainly right to reject this; because of the sense in which these facts are supposed to be objective, this construal of "looks" statements is a version of the Myth of the Given.

But Brandom thinks "looks" statements, for Sellars, should not be reports at all—in particular not reports of experiences, since Sellars is supposed to be showing us how to do without experiences in our picture of empirical knowledge. Thus, purporting to capture a point Sellars should be trying to make in §15, Brandom writes (p. 139): "it is a mistake to treat [statements to the effect that it looks to one as if something is *F*] as reports at all—since they *evince* a disposition to call something *F*, but may not happily be thought of as *saying that* one has such a disposition." This general rejection of the idea that "looks" statements are reports does not fit what Sellars actually

---

2. In *Science and Metaphysics: Variations on Kantian Themes*, Sellars allows for a version of "looks" statements in the pre-Jonesian language. He says (p. 159): "This locution ['*x* looks red to me'] must . . . be interpreted as having, roughly, the sense of '*x* causes me to be disposed to think-out-loud: Lo! This is red, or would cause me to have this disposition if it were not for such and such considerations.'" If one said that, one would be explicitly attributing a disposition to oneself, rather than evincing one, as in Brandom's picture. But what we have here is just a different way of exploiting the conceptual apparatus Brandom confines himself to. The passage brings out that the materials for Brandom's account of "looks" statements are available before Jones has done his work, and hence before Sellars has in hand the materials that he makes it clear he needs for *his* account of "looks" statements.

says, and Brandom tries to accommodate that by saying Sellars "wavers" on the point. But a glance at the text shows Sellars to be unwaveringly clear that "looks" statements *are* reports—not, certainly, of dispositions, the only candidate Brandom considers, but of *experiences*, and in particular of their intentional content. §15 ends like this:

> Let me begin by noting that there certainly seems to be something in the idea that the sentence "This looks green to me now" has a reporting role. Indeed it would seem to be essentially a report. But if so, *what* does it report, if not a minimal objective fact, and if what it reports is not to be analyzed in terms of sense data?

And a couple of pages later (in §16 bis), after he has introduced the two aspects he attributes to experiences, their intentionality and their sensory character, Sellars answers that question—he tells us what "looks" statements report:

> Thus, when I say "X looks green to me now" I am *reporting* the fact that my experience is, so to speak, intrinsically, *as an experience*, indistinguishable from a veridical one of seeing that x is green. Included in the report is the ascription to my experience of the claim 'x is green'; and the fact that I make this report rather than the simple report "X is green" indicates that certain considerations have operated to raise, so to speak in a higher court, the question 'to endorse or not to endorse'.

This is not wavering. It is a straightforward, indeed emphatic, statement of something Brandom thinks Sellars should be denying, that "looks" statements are reports: not (to repeat) of dispositions, but of the intentional (claim-containing) and, implicitly, the sensory character of experiences. When Sellars discharges the promissory note of §16, the culminating move (in §59) is precisely to provide for a *reporting* role for self-attributions of "thoughts", which include experiences *qua* characterizable as having intentional content.

If one goes no further than reporting one's experience as containing the claim that things are thus and so, one still has to determine whether to endorse that claim oneself. If one endorses it, one claims to see that things are thus and so (if the experience is a visual experience). If not, one restricts oneself to saying it looks to one as if things are thus and so. In a "looks" statement, that is, one withholds one's endorsement of the claim one reports one's experience as containing.

Now Brandom seizes on this withholding of endorsement, and exploits it in an explanation, which he attributes to Sellars, for the incorrigibility of "looks" statements. Brandom writes, on Sellars's behalf (p. 142): "Since asserting 'X looks *F*' is not undertaking a propositional commitment—but only expressing an overrideable disposition to do so—there is no issue as to whether or not that commitment (which one?) is correct."

But this reflects Brandom's failure to register the Sellarsian idea I have been documenting, the idea that when one says something of the form "X looks *F*" one reports the claim-containing character of one's experience. That one's experience contains a certain claim—in Brandom's schematic example, the claim that X is *F*—is an assertoric commitment one *is* undertaking when one says how things look to one, even though one withholds commitment to the claim one reports one's experience as containing. Brandom's question "Which one?" is meant to be only rhetorical, but it has an answer: commitment to the proposition that one's experience contains a certain claim. Brandom's explanation of the incorrigibility of "looks" statements is not Sellarsian at all. For an authentically Sellarsian account of first-person authority in saying how things look to one—"privileged access" to what one reports in such a performance—we have to wait until the culmination of the first phase of the myth of Jones; Sellars addresses the issue in §59.[3]

6. Commenting on §§19 and 20, Brandom remarks (p. 147): "These sections do not present Sellars's argument in a perspicuous, or even linear, fashion." This reflects the fact that what he thinks Sellars *should* be doing in Part III is expounding the "two-ply" picture of observational knowledge, in which observation reports are explained in terms of reliable differential responsive dispositions whose outputs are constituted as conceptually contentful by their position in an inferentially articulated practice.

---

3. In his enthusiasm for the explanatory power of the idea of withholding endorsement, Brandom is led into a clearly wrong characterization of Sellars's treatment of generic looks in §17. Brandom says (p. 145): "Sellars's account is in terms of scope of endorsement. One says that the plane figure looks 'many-sided' instead of '119-sided' just in case one is willing only to endorse (be held responsible for justifying) the more general claim." (For a similar statement, see *Making It Explicit*, p. 293.) But on Sellars's account, if one says a plane figure looks many-sided, one exactly does *not* endorse the claim that it is many-sided. Sellars's account of generic looks is not in terms of scope of endorsement, but in terms of what is up for endorsement. The claims that experiences contain, like claims in general, can be indeterminate in content.

But it is questionable exegetical practice to insist that a text contains something one wants to find in it, even though that requires one to criticize its perspicuity. One should pause to wonder whether it does something else, perhaps with complete perspicuity.

And that is how things are here. In Part III, and in particular in §§19 and 20, Sellars is not unperspicuously presenting Brandom's "two-ply" picture. He is, quite perspicuously, giving a preliminary account of how the knowledge-yielding capacity of experience—even experience of something as simple as colour—presupposes knowledge of matters of fact other than those non-inferentially knowable by enjoying experiences of the kind in question. The presupposed knowledge is exactly not inferentially related to the knowledge that presupposes it; that is Sellars's point in Part VIII.

Brandom says "endorsement" is Sellars's term for the second element in the "two-ply" picture (p. 140). He thinks Sellars's talk of endorsement is directed at entitling him to talk of claims at all, by placing what he is only thereby permitted to conceive as conceptually contentful commitments in an inferentially organized deontic structure.

But Sellars introduces the idea that experiences contain claims without any hint that he feels obliged to concern himself—here—with the question what claims are. His initial account of "looks" statements is promissory because he needs Jones to extend the idea of claims from its primary application, which is to a certain sort of overt linguistic performance, before it can be used in attributing intentional content to inner episodes. For these purposes, the primary application is unproblematic. Sellars's talk of endorsement is not code for the idea of taking up what would otherwise be mere responses into a deontically structured practice, so that they can be understood to have conceptual content. "Endorsement" just means *endorsement*. Once we are working with the idea that experiences contain claims, it is routinely obvious that the subject of an experience faces the question whether to endorse the claim her experience contains. The idea that the outputs of some responsive dispositions are constituted as conceptually contentful by inferential articulation is not relevant to any point Sellars has occasion to make in this part of the essay.

Or, I believe, anywhere in "Empiricism and the Philosophy of Mind". I mentioned earlier that before he puts Jones to work, Sellars adds concepts of overt linguistic performances, with their conceptual content, to the

"Rylean" resources that are already in place (§49). He does that quickly and without fanfare. In this essay Sellars is not in the business of giving an "inferentialist" account of what it is for overt performances to have conceptual content at all, the thesis that is the second element in Brandom's "two-ply" picture. Not that he offers some other kind of account. His purposes here generate no need to concern himself with the question to which "inferentialism" is a response.

After his remark that Sellars's presentation in §§19 and 20 is not perspicuous, Brandom says "the argument is repeated in a more satisfactory form in [§§33–37]". He means that those sections, the central sections of Part VIII, give a better formulation of the "two-ply" picture. But this reflects the fact that he misreads those sections too.

Brandom thinks the point of §§33–37 is to expound the second element in the "two-ply" account, the idea that the outputs of the responsive dispositions that issue in observation reports are constituted as conceptually contentful by their position in an inferentially articulated practice. Against this background, he argues that those sections bring out a problem for Sellars's epistemological internalism.

Sellars holds that for a claim to express observational knowledge, two conditions must be met (§35, the two hurdles). First, the claim must issue from a capacity whose outputs are reliably correct. And second, the person who makes the claim must be aware that her pronouncements on such matters have that kind of authority. As Sellars notes, the idea of reliability can be explicated in terms of there being a good inference—what Brandom calls "the reliability inference"—from the person's making a claim (in the circumstances in which she makes it) to things being as she says they are.

Brandom thinks this puts Sellars's second condition in tension with the thesis that observational knowledge is non-inferential. He thinks the condition would imply that one arrives at an observation report by persuading oneself, via the "reliability inference", that things are as one would be saying they are if one indulged an inclination one finds in oneself to make a certain claim. That would imply that the knowledge expressed in the report is inferential. So Brandom concludes that we must reject the second condition if we are to hold on to Sellars's own thought that observational knowledge is not inferential. To be better Sellarsians than Sellars himself, we should insist that an observational knower can invoke her own reliability at most *ex post facto*.[4] And it is a short step from there to claiming, as Brandom does, that there can be cases of observational knowledge in which the knower cannot invoke her own reliability even *ex post facto*. It is enough if someone else, a scorekeeper, can justify a belief as the conclusion of the "reliability inference", even if the believer herself cannot do that.[5]

But here Brandom misses what Sellars, in §32, signals as the central point of Part VIII: to bring into view the second dimension of dependence. One bit of knowledge can depend on another in this dimension without any threat to the thesis that it is non-inferential.

We have already considered the example of this that Sellars elaborates in Part III. (He refers back to Part III, in particular to §19, in §37.) Claims about the colours of things, made on the basis of experience, depend in the second dimension on knowledge about the effects of different kinds of illumination on colour appearances. I might support my entitlement to the claim that something is green by saying "This is a good light for telling what colour something is". The relevance of this to my observational authority about the thing's colour belongs in the second dimension, which is not to be spelled out in terms of inference. I do not cast what I say about the light as a premise in an inferential grounding for what I claim to know about the colour of the thing.

Similarly with Sellars's second hurdle. I might support my entitlement to the claim that something is green by invoking—not just *ex post facto*, but at the time—my reliability on such matters. I might say "I can tell a green thing when I see one (at least in this kind of light)". I must be aware of my reliability, to be able to cite it like this, in support of the authority of my claim. And here too, the support is in the second dimension, which Sellars carefully separates from the dimension in which one bit of knowledge provides inferential grounding for another.

It is true that the concept of reliability can be explicated in terms of the goodness of the "reliability inference". But that is irrelevant to the present point. To say that a claim depends for its authority, in the second dimension, on the subject's reliability (in a way that requires her to be aware of her reliability) is not to say that it depends in the first dimension, the inferential dimension, on her inclination to make it, via the "reliability inference".

4. For the idea of *ex post facto* inferential justifications of non-inferential beliefs, see "Insights and Blind Spots of Reliabilism", especially at pp. 103–4 and 211, n. 3.

5. See *Making It Explicit*, pp. 217–21. The idea is hinted at in the Study Guide; see pp. 157, 159.

In Brandom's treatment of Part III, taking Sellars to be concerned to expound the "two-ply" picture of observation knowledge led to a baseless accusation of lack of perspicuity. Here it leads him to miss, nearly completely, what Sellars signals as the central point he wants to make in Part VIII.

With his fixation on the "two-ply" picture, Brandom makes almost nothing of Sellars's point about the second dimension. He almost exclusively explains Sellars's moves in Part VIII in terms of a requirement for *understanding* the forms of words that are uttered in observation reports, that one be able to use them not only in making observation reports but also as premises and conclusions of inferences. There surely is such a requirement, but there is nothing to indicate that it is Sellars's concern here (or, as I have urged, anywhere else in this essay). Sellars's concern is with a requirement for claims to be expressive of observational knowledge, with the distinctive *authority* that that implies. Understanding what it is that one is claiming—in this case with that distinctive authority—is not what is in question. The point of Sellars's second hurdle is not to cite the "reliability inference" as part of the inferentially articulated structure in which forms of words must stand if they are to have conceptual content at all. Sellars's thesis is that *observational authority* depends on the subject's own reliability in the second dimension, and this dependence requires that the subject be aware of her own reliability. He invokes the "reliability inference" only as a gloss on the idea of reliability. (That it is a good gloss is obvious. This is not a first move in giving a contentious "inferentialist" account of conceptual content *überhaupt*.) The second hurdle stands in no tension with the thesis that observational knowledge is non-inferential.

At one place in the Study Guide (p. 162, expounding §38), Brandom—as it were in spite of himself—lets a glimpse of Sellars's real point emerge, when he says that observation reports "themselves rest (not inferentially but in the order of *understanding* and sometimes of justification) on other sorts of knowledge". But the stress on the order of understanding—by which Brandom means the inferential structure that forms of words must belong to if they are to be conceptually contentful at all—is, as I have been urging, irrelevant to Sellars's point. Sellars's case against traditional empiricism relates entirely to the order of justification, the order of responses to the Kantian question *"Quid iuris?"*. His point is that observational knowledge *always* (not sometimes) rests in the order of justification—in the non-inferential second dimension—on other sorts of knowledge. That is why it is not foundational in the sense envisaged by traditional empiricism.

I have put this in the terms Brandom uses. But we could express Sellars's central point in Part VIII by saying that this talk of *the* order of justification is misleading. One way of placing an episode or state in the space of reasons—as Sellars says we do when we classify it as an episode or state of knowing (§36)—is to give grounds for accepting that its content is true, premises from which there is a sufficiently good inference to the truth of what the putative knower claims or would claim. Sellars's point in introducing the second dimension is that there is another way of responding to the question *"Quid iuris?"*, in which what one says in response relates quite differently to the claim whose candidacy to be recognized as knowledgeable is under discussion. In a response of this second kind, one does not offer grounds for endorsing a claim that purports to express knowledge. What one addresses, in the first instance, is not the truth of the particular thing the subject says but her authority, in the circumstances, to say something—anything—of the relevant sort: for example her authority, in the prevailing illumination, to make a claim about something's colour. Of course if we accept that she is in a position to speak with authority on the matters in question, that supplies us with material that could serve in an inferential grounding for the particular thing she says, using the fact that she says it, plus the consideration we have accepted as bearing on her authority in saying things of the relevant kind, as premises. But the consideration that bears on her authority is directly relevant to whether the claim she makes is knowledgeable, not by way of its capacity to figure in an inferential grounding for the claim, an argument to its truth. We convince ourselves that it is true on the ground that her saying it is expressive of knowledge; its truth does not figure in our route to the conviction that she is a knower.[6]

I have been insisting that Sellars's aim in introducing the second dimension is *epistemological*. The second dimension pertains to what is required for claims to have the authority that belongs to expressions of knowledge. But

---

6. In the context in which Sellars identifies the space of reasons as the space in which one places episodes or states when one classifies them as episodes or states of knowing, he describes it as the space "of justifying and being able to justify what one says" (§36). What I have said about the second dimension implies that this description is not completely felicitous. A second-dimension response to the question *"Quid iuris?"* justifies *what one says* only indirectly. Its direct aim is to characterize one's right to speak with authority on the topic one speaks on. It does that independently of what, in particular, one says.

the point is not epistemological in a way that excludes *semantical* significance. Concepts of, say, colour—in their usual form, as opposed to the versions of them that might be available to the congenitally blind—can be employed in claims (or judgments) with the distinctive authority that attaches to observation reports, and that fact is partly constitutive of the kind of content the concepts have.

But this semantical significance is quite distinct from the "inferentialism" that is the second element of Brandom's "two-ply" account. The point does not concern an inferential dependence between *claimables*, constituted as such only by there being inferential relations between them, as in Brandom's picture. It concerns a non-inferential dependence thanks to which certain *claimings* can have the authority of observational knowledge. As I said, there is a semantical aspect to this, because the forms of words uttered in these claimings would not have the distinctive kind of conceptual content they do if they were not able to figure in claimings with that distinctive authority. But this is not a first step into "inferentialism". The relevant dependence is, as I have followed Sellars in insisting, not inferential. And anyway, since the dependence is exemplified only by observation reports, not by claims in general, the semantical thought here is not, as in Brandom's "inferentialism", one about conceptual contentfulness *überhaupt*.

7. As I said at the beginning, when Brandom argues that Sellars's aim is to dismantle empiricism, he considers and dismisses a passage that might seem to point in a different direction. I promised to come back to this.

The passage is §6, where Sellars embarrasses classical sense-datum theorists with commitment to an inconsistent triad, of which one element is the thesis that "the ability to know facts of the form *x is φ* is acquired". One could avoid the inconsistency by giving up that thesis. But against that option Sellars says it would "do violence to the predominantly nominalistic proclivities of the empiricist tradition". As Brandom acknowledges, the thesis that the ability to have classificatory knowledge is acquired is part of the "psychological nominalism" Sellars is going to espouse in his own voice (see §§ 29, 30, 31). So it is tempting to suppose we are intended to recognize a convergence with that Sellarsian doctrine when, spelling out the nominalistic proclivities of the empiricist tradition, he says:

> [M]ost empirically minded philosophers are strongly inclined to think that all classificatory consciousness, all knowledge *that something is thus-and-so,*

or, in logicians' jargon, all subsumption of particulars under universals, involves learning, concept formation, even the use of symbols.

But Brandom insists that Sellars is not indicating any sympathy with the empiricist tradition. Brandom implies (p. 169) that Part VI deals with some nominalistic proclivities, distinctive to the empiricist tradition, in which Sellars himself does not indulge, even though Sellars agrees with the empiricists that the ability to have classificatory knowledge is acquired.

There are two things that are unsatisfactory about this.

First, Part VI does not depict the classical empiricists as having their thinking shaped by nominalistic proclivities not indulged in by Sellars. Sellars's point about the classical empiricists is that they take themselves to have a problem of universals only in connection with *determinable* repeatables. Where *determinate* repeatables are concerned, they proceed as if the ability to know facts of the form *x is φ* is a concomitant of mere sentience, not something that needs to be acquired. That is, the classical empiricists are only imperfectly faithful to the nominalism Sellars ascribes to their tradition in §6. As far as this goes, the nominalistic proclivities Sellars ascribes to the empiricist tradition can perfectly well be the nominalistic proclivities he is going to espouse for himself.

Second, on Brandom's account the argument Sellars deploys, to exclude that option for avoiding the inconsistent triad, is purely *ad hominem*. And this does not fit comfortably with the importance the argument has in the structure of the essay.

The nominalistic proclivities of the empiricist tradition are essential for justifying what Sellars says at the beginning of §7:

> It certainly begins to look as though the classical concept of a sense datum were a mongrel resulting from a crossbreeding of two ideas:
>
> (1) The idea that there are certain inner episodes—e.g. sensations of red or of C#—which can occur to human beings (and brutes) without any prior process of learning or concept formation; and without which it would *in some sense* be impossible to *see*, for example, that the facing surface of a physical object is red and triangular, or *hear* that a certain physical sound is C#.
>
> (2) The idea that there are certain inner episodes which are the noninferential knowings that certain items are, for instance, red or C#; and that these episodes are the necessary conditions of empirical knowledge as providing the evidence for all other empirical propositions.

Why must these two kinds of episodes be distinguished? Those described under (1) do not require a prior process of learning or concept formation. But those described under (2), non-inferential knowings that . . . , do. And why should we accept that they do? The only ground so far on offer is that this is implied by the nominalism Sellars attributes to the empiricist tradition. His own nominalism, which Brandom says is different, has not yet been explicitly introduced.

Sellars repeats this diagnosis of classical sense-datum theory at the beginning of Part III, in §10. And there he goes on as follows:

> A reasonable next step would be to examine these two ideas and determine how that which survives criticism in each is properly to be combined with the other. Clearly we would have to come to grips with the idea of *inner episodes*, for this is common to both.

This sets the agenda for the rest of the essay. In §16 and §16 bis Sellars begins to explain experience as involving episodes of the two kinds conflated into a mongrel by classical sense-datum theory. And that continues to be his project until the end. The myth of Jones serves the purpose of coming to grips with the idea of inner episodes—episodes of those two kinds in particular.

Now it would be a structural weakness if this agenda-setting move were motivated by an argument that is purely *ad hominem*, an argument that should seem cogent only to adherents of the empiricist tradition, supposedly not including Sellars himself. The structure of the essay looks stronger if the argument in §6 is meant to be already, as formulated there, convincing to right-thinking people. It is true that the argument is explicitly directed *ad hominem*. It points out that a certain escape from the inconsistent triad is unavailable to classical sense-datum theorists, who belong to the empiricist tradition if anyone does. But the argument's role in motivating what becomes the programme for the rest of the essay recommends that we not understand it as exclusively *ad hominem*. We should take Sellars to be intending to exploit the convergence between the nominalism of §6 and his own nominalism, so as to indicate that he himself belongs to the empiricist tradition.

That fits with understanding "Empiricism and the Philosophy of Mind" as aiming to recall empiricism to its better wisdom, in an argument that hinges on its nominalistic proclivities. As Part VI points out, the canonical empiricists lapse from the nominalism of their tradition in their picture of our dealings with determinate observable qualities. To avoid the Myth of the

Given in the form it takes in traditional empiricism, what we need is an empiricism that keeps faith with the nominalism only imperfectly conformed to by traditional empiricism. And that is just what Sellars provides.

8. So far I have argued exclusively from the text of "Empiricism and the Philosophy of Mind". I shall end with a piece of evidence from elsewhere.

At one point in "Imperatives, Intentions, and the Logic of 'Ought'",[7] Sellars considers a Jonesian account of intentions, in which "shall" thoughts are conceived as inner episodes modelled on certain overt utterances. He introduces the idea like this (p. 195):

> There is a consideration pertaining to intentions and their expression which, though not strictly a part of the argument of this paper, indicates how it might fit into the broader framework of an empiricist philosophy of mind.

And in an endnote he says (p. 217):

> For an elaboration of such a framework, see my "Empiricism and the Philosophy of Mind,". . . .

Here Sellars is explicit that "Empiricism and the Philosophy of Mind" puts forward an empiricist philosophy of mind. He is talking about the Jonesian approach to the mental in general, rather than the epistemological and transcendental implications of the way "Empiricism and the Philosophy of Mind" deals with perceptual experience in particular. But it is clear that the label "empiricist" is—to put it mildly—not one he is keen to disown. And it is natural to extend this to his discussion of experience itself.

This passage encourages me in answering my question in the way I have been urging. Why does "empiricism" figure in the title of "Empiricism and the Philosophy of Mind"? Because a major purpose of the essay is to propound an empiricism free from the defects of traditional empiricism.

7. Thanks to Joshua Stuchlik for drawing my attention to this passage.

ESSAY **13**

Sellars's Thomism

1. Wilfrid Sellars was an important systematic philosopher, not a historian of philosophy. But his own thinking was pervasively shaped by his broad and profound study of the great tradition in philosophy. And in many places he found it natural to expound his own thinking by way of discussing his predecessors. The most obvious example is his book *Science and Metaphysics*, which is subtitled, in a way that captures its character well, *Variations on Kantian Themes*. But there are many smaller-scale exploitations of the mighty dead in Sellars's systematic writings: invocations of, for instance, Leibniz, the British empiricists, and Wittgenstein. In this essay I am going to consider a case of this use of history to expound his own thinking that is perhaps surprising in the light of the kind of philosophy Sellars went in for. I am going to consider a paper called "Being and Being Known", in which Sellars explains and recommends a central feature of his own thinking by commending, but also taking issue with, something he finds in Aquinas. Aquinas will come into view here only through Sellars, so I shall be engaging in the history of philosophy only at one remove (unless considering Sellars already counts as engaging in the history of philosophy). My interest in the topic comes from trying to understand Sellars himself rather than his historical foil. But by the end I shall be in a position to say something general about the kind of history of philosophy that Sellars is doing in this work.[1]

2. One of Sellars's central doctrines is that the intentionality—the aboutness—of episodes of thought should be modelled on, understood as an extension from, our understanding of the way linguistic performances are meaningful.

---

1. This essay was given as a Charles McCracken Lecture in the history of philosophy at Michigan State University.

It may help to bring out the flavour of this conception if I mention P. T. Geach's presentation of the same fundamental idea, in the guise of an account of judging, which Geach discusses as a paradigmatic mental act. Geach works with an idiom he finds in more than one place in the Old Testament. He focuses on an example from the Psalms: "The fool hath said in his heart: there is no God."[2] (The passage is of course familiar from Hobbes's *Leviathan*, where the same fool says in his heart: there is no such thing as Justice.)[3] What the psalm tells us, differently put, is that the fool has judged that there is no God. The fool has not expressed his judgment overtly, so as to let others know of it. Perhaps we can count saying things, literally, as judging out loud, but we are told that the fool's saying is kept in his heart. However, the psalm's idiom clearly models the inner, non-overt performance that the fool goes in for on an outer, overt performance of saying out loud, not in one's heart, "There is no God", or words to that effect, perhaps in a different language—the description works just as well in English as it did in Hebrew.

The suggestion is not that what it is to think a thought is to have words sounding in one's mind's ear, so to speak, or to be rehearsing in the imagination a performance in which one would be speaking the words out loud. No doubt thinking sometimes involves verbal imagery, but the suggestion is not that this always happens when one thinks. The proposal is not about the phenomenology of thought episodes. In fact it is not a recommendation of any conception, phenomenological or otherwise, of what thought episodes, considered in themselves, in abstraction from their content, might be. What the proposal concerns is how to understand, precisely, the *content* of thought episodes, their directedness at external reality. The proposal is that we should start with an understanding of how overt speech has its bearing on its subject matter, and use that understanding as a basis on which to form a parallel conception of how thinking has its bearing on a reality external to thinking. That is, we should take it that the very idea of judging that such-and-such is the case—a paradigmatic example of episodic thought—is formed by analogy with the idea of saying that such-and-such is the case. The very idea of judging embodies a kind of metaphor.

3. Now it is well known that Thomism includes a version of what Sellars calls "the doctrine of the mental word" ("Being and Being Known", p. 43).

---

2. Psalms, xiv.1; see Geach, *Mental Acts*.
3. *Leviathan*, Part I, chapter 15: p. 203 in the Macpherson edition.

In Thomistic parlance, to have, say, the concept of being a man—to have the capacity to engage in intellectual acts in which, for instance, something is thought of as being a man—is to have one's intellect in first act, or first actuality, with respect to the mental word · man ·; that is, to have that mental word in one's intellectual repertoire. This first actuality is one step above the mere potentiality to acquire the concept, but it is obviously still in its way a potentiality. But when one actually engages in an intellectual act in which one thinks of something as being a man, one's intellect is in second act, or second actuality, with respect to the mental word · man ·. The difference between first actuality and second actuality is the difference between having the capacity to use the word and actually using it.

I have been paraphrasing Sellars's sketch of this Thomistic way of talking. It will not have been apparent to the ear that Sellars uses dot quotes to cite the mental word that serves as an example in his exposition. In Sellars's usual way of employing the dot-quote convention, any expression, in any language, that has—nearly enough—the same role in the language it belongs to as the word "man" has in English is a · man ·. As the construction with the indefinite article indicates, "· man ·" is like "lion" in being a classificatory term, a term for things that belong to a kind. The instances of the kind, each of which is a · man ·, are words, and they belong to the kind by virtue of their having matching roles—nearly enough—in the languages they belong to. So for instance "Mensch", in German, is a · man ·, and so is "homme", in French. Of course "man" in English is itself a · man ·. We need "nearly enough" in the account of what it is for something to be a · man · for the obvious reason that the roles of words in different languages cannot be expected to match perfectly.

Now as I said, in his exposition of Thomism, Sellars equates the dot-quoted expression with the mental word. Thereby he indicates two things. First, the mental word he is talking about is (to put the point by using the dot-quoted expression in his more usual way) a · man ·; it has—nearly enough—the same role in the mental language as the English word "man" has in English. Second, it is not to be identified with a word of any particular ordinary language. We might say the identity of the mental word is exhausted by the fact that it is a · man ·, whereas in the case of an ordinary example of something that is a · man ·, it is also true of it that it is a particular word in a particular language, say "homme" or "Mensch".

Brushing past these complications, and putting the Thomistic doctrine without the scholastic-Aristotelian apparatus of grades of actuality, we can say that what it comes to is that intellectual episodes, for instance acts of judgment, are conceived as exercises of competence with mental words.

So far, this sounds like an anticipation of Sellars's own account, and that is surely why Sellars is interested in the Thomistic doctrine at all. However, in Sellars's reading the Thomistic version of the doctrine of the mental word lacks a feature that is essential to his own version. In Sellars's own version, the analogy between non-overt acts of the intellect and overt linguistic performances is essential for explaining the idea that thought has content. That was what I stressed when I set out the Geach-Sellars proposal. But according to Thomism as Sellars reads it, "the nature of a mental word can be understood independently of this analogy" (p. 44). On Sellars's interpretation, when Aquinas depicts intellectual acts as inner uses of mental words, he is giving expression to an understanding of how intellectual acts relate to their subject matter that does not turn on an analogy with the way overt linguistic performances relate to their subject matter.

This is on the face of it a somewhat surprising reading. It seems obvious that any idea of a mental word would need to involve an analogy with the idea of a word of the ordinary kind, a word one might use or encounter in speech or writing. It will take some explaining to bring out how Sellars understands the Thomistic doctrine so that the analogy that the idea of mental words certainly does carry on its surface is nevertheless not the crucial thing about the idea, as it is in Sellars's own story.

4. What we have seen so far of the Thomistic conception of intellectual acts, as Sellars understands it, is that in an intellectual episode in which the concept of being a man is involved, the intellect is in second actuality with respect to a mental word that corresponds to our word "man".

There is a complication that I shall mention only to set it aside. No doubt in any such episode the intellect must be in second actuality with respect to other mental words as well. These other actualizations must be combined with the actualization we have singled out, the actualization with respect to the word ·man·, in a way that mirrors the logical syntax of a perspicuous expression of a whole thought. When we focus on uses of the one mental word, we exploit a way of talking all at once about a whole set of possible intellectual acts, all those that involve the concept of being a man. The members of the set differ in what other concepts they involve. Sellars notes the fact that a full picture of the mental word needs an analogue to syntax

(p. 43), but there is no need for him, or us, to go into it. It makes no difference to his argument about Thomism.

The first new point that we do need to take account of, in order to work towards an understanding of Sellars's treatment of Thomism, is this. In Aquinas, as Sellars reads him, the picture as we have it so far, according to which intellectual acts involving the concept of being a man are inner uses of the mental equivalent of our word "man", is another way of formulating a standard scholastic-Aristotelian conception of acts of the intellect. This standard scholastic-Aristotelian conception exploits apparatus that also figures in a characterization of the realm of being. We can illustrate the application to the realm of being by saying that *what it is to be a man*, for instance, is a form, and when suitable matter is informed by that form, the result is a man. That is the hylomorphic, or matter-form, conception of substances. And now the application to the intellect goes like this. For an intellect to be in first act with respect to the mental word · man ·, to have that word in its repertoire, is for that same form—what it is to be a man—to inform the intellect, not of course in the way in which it informs matter so as to constitute actual men, but in a way suitable to this different informing that it can also do. And for an intellect to be in second act with respect to the mental word · man ·, for an intellect to be actually engaged in an intellectual performance involving the concept of being a man, is for that same form—what it is to be a man—to inform the intellect, again not of course in the way in which it informs matter so as to constitute actual men, but in yet another suitable way.

These are both cases of *isomorphism* between the intellect and the extra-intellectual realities it can think about. Isomorphism is sameness of form, and that is exactly what there is between the intellect and the things it thinks about, according to this way of talking. The same form informs both matter and, in suitable different ways, the intellect. To have the concept of being a man is for one's intellect to be informed, in the appropriate way, by the same form that informs actual men. And to exercise the concept of being a man is for one's intellect to be informed, in a different appropriate way, by the same form that informs actual men. So both an intellect that can think of men and an intellect that is actually thinking of men are, in their different ways, isomorphic with actual men, in a sense that precisely fits the etymology of the word "isomorphic" (an equivalent might be "equiform").

Sellars introduces the general idea of Aristotelian isomorphism, as it is exploited by Thomism, in connection with the first of the two isomorphisms I have just described, the isomorphism between the intellect as capable of thinking about men, on the one hand, and actual men, on the other (p. 44). But it is the second isomorphism, the isomorphism between the intellect as actually thinking about men, on the one hand, and actual men, on the other, that really matters for his argument, and that is the one I shall concentrate on.

This Aristotelian isomorphism between intellectual acts and extra-intellectual actualities is an isomorphism of the knower with the known at the intellectual level. That is one of the ways in which Sellars describes it (p. 41). He also considers an isomorphism of the knower with the known at the level of sense, but I shall ignore this.[4]

Now Sellars agrees with Thomism that there is an isomorphism between the intellect and the real. But in Sellars's view the Thomistic conception of the isomorphism between the intellect and the real is "oversimplified" (p. 41). I think understanding this assessment is the key to seeing why Sellars thinks Thomism cannot exploit, as he can, the analogical character of the idea of the mental word in order to cast light on the intentionality of thought.

5. To explain this, I need to say a bit about Sellars's own conception of the isomorphism between the intellect and the real. This requires venturing into a region of Sellars's thought that tends to daunt even his most ardent devotees, but I think its general lines are not too difficult to make out.

An isomorphism between the intellect and the real would be a *relation* between the intellect and the real. Or perhaps we should say that describing such an isomorphism would be a compendious way of capturing a system of relations between particular intellectual acts and the real. Now in Sellars's own view, as I have said, there is indeed such an isomorphism; there are indeed relations, of the structural sort that the word "isomorphism" suggests, between intellectual episodes and items in the real order. He describes these relations by saying that intellectual episodes *picture* the world, or parts of it.

Picturing relations are relevant to the significance of intellectual words, the intentionality of intellectual episodes. But Sellars thinks it is crucially

---

4. Sellars's main purpose in talking about the isomorphism at the level of sense is to affirm his view that there is no intentionality in sensory events. (See especially "Empiricism and the Philosophy of Mind".) It is unclear to me whether it is fair for him to interpret Thomism as needing to be corrected on this point. But I shall not try to make anything of this part of Sellars's discussion.

important not to conflate the significance of ordinary words or the intentionality of intellectual episodes, the significance of mental words, with their standing in picturing relations to things in the real order. Picturing relations are, as I stressed, *relations*, between items that are linguistic, whether literally or in the metaphorical sense in which intellectual episodes are linguistic, on the one hand, and things that belong to the real order, the extra-linguistic order, on the other. And Sellars insists that the significance of linguistic items, literally or in the extended sense in which talk of the significance of linguistic items is a way of capturing the "aboutness" of inner episodes, does not consist in their standing in relations to things in the real order. In *Science and Metaphysics* (p. ix) he goes so far as to describe "the non-relational character of 'meaning' and 'aboutness'" as "the key to a correct understanding of the place of mind in nature". Since picturing is relational, this amounts to saying that the key to a correct understanding of the place of mind in nature is that we must not conflate significance or intentionality with picturing.

6. It will be easiest to grasp what Sellars is driving at here if we work with the base case, from which we are supposed to proceed by analogy in order to understand the intentionality of intellectual episodes. The base case is the significance of bits of language ordinarily so called. If we can understand the base case, we can exploit the Geach-Sellars conception of acts of the intellect in order to extend our understanding to the significance of mental words, the intentionality of intellectual episodes.

A statement that captures the significance of a bit of language, say a word, must deal with the word *qua* possessor of significance. So it must deal with the word in its guise as an element in the norm-governed practice of speaking meaningfully in the language the word belongs to. That is what, in Sellars's view, excludes the idea that meaning consists in relations to elements in extra-linguistic reality. According to Sellars, a statement of significance about, say, a word would have to capture a match between the norm-governed role of the word, in the language it belongs to, and the nearly enough corresponding norm-governed role of some other word, in a language that anyone to whom the statement is addressed can be presupposed to understand. Statements of significance relate items in the linguistic order or the order of signification, not to items in the real order, but to other items in the linguistic order or the order of signification. For instance, Sellars offers the following as exemplifying a suitable form for statements of significance, properly understood: " 'Mensch' (in German) has the same use as *your* word 'man' ".[5]

When, by contrast, we speak of linguistic episodes as standing in picturing relations to things in the real order, we abstract from the fact that the bits of language that figure in them are governed by the norms that form the frame within which those bits of language would stand revealed as signifi-cant. In considering picturing relations between language and the world, we conceive linguistic episodes as happenings in the norm-free realm of nature—as vocalizations or inscribings, possessing their natural causes and effects, but not conceived in terms of the significance of the words that figure in them. Sellars calls linguistic objects, conceived in this abstracting way, "natural-linguistic objects".[6]

Natural-linguistic objects as such are of course related in various ways to objects that are not linguistic at all, for instance men. For instance, a situa-tion involving a man might cause a vocalization that includes an utterance of the word "man". That would be a one-off relation. But we can also con-sider relations that hold in general between natural-linguistic objects of cer-tain types and extra-linguistic situations of certain types. Vocalizations that include utterances of the word "man" on the part of a certain set of speakers—those who are competent in the use of English—are involved in complex regular connections, uniformities that could be stated in *ceteris paribus* generalizations, with situations in which men figure. These unifor-mities reflect the norms that govern the use of the word, conceived as equipped with its significance, by way of a fact Sellars expresses by saying that "espousal of principles"—that is, allegiance to norms—"is reflected in uniformities of performance".[7] But in statements of these uniformities the utterances would figure as natural-linguistic objects, abstracted from those norms and so abstracted from the fact that the word "man" has the signifi-

---

5. "Being and Being Known", p. 55. The statement is explicitly addressed to someone who has the word "man" in her repertoire. This is to avoid a problem that applies to the most obvious way of aligning items in the linguistic order in respect of their use, which would be a statement on the lines of " 'Mensch' in German has the same use as the English word 'man' ". The problem is that because the word "man" is only mentioned in this state-ment, someone could understand the statement without thereby being enabled to grasp the significance that it would be intended to explain—so it cannot be right to suppose that it actually *states* the significance of the German word.

6. See "Truth and 'Correspondence' ", p. 212.

7. "Truth and 'Correspondence' ", p. 216.

cance it has. Though they reflect the norms that govern the practice of using the word with its significance, the regularities themselves are matter-of-factual regularities in the realm of nature, on a level with (though surely more complicated than) the regularities that link, for instance, flashes of lightning with claps of thunder.

I have been talking about matter-of-factual regularities that connect utterances of the word "man" with situations involving men. But the idea is quite general. Uniformities of performance of this kind hold throughout a language. They combine to constitute a systematic structural correspondence between performances in the language considered as natural-linguistic objects, on the one hand, and situations in extra-linguistic reality, on the other. This is the isomorphism Sellars thinks there is between language and extra-linguistic reality. This is what generates picturing relations between linguistic performances, considered as elements in the realm of nature, and configurations of extra-linguistic objects.

I have so far focused on one of the two ways in which Sellars thinks picturing relations are connected with significance: picturing relations are generated by matter-of-factual regularities, regularities in the realm of nature, that reflect the fact that the natural-linguistic objects that figure in picturing relations are produced by speakers who are engaged in the norm-governed practice of speaking significantly in a language. So the norms that underlie significance are reflected in the matter-of-factual relations that constitute the fact that language pictures extra-linguistic reality.

There is another connection between picturing and significance, in the opposite direction: Sellars holds that the isomorphism that generates picturing relations between linguistic episodes and situations in the extra-linguistic world is a necessary condition for bits of language to have meaning at all.[8] As I explained, statements of the significance of words, according to Sellars, do not relate the words whose significance they capture to things in the extra-linguistic order. But if something is to be recognizable as capturing the significance of a word, it would have to be able to help make sense of how linguistic performances in which the word occurs are determinately directed at their extra-linguistic subject matter. And it would be unintelligible how a statement that does no more than align one element

---

8. See "Being and Being Known", p. 50. The claim is made there (§31) in terms of the intentionality of the intellect, but Sellars goes on to spell it out—as the Geach-Sellars thought allows—in terms of the significance of language in the ordinary sense.

in the order of signification with another element in the order of signification, without so much as mentioning things in extra-linguistic reality, could
do that if there were not a relatedness to elements in the extra-linguistic
order at some point in the complete story about language. So in Sellars's
view such relatedness, though it must be distinguished from what it is for
words to have the significance they do, needs to be acknowledged as a necessary condition for words to have their significance.

7. Bits of language figure in this Sellarsian account in two different guises.
In statements of significance bits of language figure as elements in the
norm-governed practice of making sense, and hence as elements in the
order of signification, related only to other elements in the order of signification. In statements of picturing bits of language figure as elements in
natural-linguistic occurrences, and hence as elements in the real order, not
in the order of signification, related by picturing relations to other elements
in the real order.

    This structure carries over, by way of the Geach-Sellars analogy, to intel-
lectual episodes. Considered as cases of intentionality or aboutness, intellectual episodes are analogous to linguistic performances considered as meaningful. They are elements in the order of signification in the extended sense
that is underwritten by the Geach-Sellars analogy. Statements that deal
with them as cases of intentionality or aboutness, like statements of the significance of ordinary words, relate them only to other elements in the order
of signification. But just as the significance of bits of language, in the ordinary sense, reflects and requires picturing relations between linguistic performances considered in a way that abstracts from their significance, as elements in the real order, and other elements in the real order, so with
intellectual episodes. Their intentionality or aboutness reflects and requires
picturing relations to the real order on the part of things that are in fact intellectual episodes, but considered in another guise that abstracts from their
character as possessing intentionality or aboutness—considered as occurrences in the realm of nature. This is the analogue to conceiving speech acts,
which are in fact meaningful, in abstraction from their meaningfulness, as
natural-linguistic objects.

    So intellectual episodes figure in the complete Sellarsian account of them
in two guises, just as linguistic performances in the ordinary sense do. First,
intellectual episodes are available to introspection in their guise as elements in the order of signification, in the extended sense of "signification"

exploited by the Geach-Sellars analogy. They figure in consciousness under specifications that need to be understood in terms of the analogy with uses of words in the ordinary sense.[9] But when we speak of what are in fact intellectual episodes as relata of the picturing relations they must bear to elements in the real order, if they are to be capturable by those analogical specifications, they figure, as Sellars puts it, *"in propria persona"* ("Being and Being Known", p. 58), as themselves elements in the real order.

This raises the question (p. 59): "What sort of thing is the intellect as belonging to the real order?" And Sellars responds by suggesting that the intellect, as belonging to the real order, is the central nervous system. It is "cerebral patterns and dispositions" that "picture the world". His idea is that what figure in consciousness under analogical specifications, as intellectual episodes with their intentionality, are, considered in themselves, as they must be if they are to be considered in the guise in which they figure in relations of picturing, neurophysiologically specifiable goings-on.

8. We are now in a position, at last, to understand why Sellars thinks that for Thomism the nature of the mental word must be conceived as intelligible independently of the analogy with words in the ordinary sense.

If we describe intellectual acts involving the concept of being a man as isomorphic, in their special way, with actual men, we describe them as standing in a certain *relation* to actual men. By Sellars's lights, that means that, although Thomism offers a description in terms of the Aristotelian isomorphism between intellectual acts and extra-mental actualities as characterizing intellectual acts *qua* bearers of intentionality, it is really suited to characterize them only *qua* picturing the real order. As I said, Sellars holds that intentionality does not consist in relations to the real order, and picturing does. Describing certain intellectual acts as isomorphic to actual men is describing them in terms of a way in which they are related to the real order. So in Sellars's view Thomism conflates intentionality with picturing. It offers something that could only describe intellectual acts in their guise as

---

9. Sellars ("Being and Being Known", p. 48) reads Descartes as holding that "the reflexive awareness of a mental act" is "an adequate (i.e. among other things non-analogical) grasp of the act as being of a certain determinate kind of species". So he represents his conception, according to which intellectual acts are available to introspection under analogical specifications, as requiring him to take issue with Descartes. (See also pp. 58–9.) I do not know what Sellars's ground is for his claim that the Cartesian idea of an adequate understanding excludes an analogical character.

subjects of picturing relations, as if it could serve as an account of their intentionality.

And if describing intellectual acts in terms of how the intellect is informed, in its own special way, by the forms that also inform material substances is really suited to represent intellectual acts only as relata of picturing relations, that mode of representation of intellectual acts would have to be such that, if correct, it would capture what they are, not in the order of signification, but in the real order. It would have to be such as to capture what intellectual acts are *in propria persona*.

For Thomism, then, describing intellectual acts in terms of the Aristotelian isomorphism would supposedly capture what they are *qua* bearers of intentionality. But these descriptions would have to purport to characterize intellectual acts as they are in themselves, in the real order, since it is as what they are in the real order, not as what they are in the order of signification, that intellectual acts figure in the picturing relations that are all that the Aristotelian isomorphism can really encompass. Putting this together: for Thomism, the intentionality of intellectual acts can be revealed by descriptions of them as isomorphic with elements in the real order, and those descriptions purport to display intellectual acts as what they are in themselves.

Now suppose that is how someone sees things. For such a person, it will be only a second best if we can also characterize the intentionality of intellectual episodes in a merely analogical way. How could it be essential to resort to an analogical characterization, if we have at our disposal descriptions that display the intentionality of intellectual episodes precisely by capturing their intrinsic nature—what they are in the real order? So according to this way of thinking, the analogy with the significance of ordinary bits of language cannot be essential to explaining the intentionality of intellectual episodes. Describing intellectual episodes as employments of mental words certainly exploits an analogy, but that style of description of intellectual episodes can only be secondary. The description in terms of the Aristotelian isomorphism says how things literally are when the metaphor of mental words is appropriate. It explains the force of the metaphor, and the metaphor can drop out as inessential.

In Sellars's own account intentionality can be understood only by analogical extension from an independent understanding of the significance of ordinary words. But in Sellars's reading of Thomism understanding is transmitted in the other direction. What the analogical talk of mental words amounts to is supposedly independently intelligible, since the Aristotelian isomorphism yields a characterization of what intellectual acts are *in propria persona*. And then we can explain what it is for ordinary words to be meaningful in terms of this understanding of what it is for mental words to be meaningful. This is the reverse of the order of explanation envisaged in the Geach-Sellars conception.

9. This reading of Thomism is controlled by Sellars's doctrine that anything whose character is capturable in terms of *relations* in which it stands to elements in the real order cannot be, in the guise in which it figures when it is described in those terms, an element in the order of signification. Things that belong to the order of signification—words considered as meaningful, to focus on the primary case—have their identity as elements in the order of signification constituted by their position in the norm-governed practice of speaking a language. And Sellars thinks it follows that statements that capture what words are in the order of signification cannot do so by relating them to things in the real order. Statements of significance can work only by aligning words as elements in the order of signification with other elements in the order of signification, with sufficiently closely matching positions in the norm-governed practice of speaking a language, perhaps a different language. That is the ground on which Sellars thinks he can accuse Thomism of conflating intentionality, position in the order of signification in the extended sense, with picturing. That is why Sellars thinks Thomism offers, as if it could display intellectual episodes in their guise as possessors of intentionality, a form of description that could really capture them only in their guise as elements in the real order, standing in picturing relations to other elements in the real order.

But this basis for Sellars's reading of Thomism seems simply wrong. Consider this statement: the English word "man", or (better) the English expression "... is a man" (or its various syntactic transformations: "... are men" and so forth), is related to men in that it is true of them. Or this: the English word "snow" is related to snow in that the result of concatenating it with "... is white" is true if and only if snow is white. I have formulated these examples so as to emphasize that they state relations between linguistic expressions and extra-linguistic realities: between "... is a man" and men, between "snow" and snow. This should be impossible by Sellars's lights, because the statements deal with the linguistic expressions they are about in their guise as meaningful, as caught up in the norm-governed practice of speaking significantly in English—not merely in their guise as delineating acoustic or inscriptional features of occurrences that are in fact linguistic, though seeing them in merely acoustic or inscriptional terms abstracts from that fact. The statements deal with the expressions they are about as elements in the order of signification, not as natural-linguistic objects—the only guise in which Sellars's thinking allows for relations between linguistic items and elements in the real order. It is a blind spot on Sellars's part that he does not contemplate the evident possibility of statements that both deal with expressions as meaningful and relate the expressions to things in the real order.

The Thomistic style of description depicts intellectual episodes that involve the concept of being a man as related, by Aristotelian isomorphism, to actual men. This is the ground on which Sellars thinks the Thomistic conception of intellectual episodes can really only be a competitor with his conception of what intellectual episodes are in their guise as elements of the real order, goings-on in the central nervous system. But this is undermined when we note Sellars's blind spot. It is certainly true that the Thomistic form of description describes intellectual episodes in terms of relations to elements in the real order. But it does not follow, as Sellars thinks, that descriptions in the Thomistic style cannot depict the acts as possessors of intentionality, elements in the order of signification in the extended sense—any more than it follows, from the fact that the statement I gave about "snow" relates it to snow, that the statement cannot deal with "snow" as an element in the order of signification.

When Thomism describes intellectual episodes in which, say, something is thought of as a man in terms of the intellect's being informed, in a special way, by the form that, when it informs suitable parcels of matter, constitutes actual men, that need not be taken as purporting to *explain* the fact that "man" figures in a specification of the intentional content of the episodes, by giving an account of what they are, considered in themselves, that is supposed to be autonomously intelligible. Talk of the intellect's being informed, in its special way, by the form that informs actual men need be no more than another wording for the idea of intentional content in whose specification "man" would figure. It need not be construed as purporting to capture in literal terms what is captured only metaphorically by talk of employment of mental words. Once we clear away the result of Sellars's blind spot, we can see things the other way around. The analogical specification of intellectual episodes, in terms of employment of mental words, is the best explanation there could be for the special mode of informing that is invoked when we speak of the intellect as informed by the forms that also constitute material actualities. What it is for the intellect to be informed, in the relevant way, by the form that, in a different way, informs actual men is for the intellect to be employing the mental word · man ·. So Sellars is wrong to think Thomism necessarily stands in opposition to the Geach-Sellars proposal for how to understand intentionality.

As I said, Sellars thinks acknowledging that intentionality is non-relational is the key to understanding the place of mind in nature. In a correct account of the place of mind in nature, on his view, intellectual acts, considered as elements in the real order, are goings-on in the central nervous system. Here Sellars's conviction that what things are as elements in the order of signification cannot be captured by describing them in terms of relations to extra-mental actualities helps to make it look compulsory to place the mind in nature, in the sense of identifying intellectual episodes with something we can find in the world as it comes into view in the pursuit of the natural sciences. In their guise as denizens of the natural world the episodes *can* be related to extra-mental actualities. And if intentionality is non-relational, there must surely be some guise in which its possessors are related to extra-mental actualities, even if it is not their guise as possessors of intentionality. Otherwise we risk making it a mystery what possessors of intentionality have to do with the extra-mental actualities that they are, as we say, directed towards.

But if significance does not have to be non-relational, intentionality does not either. The Thomistic style of specification of intellectual episodes, which relates them by an Aristotelian isomorphism to material actualities, can legitimately be taken to fit the episodes in their guise as possessors of intentionality. As I suggested, the mode in which the intellect is said to be informed can be explained in terms of the avowedly analogical idea of employing mental words. There is no need for a different level of specification, supposedly capturing the episodes as what they are in the real order, in which guise alone they can be seen as related to extra-mental actualities. They are already seen as related to extra-mental actualities in their guise as possessors of intentionality.

And now it begins to look like a mere scientistic prejudice, not something dictated by a correct conception of meaning and aboutness, to suppose that what are in fact intellectual episodes, possessors of intentionality, must be in view, though in a different guise, when the world is viewed through the conceptual apparatus of the natural sciences, so as to be able to be described as standing in picturing relations to other elements in the world so viewed. If one assumes something on those lines, the conceptual apparatus of neurophysiology certainly looks like the likeliest candidate for capturing intellectual episodes in this supposedly necessary further guise. But if the general assumption is unwarranted, that is beside the point.[10]

10. It is sometimes suggested that a genuinely historical approach to past philosophers would stand in contrast with the practice of, for instance, Jonathan Bennett. Bennett describes his practice as studying old texts "in the spirit of a colleague, an antagonist, a student, a teacher". He quotes H. P. Grice saying: "I treat those who are great but dead as if they were great but living, as persons who have something to say to us *now*."[11]

It is hard to draw a sharp contrast between Bennett's approach and a more antiquarian stance. For one thing, however keen we are to stress the pastness of past philosophers, we cannot cleanly separate a concern with what they had to say from a willingness to treat them as interlocutors in a conversation, in which the living parties had better be at least open to the possibility that they might have something to learn from the dead. And on the other side, a responsible concern with what the dead may have to say to us now, as Grice puts it, cannot allow us to forget differences between the milieu from which a dead philosopher as it were addresses us and the milieu from which we aim to understand him.

Now the spirit in which Sellars approaches Aquinas is approximately the spirit Bennett expresses. Sellars treats Aquinas as a colleague and as an antagonist. And as I have suggested, something on these lines seems, nearly enough, inevitable if we are to be genuinely concerned to say, necessarily in our own terms, what a past philosopher had to say.[12]

But as I have explained it, Sellars's treatment of Aquinas neatly exemplifies a standing risk posed by such an approach to a historical figure, and I shall end with a remark about that.

As I said, Sellars's reading of Aquinas is shaped by a doctrine of his own, that meaning and intentionality are non-relational. We cannot avoid reading

10. Much more would need to be said about this in a fuller treatment of Sellars. For helpful remarks on what I am depicting as a scientistic prejudice, see several of the papers in Jennifer Hornsby, *Simple Mindedness*.

11. *Learning from Six Philosophers*, p. 1.

12. For an extensive defence of this kind of approach to the history of philosophy, see Part One of Robert B. Brandom, *Tales of the Mighty Dead*.

in the light of our own convictions if we are to bring past philosophers into a conversation with ourselves. But if we allow the dialogue to be shaped by a doctrine that reflects a blind spot on our part, the result will be a distortion—except, perhaps, if the blind spot is shared between us and our target.

It is surely obvious that we risk going astray in the attempt to understand others if we go astray in the philosophical assumptions that we bring to the exercise. But I think something more specific, and more interesting, than that is exemplified in Sellars's reading of Aquinas.

What I have described as a blind spot is not a mere oversight on Sellars's part. I think it reflects Sellars's attempt to combine two insights: first, that meaning and intentionality come into view only in a context that is normatively organized, and, second, that reality as it is contemplated by the sciences of nature is norm-free. The trouble is that Sellars thinks the norm-free reality disclosed by the natural sciences is the only location for genuine relations to actualities. That is what leads to the idea that placing the mind in nature requires abstracting from aboutness.

Now Aquinas, writing before the rise of modern science, is immune to the attractions of that norm-free conception of nature. And we should not be too quick to regard this as wholly a deficiency in his thinking. (Of course in all kinds of ways it is a deficiency.) There is a live possibility that, at least in one respect, Thomistic philosophy of mind is superior to Sellarsian philosophy of mind, just because Aquinas lacks the distinctively modern conception of nature that underlies Sellars's thinking. Sellars allows his philosophy to be shaped by a conception that is characteristic of his own time, and so misses an opportunity to learn something from the past.

Avoiding the Myth
of the Given

1. What is the Myth of the Given?

Wilfrid Sellars, who is responsible for the label, notoriously neglects to explain in general terms what he means by it. As he remarks, the idea of givenness for knowledge, givenness to a knowing subject, can be innocuous.[1] So how does it become pernicious? Here is a suggestion: Givenness in the sense of the Myth would be an availability for cognition to subjects whose getting what is supposedly Given to them does not draw on capacities required for the sort of cognition in question.

If that is what Givenness would be, it is straightforward that it must be mythical. Having something Given to one would be being given something for knowledge without needing to have capacities that would be necessary for one to be able to get to know it. And that is incoherent.

So how can the Myth be a pitfall? Well, one could fall into it if one did not realize that knowledge of some kind requires certain capacities. And we can see how that might be a real risk, in the context in which Sellars mostly discusses the Myth, by considering a Sellarsian dictum about knowledge.

Sellars says attributions of knowledge place episodes or states "in the logical space of reasons".[2] He identifies the logical space of reasons as the space "of justifying and being able to justify what one says". Sellars means to exclude an externalistic view of epistemic satisfactoriness, a view according to which one can be entitled to a belief without being in a position to know what entitles one to it. Knowing things, as Sellars means his dictum, must draw on capacities that belong to reason, conceived as a faculty whose exercises include vindicating one's entitlement to say things. Such a faculty acquires its

---

1. "Empiricism and the Philosophy of Mind", §1.
2. "Empiricism and the Philosophy of Mind", §36.

first actuality, its elevation above mere potentiality, when one learns to talk. There must be a potential for self-consciousness in its operations.

Now consider how this applies to perceptual knowledge. Perceptual knowledge involves sensibility: that is, a capacity for differential responsiveness to features of the environment, made possible by properly functioning sensory systems. But sensibility does not belong to reason. We share it with non-rational animals. According to Sellars's dictum, the rational faculty that distinguishes us from non-rational animals must also be operative in our being perceptually given things to know.

This brings into view a way to fall into the Myth of the Given. Sellars's dictum implies that it is a form of the Myth to think sensibility by itself, without any involvement of capacities that belong to our rationality, can make things available for our cognition. That coincides with a basic doctrine of Kant.

Note that I say "for *our* cognition". It can be tempting to object to Sellars's dictum on the ground that it denies knowledge to non-rational animals. It is perfectly natural—the objection goes—to talk of knowledge when we say how the sensibility of non-rational animals enables them to deal competently with their environments. But there is no need to read Sellars, or Kant, as denying that. We can accept it but still take Sellars's dictum, and the associated rejection of the Myth, to express an insight. Sellars's dictum characterizes knowledge of a distinctive sort, attributable only to rational animals. The Myth, in the version I have introduced, is the idea that sensibility by itself could make things available for the sort of cognition that draws on the subject's rational powers.

2. A knowledgeable perceptual judgment has its rational intelligibility, amounting in this case to epistemic entitlement, in the light of the subject's experience. She judges that things are thus and so because her experience reveals to her that things are thus and so: for instance, she sees that things are thus and so. The intelligibility displayed by such an explanation belongs to a kind that is also exemplified when a subject judges that things are thus and so because her experience merely seems to reveal to her that things are thus and so. These uses of "because" introduce explanations that show rationality in operation. In the kind of case I began with, rationality enables knowledgeable judgments. In the other kind of case, reason leads its possessor astray, or at best enables her to make a judgment that merely happens to be true.

In Kant, the higher faculty that distinguishes us from non-rational animals figures in experience in the guise of the understanding, the faculty of concepts. So to follow Kant's way of avoiding the Myth of the Given in this context, we must suppose capacities that belong to that faculty—conceptual capacities—are in play in the way experience makes knowledge available to us.

For the moment, we can take this introduction of the idea of conceptual capacities quite abstractly. All we need to know so far is that they must be capacities that belong to a faculty of reason. I shall try to be more specific later.

I have invoked the idea of judgments that are rationally intelligible in the light of experience, in the best case to the extent of being revealed as knowledgeable. There is an interpretation of this idea that I need to reject.

The idea is not just that experience yields items—experiences—to which judgments are rational responses. That would be consistent with supposing that rational capacities are operative only in responses to experiences, not in experiences themselves. On this view the involvement of rational capacities would be entirely downstream from experiences.

But that would not do justice to the role of experience in our acquisition of knowledge. As I noted, even for Sellars there is nothing wrong with saying things are given to us for knowledge. The idea of givenness becomes mythical—becomes the idea of Givenness—only if we fail to impose the necessary requirements on getting what is given. And it is in experiencing itself that we have things perceptually given to us for knowledge. Avoiding the Myth requires capacities that belong to reason to be operative in experiencing itself, not just in judgments in which we respond to experience.

3. How should we elaborate this picture? I used to assume that to conceive experiences as actualizations of conceptual capacities, we would need to credit experiences with *propositional* content, the sort of content judgments have. And I used to assume that the content of an experience would need to include *everything* the experience enables its subject to know non-inferentially. But both these assumptions now strike me as wrong.

4. Let me start with the second. We can question it even if, for the moment, we go on assuming experiences have propositional content.

Suppose I have a bird in plain view, and that puts me in a position to know non-inferentially that it is a cardinal. It is not that I infer that what I see is a cardinal from the way it looks, as when I identify a bird's species by comparing what I see with a photograph in a field guide. I can immediately recognize cardinals if the viewing conditions are good enough.

Charles Travis has forced me to think about such cases, and in abandoning my old assumption I am partly coming around to a view he has urged on me.[3]

On my old assumption, since my experience puts me in a position to know non-inferentially that what I see is a cardinal, its content would have to include a proposition in which the concept of a cardinal figures: perhaps one expressible, on the occasion, by saying "That's a cardinal". But what seems right is this: my experience makes the bird visually present to me, and my recognitional capacity enables me to know non-inferentially that what I see is a cardinal. Even if we go on assuming my experience has content, there is no need to suppose that the concept under which my recognitional capacity enables me to bring what I see figures in that content.

Consider an experience had, in matching circumstances, by someone who cannot immediately identify what she sees as a cardinal. Perhaps she does not even have the concept of a cardinal. Her experience might be just like mine in how it makes the bird visually present to her. It is true that in an obvious sense things look different to me and to her. To me what I see looks like (looks to be) a cardinal, and to her it does not. But that is just to say that my experience inclines me, and her similar experience does not incline her, to say it is a cardinal. There is no ground here for insisting that the concept of a cardinal must figure in the content of my experience itself.

It would be right to say I am unlike this other person in that I see that the bird is a cardinal; my experience reveals to me that it is a cardinal. But that is no problem for what I am proposing. Such locutions—"I see that . . .", "My experience reveals to me that . . ."—accept, in their "that . . ." clauses, specifications of things one's experience puts one in a position to know non-inferentially.[4] That can include knowledge that experience makes available by bringing something into view for someone who has a suitable recognitional capacity. And as I have urged, content whose figuring in such knowledge is owed to the recognitional capacity need not be part of the content of the experience itself.

---

3. Thanks to Travis for much helpful discussion.

4. These locutions can even be understood in such a way that inferential credentials are not ruled out for the knowledge in question. Consider, for instance, "I see that the mailman has not yet come today".

5. Should we conclude that conceptual capacities are not operative in having objects visually present to one, but only in what one makes of what one anyway sees? Should we drop the very idea that perceptual experiences had by rational animals have conceptual content?

That would be too drastic. Nothing in what I have said about recognitional capacities dislodges the argument that on pain of the Myth of the Given, capacities that belong to the higher cognitive faculty must be operative in experience. In giving one things to know, experience must draw on conceptual capacities. Some concepts that figure in knowledge afforded by an experience can be excluded from the content of the experience itself, in the way I have illustrated with the concept of a cardinal, but not all can.

A natural stopping point, for visual experiences, would be proper sensibles of sight and common sensibles accessible to sight. We should conceive experience as drawing on conceptual capacities associated with concepts of proper and common sensibles.

So should we suppose my experience when I see a cardinal has propositional content involving proper and common sensibles? That would preserve the other of those two assumptions I used to make. But I think this assumption is wrong too. What we need is an idea of content that is not propositional but intuitional, in what I take to be a Kantian sense.

"Intuition" is the standard English translation of Kant's "*Anschauung*". The etymology of "intuition" fits Kant's notion, and Kant uses a cognate expression when he writes in Latin. But we need to forget much of the philosophical resonance of the English word. An *Anschauung* is a having in view. (As is usual in philosophy, Kant treats visual experiences as exemplary.)

Kant says: "The same function which gives unity to the various representations *in a judgment* also gives unity to the mere synthesis of various representations *in an intuition*; and this unity, in its most general expression, we entitle the pure concept of the understanding."[5] The capacity whose exercise in judging accounts for the unity of the content of judgments—propositional unity—also accounts for a corresponding unity in the content of intuitions. Sellars gives a helpful illustration: the propositional unity in a judgment expressible by "This is a cube" corresponds to an intuitional unity expressible by "this cube".[6] The demonstrative phrase might partly capture the content of an intuition in which one is visually presented with a cube. (I shall return to this.)

---

5. *Critique of Pure Reason*, A79/B104–5.
6. *Science and Metaphysics*, p. 5.

Propositional unity comes in various forms. Kant takes a classification of forms of judgment, and thus of forms of propositional unity, from the logic of his day, and works to describe a corresponding form of intuitional unity for each. But the idea that forms of intuitional unity correspond to forms of propositional unity can be separated from the details of how Kant elaborates it. It is not obvious why Kant thinks the idea requires that to every form of propositional unity there must correspond a form of intuitional unity. And anyway we need not follow Kant in his inventory of forms of propositional unity.

Michael Thompson has identified a distinctive form of propositional unity for thought and talk about the living as such.[7] Thompson's primary point is about a form exemplified in saying what living things of certain kinds *do*, as in "Wolves hunt in packs" or "The lesser celandine blooms in spring". But Thompson's thought naturally extends to a form or forms exemplified in talk about what individual living things *are doing*, as in "Those wolves are hunting" or "This lesser celandine is coming into bloom".[8] And it would be in the spirit of Kant's conception to identify a corresponding form or corresponding forms of intuitional unity, one of which we might find in my visual experience of a cardinal. The concept of a bird, like the concept of a cardinal, need not be part of the content of the experience; the same considerations would apply. But perhaps we can say it is given to me in such an experience, not something I know by bringing a conceptual capacity to bear on what I anyway see, that what I see is an animal—not because "animal" expresses part of the content unified in the experience in accordance with a certain form of intuitional unity, but because "animal" captures the intuition's categorial form, the distinctive kind of unity it has.

The common sensibles accessible to sight are modes of space occupancy: shape, size, position, movement or its absence. In an intuition unified by a form capturable by "animal", we might recognize content, under the head of modes of space occupancy, that could not figure in intuitions of inanimate objects. We might think of common sensibles accessible to sight as including, for instance, postures such as perching and modes of locomotion such as hopping or flying.

---

7. See "The Representation of Life".

8. A form or forms: perhaps we should distinguish an animal version from a non-animal version. A special case of the animal version would be a form for talk of intentional action, which is the topic of G. E. M. Anscombe, *Intention*.

We can avoid such issues by concentrating, as Sellars often does, on visual presentness of things like coloured cubes. But even with this restricted focus, there is still a complication. If there can be visual intuitions whose content is partly specifiable by, say, "that cube", intuitions in which something's being cubic is visually given to one, then the higher cognitive faculty needs to be in our picture not just to account for the unity with which certain content figures in such an intuition, but also, in the guise of the productive imagination, to provide for part of the content itself—supplying, as it were, the rest of the cube, behind the facing surfaces. Sellars often uses the example of a pink ice cube, and one reason is presumably that it allows him not to bother with this complication, because he envisages his ice cube as translucent, so that its back can be actually in view.[9]

6. So far, conceptual capacities are on the scene only as the kind of capacities that must be in play in experience if we are to avoid the Myth: capacities that belong to rationality in a demanding sense. But I undertook to try to be more specific.

If the idea of the conceptual singles out a kind of content, it seems right to focus on the content of judgments, since judging is the paradigmatic exercise of theoretical rationality.

We can think of judgments as inner analogues to assertions. That makes it natural to count judging as a *discursive* activity, even though the idea of discourse has its primary application to overt performances.[10] In an assertion one makes something discursively explicit. And the idea of making things explicit extends without strain to judging. We can say that one makes what one judges explicit to oneself.

I said we should centre our idea of the conceptual on the content of judgments. But now that I have introduced the idea of the discursive, I can put the point like this: we should centre our idea of the conceptual on the content of discursive activity.

Now intuiting is not discursive, even in the extended sense in which judging is. Discursive content is articulated. Intuitional content is not.

9. See Willem A. deVries, *Wilfrid Sellars*, p. 305, n. 18.

10. Perhaps it is already metaphorical even in that application. See Stephen Engstrom, "Sensibility and Understanding", for some remarks on how the discursive understanding can be conceived as running about, which is what the etymology of the term indicates that it should mean.

Part of the point is that there are typically aspects of the content of an intuition that the subject has no means of making discursively explicit. Visual intuitions typically present one with visible characteristics of objects that one is not equipped to attribute to the objects by making appropriate predications in claims or judgments. To make such an aspect of the content of an intuition into the content associated with a capacity that is discursive in the primary sense, one would need to carve it out, as it were, from the categorially unified but as yet unarticulated content of the intuition by determining it to be the meaning of a linguistic expression, which one thereby sets up as a means for making that content explicit. (This might be a matter of coining an adjective. Or the expression might be one like "having that shade of colour".) Perhaps one can bypass language and directly equip oneself with a counterpart capacity that is discursive in the sense in which judging is discursive. There would be the same need to isolate an aspect of the content of the intuition, by determining it to be the content associated with a capacity to make predications in judgments.

And articulating goes beyond intuiting even if we restrict ourselves to aspects of intuitional content that are associated with discursive capacities one already has.

In discursive dealings with content, one puts significances together. This is particularly clear with discursive performances in the primary sense, whose content is the significance of a combination of meaningful expressions. But even though judging need not be conceived as an act spread out in time, like making a claim, its being discursive involves a counterpart to the way one puts significances together in meaningful speech.

I mean this to be consistent with rejecting, as we should, the idea that the contents one puts together in discursive activity are self-standing building-blocks, separately thinkable elements in the contents of claims or judgments. One can think the significance of, say, a predicative expression only in the context of a thought in which that content occurs predicatively. But we can acknowledge that and still say that in discursive activity one puts contents together, in a way that can be modelled on stringing meaningful expressions together in discourse literally so called.

That is not how it is with intuitional content. The unity of intuitional content is *given*, not a result of our putting significances together. Even if discursive exploitation of some content given in an intuition does not require one to acquire a new discursive capacity, one needs to carve out that content from the intuition's unarticulated content before one can put it together with other bits of content in discursive activity. Intuiting does not do this carving out for one.

If intuitional content is not discursive, why go on insisting it is conceptual? Because every aspect of the content of an intuition is present in a form in which it is already suitable to be the content associated with a discursive capacity, if it is not—at least not yet—actually so associated. That is part of the force of saying, with Kant, that what gives unity to intuitions is the same function that gives unity to judgments. If a subject does not already have a discursive capacity associated with some aspect of the content of an intuition of hers, all she needs to do, to acquire such a discursive capacity, is to isolate that aspect by equipping herself with a means to make that content—that very content—explicit in speech or judgment. The content of an intuition is such that its subject can analyse it into significances for discursive capacities, whether or not this requires introducing new discursive capacities to be associated with those significances. Whether by way of introducing new discursive capacities or not, the subject of an intuition is in a position to put aspects of its content, the very content that is already there in the intuition, together in discursive performances.

I said that the unity of intuitional content is *given*. Kant sometimes implies a different picture. He says, for instance, that "all combination, be we conscious of it or not, . . . is an act of the understanding *(Verstandeshandlung)*" (B130). In its context, this remark implies that we actively put content together in intuitions no less than in judgments (though with intuitions the activity has to be unconscious). And that goes badly with my claim that intuitional content is not discursive. But Kant does not need to hold that the unity of intuitional content is not given. What he really wants to insist is that it is not Given: that it is not provided by sensibility alone. In intuiting, capacities that belong to the higher cognitive faculty are in play. The unity of intuitional content reflects an operation of the same unifying function that is operative in the unity of judgments, in that case actively exercised. That is why it is right to say the content unified in intuitions is of the same kind as the content unified in judgments: that is, conceptual content. We could not have intuitions, with their specific forms of unity, if we could not make judgments, with their corresponding forms of unity. We can even say that the unity-providing function is essentially a faculty for discursive activity, a power to judge. But its operation in providing for the unity of intuitions is not itself a case of discursive activity.

Not that it is a case of prediscursive activity, at least if that means that intuiting is a more primitive forerunner of judging. The two kinds of unity
that Kant says are provided by the same function, the unity of intuitions
and the unity of judgments, are on a level with one another.

7. In a visual intuition, an object is visually present to a subject with those
of its features that are visible to the subject from her vantage point. It is
through the presence of those features that the object is present. How else
could an object be visually present to one?

The concept of an object here is formal. In Kant's terms, a category, a
pure concept of the understanding, is a concept of an object in general. A
formal concept of, as we can naturally say, a kind of object is explained by
specifying a form of categorial unity, a form of the kind of unity that characterizes intuitions. Perhaps, as I suggested, following Thompson, "animal"
can be understood as expressing such a concept.

On the account I have been giving, having an object present to one in an intuition is an actualization of capacities that are conceptual, in a sense that belongs with Kant's thesis that what accounts for the unity with which the associated content figures in the intuition is the same function that provides for
the unity of judgments. I have urged that even though the unity-providing
function is a faculty for discursive activity, it is not in discursive activity that
these capacities are operative in intuitions. With much of the content of an ordinary visual intuition, the capacities that are in play in one's having it as part
of the content of one's intuition are not even susceptible of discursive exercise. One can make use of content's being given in an intuition to acquire a
new discursive capacity, but with much of the content of an ordinary intuition, one never does that. (Think of the finely discriminable shapes and
shades of colour that visual experience presents to one.) Nevertheless an intuition's content is all conceptual, in this sense: it is in the intuition in a form in
which one *could* make it, that very content, figure in discursive activity. That
would be to exploit a potential for discursive activity that is already there in
the capacities actualized in having an intuition with that content.[11]

In an intuition, an object is present to one whether or not one exploits
this potential for discursive activity. Kant says the "I think" of apperception

---

11. Intuitional content that is not brought to discursive activity is easily forgotten. This
does not tell at all against saying it is conceptual content, in the sense I have tried to explain. See Sean Dorrance Kelly, "Demonstrative Concepts and Experience".

must be able to accompany all *Vorstellungen* that are mine, in a sense that is related to the idea of operations of the function that gives unity both to judgments and to intuitions (B131). An object is present to a subject in an intuition whether or not the "I think" accompanies any of the intuition's content. But any of the content of an intuition must be able to be accompanied by the "I think". And for the "I think" to accompany some of the content of an intuition, say a visual intuition, of mine is for me to *judge* that I am visually confronted by an object with such-and-such features. Since the intuition makes the object visually present to me through those features, such a judgment would be knowledgeable.

We now have in view two ways in which intuitions enable knowledgeable judgments.

One is the way I have just described. A potential for discursive activity is already there in an intuition's having its content. And one can exploit some of that potential in a knowledgeable judgment that redeploys some of the content of the intuition. In the kind of case that first opens up this possibility, one adds a reference to the first person. When the "I think" accompanies some content provided in an intuition, that yields a knowledgeable judgment that I am confronted by an object with such-and-such features. But being in a position to make such a judgment is being in a position to judge that there is an object with such-and-such features at such-and-such a location. One need not explicitly refer to oneself in a judgment whose status as knowledgeable depends on its being a discursive exploitation of some of the content of an intuition.

The other way intuitions make knowledge possible is the way I illustrated with my knowledge that a bird I see is a cardinal. Here a knowledgeable judgment enabled by an intuition has content that goes beyond the content of the intuition. The intuition makes something perceptually present to the subject, and the subject recognizes that thing as an instance of a kind. Or as an individual; it seems reasonable to find a corresponding structure in a case in which an experience enables one to know non-inferentially who it is that one is perceptually presented with.

8. Travis urges that experiences do not represent things as so.[12] If experiences are intuitions, he is strictly correct. Anything that represents things as

---

12. See "The Silence of the Senses".

so has propositional content, and I have been spelling out a conception of intuitions on which they do not have propositional content. But though Travis is right about the letter of the thesis that experiences represent things as so, he is wrong about the spirit, as we can see by considering the first of those two ways in which intuitions enable judgments that are knowledgeable. Though they are not discursive, intuitions have content of a sort that embodies an immediate potential for exploiting that same content in knowledgeable judgments. Intuitions immediately reveal things to be the way they would be judged to be in those judgments.

When Sellars introduces the conceptual character he attributes to experiences, he describes experiences as "so to speak, making" claims or "containing" claims.[13] If experiences are intuitions, that is similarly wrong in the letter but right in spirit. Intuitions do not have the sort of content claims have. But intuitions immediately reveal things to be as they would be claimed to be in claims that would be no more than a discursive exploitation of some of the content of the intuitions.

When Travis says experiences do not represent things as so, he does not mean that experiences are intuitions in the sense I have been explaining. He says experience is not a case of intentionality, and I think it is fair to understand him as denying that conceptual capacities are in play in experience at all. Visual experiences bring our surroundings into view; that should be common ground. Travis's idea is that the way experience makes knowledge available can be understood, across the board, on the model of how an experience might enable me to know that what I see is a cardinal. In Travis's picture conceptual capacities are in play only in our making what we can of what visual experiences anyway bring into view for us, independently of any operation of our conceptual capacities.[14] In Travis's picture, having things in view does not draw on conceptual capacities. And if it does not draw on conceptual capacities, having things in view must be provided for by sensibility alone.

The trouble with this is that it is a form of the Myth of the Given. We do not fall into the Myth just by supposing that features of our surroundings are given to us in visual experience. But in Travis's picture that givenness becomes a case of Givenness.

---

13. "Empiricism and the Philosophy of Mind", §16.

14. "In making out, or trying to, what it is that we confront": "The Silence of the Senses", p. 65.

Travis thinks the idea that experiences have content conflicts with the idea that experience directly brings our surroundings into view. He is not alone in this.[15] Wanting, as is reasonable, to keep the idea that experience directly brings our surroundings into view, he is led to deny that experiences have content. But there is no conflict. Intuitions as I have explained them directly bring objects into view through bringing their perceptible properties into view. Intuitions do that precisely by having the kind of content they have.

If intuitions make knowledge available to us, merely seeming intuitions merely seem to make knowledge available to us. It is often thought that when people urge that experiences have content, they are responding to a felt need to accommodate the fact that experience can mislead us.[16] But the proper ground for crediting experiences with content is that we must avoid the Myth of the Given. Making room for misleading experiences is a routine by-product.

9. Donald Davidson claims that "nothing can count as a reason for holding a belief except another belief".[17] His point is to deny that beliefs can be displayed as rational in the light of episodes or states in sensory consciousness—unless that means they can be displayed as rational in the light of *beliefs about* episodes or states in sensory consciousness. That would put the potential rational relevance to beliefs of episodes or states in sensory consciousness on a level with the potential rational relevance to beliefs of anything at all that one might have beliefs about.

In previous work, I took it that Davidson's slogan reflects an insight: that conceptual capacities must be in play not only in rationally forming beliefs or making judgments, but also in having the rational entitlements one exploits in doing that. But I urged that the insight, so understood, permits judgments to be displayed as rational in the light of experiences themselves, not just in the light of beliefs about experiences, since we can understand experiences as actualizations of conceptual capacities.[18]

Trying to spell out this possibility, which I found missing from Davidson's picture, I made one of the assumptions I have here renounced: that if experiences are actualizations of conceptual capacities, they must have propositional content. That gave Davidson an opening for a telling response.

---

15. See, e.g., Bill Brewer, "Perception and Content".

16. See Brewer, "Perception and Content".

17. "A Coherence Theory of Truth and Knowledge", p. 141.

18. See, e.g., *Mind and World*.

Davidson argued that if by "experience" we mean something with propositional content, it can only be a case of taking things to be so, distinctive in being caused by the impact of the environment on our sensory apparatus. But of course his picture includes such things. So I was wrong, he claimed, to suppose there is anything missing from his picture.[19]

I want to insist, against Davidson, that experiencing is not taking things to be so. As Travis urges, our visual experiences bring our surroundings into view. Some of what we are thereby entitled to take to be so, in judgments that would be rational given what is visually present to us, we do take to be so. But even when we detach belief-acquisition from explicitly judging things to be so, as we should, we would exaggerate the extent of the doxastic activity experience prompts in us if we were to suppose we acquire all the beliefs we would be entitled to by what we have in view.

So I agree with Travis that visual experiences just bring our surroundings into view, thereby entitling us to take certain things to be so, but leaving it a further question what, if anything, we do take to be so. But as I have argued, Travis's version of that thought falls into the Myth of the Given. And if we avoid the Myth by conceiving experiences as actualizations of conceptual capacities, while retaining the assumption that that requires crediting experiences with propositional content, Davidson's point seems well taken. If experiences have propositional content, it is hard to deny that experiencing is taking things to be so, rather than what I want: a different kind of thing that entitles us to take things to be so.

If experience comprises intuitions, there is a way between these positions. Intuitions bring our surroundings into view, but not in an operation of mere sensibility, so we avoid Travis's form of the Myth of the Given. But the conceptual content that allows us to avoid the Myth is intuitional, not propositional, so experiencing is not taking things to be so. In bringing our surroundings into view, experiences entitle us to take things to be so; whether we do is a further question.

As I said, there are two ways in which experience, conceived as comprising intuitions, entitles us to moves with discursive content. It entitles us to judgments that would exploit some of the content of an intuition, and it

---

19. For a particularly clear expression, see "Reply to John McDowell". Berkeley colleagues of Davidson's have weighed in a similar vein. See Barry Stroud, "Sense-Experience and the Grounding of Thought", and Hannah Ginsborg, "Reasons for Belief". For a similar view, independent of Davidson, see Kathrin Glüer, "On Perceiving That".

figures in our entitlement to judgments that would go beyond that content in ways that reflect capacities to recognize things made present to one in an intuition. But as I have insisted, in intuiting itself we do not deal discursively with content.

I mentioned Sellars's proposal that the content of an intuition might be captured, in part, by a form of words like "this red cube". Content so expressed would be fragmentary discursive content. It might be part of the content of a judgment warranted in the second of those two ways, where what one judges includes, over and above content contained in the intuition itself, concepts whose figuring in the judgment reflects recognitional capacities brought to bear on something the intuition makes present to one. Thus, a bit of discourse that begins "This red cube . . ." might go on ". . . is the one I saw yesterday".

I think this indicates that Sellars's proposal is useful only up to a point. It might seem to imply that intuitional content is essentially fragmentary discursive content. But intuitional content is not discursive content at all. Having something in view, say a red cube, can be complete in itself. Having something in view can enable a demonstrative expression, or an analogue in judgment, that one might use in making explicit something one takes to be so, but the potential need not be actualized.

10. Davidson's slogan as it stands restricts the way beliefs can be displayed as rational to exploitations of *inferential* structures. It implies that giving a reason for holding a belief is depicting the content of the belief as the conclusion of an inference with the content of another belief as a premise.

I proposed to modify Davidson's slogan by saying that not only beliefs but also experiences can be reasons for belief. And according to my old assumption experiences have the same kind of content as beliefs. So it was understandable that I should be taken to be recommending an inferential, or at least quasi-inferential, conception of the way experience entitles us to perceptual beliefs.[20]

That was not what I intended. I did not mean to imply that experience yields premises for inferences whose conclusions are the contents of perceptual beliefs. On the contrary, I think experience directly reveals things to be as they are believed to be in perceptual beliefs, or at least seems to do that. But it is hard to make that cohere with supposing experiences have the

---

20. See Crispin Wright, "Human Nature?".

same kind of content as beliefs. That is just a way of registering how persuasive Davidson's "Nothing is missing" response is, so long as we do not question the assumption that conceptual content for experiences would have to be propositional.

Taking experience to comprise intuitions, in the sense I have explained, removes this problem. It should not even seem that the way intuitions entitle us to beliefs involves an inferential structure. If an object is present to one through the presence to one of some of its properties, in an intuition in which concepts of those properties exemplify a unity that constitutes the content of a formal concept of an object, one is thereby entitled to judge that one is confronted by an object with those properties. The entitlement derives from the presence to one of the object itself, not from a premise for an inference, at one's disposal by being the content of one's experience.

On the interpretation I offered at the beginning, Sellars's view of the Given as a pitfall to be avoided, in thinking about experience, is an application of his thought that knowledge, as enjoyed by rational animals, draws on our distinctively rational capacities. I have just explained how that does not imply that the warrant for a perceptual judgment is quasi-inferential.[21]

Finding such an implication is of a piece with thinking Sellars's Kantian understanding of what knowledge is for rational animals over-intellectualizes our epistemic life.[22] This needs discussion, but I shall end by briefly arguing that it is the very reverse of the truth.

An intellectualistic conception of the human intellect regards it as something distinct from our animal nature. The best antidote is to see capacities of reason as operative even in our unreflective perceptual awareness.

It is utterly wrong to think Sellars's conception implies that all of our epistemic life is actively led by us, in the bright light of reason. That rational capacities are pervasively in play in human epistemic life is reflected in the fact that any of it *can* be accompanied by the "I think" of explicit self-consciousness. But even though all of our epistemic life is able to be accompanied by the "I think", in much of it we unreflectively go with the flow.

I said that all of our epistemic life can be accompanied by the "I think". Sub-personal occurrences in our cognitive machinery are not a counter-example

---

21. For the idea that Sellars's rejection of the Given amounts to the thesis that the warrant for perceptual judgments is inferential or quasi-inferential, see Daniel Bonevac, "Sellars vs. the Given".

22. See Tyler Burge, "Perceptual Entitlement".

to this claim. They are not, in the relevant sense, part of our epistemic life. No doubt knowledge of how our cognitive machinery works is essential for a full understanding of how it can be that our epistemic capacities are as they are. But having a standing in the space of reasons—for instance, being in a position to see that things are thus and so—is not a sub-personal matter. It is true that the sub-personal machinery that enables us to have such standings operates outside the reach of our apperception. And there are, unsurprisingly, similarities between our sub-personal cognitive machinery and the cognitive machinery of non-rational animals. But that does not threaten the idea that rational animals are special in having epistemic standings to which it is essential that they are available to apperception.

What makes Sellars's internalistic conception appropriate for our perceptual knowledge is not that in perception we engage in rational activity on the lines of reasoning—something that might be regarded as separate from our animal nature, specifically, for present purposes, our sentient nature. That *would* be over-intellectualizing our perceptual knowledge. But the reason why internalism is correct about our perceptual knowledge is that rational capacities, and hence availability to apperception, permeate our experience itself, including the experience we act on unreflectively in our ordinary coping with our surroundings. Such is the form that animal engagement with the perceptible environment takes in the case of rational animals.

BIBLIOGRAPHY

CREDITS

INDEX

Bibliography

Allison, Henry E., *Kant's Transcendental Idealism* (New Haven: Yale University Press, 1983).

Anscombe, G. E. M., *Intention* (Cambridge, Mass.: Harvard University Press, 2000).

Aquila, Richard E., *Matter in Mind: A Study of Kant's Transcendental Deduction* (Bloomington: Indiana University Press, 1989).

Ayers, Michael, "Sense Experience, Concepts, and Content—Objections to Davidson and McDowell", in Ralph Schumacher, ed., *Perception and Reality: From Descartes to the Present* (Paderborn, Germany: mentis, 2004).

Bennett, Jonathan, *Learning from Six Philosophers: Descartes, Spinoza, Leibniz, Locke, Berkeley, Hume*, vol. 1 (Oxford: Oxford University Press, 2001).

Bonevac, Daniel, "Sellars vs. the Given", *Philosophy and Phenomenological Research* 64 (2002).

Brandom, Robert B., "The Centrality of Sellars's Two-Ply Account of Observation to the Arguments of 'Empiricism and the Philosophy of Mind' ", in Brandom, *Tales of the Mighty Dead: Historical Essays in the Metaphysics of Intentionality* (Cambridge, Mass.: Harvard University Press, 2002).

———, "Insights and Blind Spots of Reliabilism", in Brandom, *Articulating Reasons: An Introduction to Inferentialism* (Cambridge, Mass.: Harvard University Press, 2000).

———, *Making It Explicit: Reasoning, Representing, and Discursive Commitment* (Cambridge, Mass.: Harvard University Press, 1994).

———, "Replies", in *Philosophy and Phenomenological Research* 57 (1997).

———, "Some Pragmatist Themes in Hegel's Idealism: Negotiation and Administration in Hegel's Account of the Structure and Content of Conceptual Norms", in Brandom, *Tales of the Mighty Dead: Historical Essays on the Metaphysics of Intentionality* (Cambridge, Mass.: Harvard University Press, 2002).

———, "Study Guide", in Wilfrid Sellars, *Empiricism and the Philosophy of Mind* (Cambridge, Mass.: Harvard University Press, 1997).

Brewer, Bill, "Perception and Content", *European Journal of Philosophy* 14 (2006).

Burge, Tyler, "Perceptual Entitlement", *Philosophy and Phenomenological Research* 67 (2003).

Collins, Arthur W., "Beastly Experience", *Philosophy and Phenomenological Research* 58 (1998).

Davidson, Donald, "Afterthoughts" to "A Coherence Theory of Truth and Knowledge", in Alan Malachowski, ed., *Reading Rorty* (Oxford: Blackwell, 1990).

———, "A Coherence Theory of Truth and Knowledge", in Davidson, *Subjective, Intersubjective, Objective* (Oxford: Clarendon Press, 2001).

———, "In Defence of Convention T", in Davidson, *Inquiries into Truth and Interpretation* (Oxford: Clarendon Press, 1984).

———, "Mental Events", in Davidson, *Essays on Actions and Events* (Oxford: Clarendon Press, 1980).

———, "The Myth of the Subjective", in Michael Krausz, ed., *Relativism: Interpretation and Confrontation* (Notre Dame, Ind.: Notre Dame University Press, 1989).

———, "A Nice Derangement of Epitaphs", in Ernest LePore, ed., *Truth and Interpretation: Perspectives on the Philosophy of Donald Davidson* (Oxford: Blackwell, 1986).

———, "On the Very Idea of a Conceptual Scheme", in Davidson, *Inquiries into Truth and Interpretation* (Oxford: Clarendon Press, 1984).

———, "Reply to John McDowell", in L. E. Hahn, ed., *The Philosophy of Donald Davidson* (Chicago: Open Court, 1999).

DeVries, Willem A., *Wilfrid Sellars* (Chesham, Bucks: Acumen, 2005).

Engstrom, Stephen, "Sensibility and Understanding", *Inquiry* 49 (2006).

Evans, Gareth, *The Varieties of Reference* (Oxford: Clarendon Press, 1982).

Flay, Joseph C., *Hegel's Quest for Certainty* (Albany: SUNY Press, 1984).

Friedman, Michael, "Exorcising the Philosophical Tradition: Comments on John McDowell's *Mind and World*", *Philosophical Review* 105 (1996).

Gadamer, Hans-Georg, "Hegel's Dialectic of Self-Consciousness", in *Hegel's Dialectic: Five Hermeneutical Studies*, trans. P. Christopher Smith (New Haven: Yale University Press, 1976).

Geach, P. T., *Mental Acts* (London: Routledge and Kegan Paul, 1957).

Ginsborg, Hannah, "Reasons for Belief", *Philosophy and Phenomenological Research* 72 (2006).

Glüer, Kathrin, "On Perceiving That", *Theoria* 70 (2004).

Hegel, G. W. F., *Faith and Knowledge*, trans. Walter Cerf and H. S. Harris (Albany: SUNY Press, 1977).

———, *Hegel's Phenomenology of Spirit*, trans. A. V. Miller (Oxford: Oxford University Press, 1977).

———, *Hegel's Science of Logic*, trans. A. V. Miller (New York: Humanities Press, 1976).

Heidegger, Martin, *Kant and the Problem of Metaphysics*, trans. Richard Taft (Bloomington: Indiana University Press, 1990 [fourth edition]).

Henrich, Dieter, "Zwei Naturalismen auf Englisch", *Merkur* 565 (1996).

Hobbes, Thomas, *Leviathan*, C. B. Macpherson, ed. (Harmondsworth: Penguin, 1968).

Hornsby, Jennifer, *Simple Mindedness* (Cambridge, Mass.: Harvard University Press, 1997).

Hyppolite, Jean, *Genesis and Structure of Hegel's Phenomenology of Spirit*, trans. Samuel Cherniak and John Heckman (Evanston, Ill.: Northwestern University Press, 1977).

Kant, Immanuel, *Correspondence*, trans. Arnulf Zweig (Cambridge: Cambridge University Press, 1999).

———, *Critique of Pure Reason*, trans. Norman Kemp Smith (London: Macmillan, 1929).

Kelly, George Armstrong, "Notes on Hegel's 'Lordship and Bondage' ", in Jon Stewart, ed., *The Phenomenology of Spirit Reader* (Albany: SUNY Press, 1998).

Kelly, Sean Dorrance, "Demonstrative Concepts and Experience", *Philosophical Review* 110 (2001).

Longuenesse, Béatrice, "Point of View of Man or Knowledge of God: Kant and Hegel on Concept, Judgment, and Reason", in Sally Sedgwick, ed., *The Reception of Kant's Critical Philosophy: Fichte, Schelling, and Hegel* (Cambridge: Cambridge University Press, 2000).

McDowell, John, "Aesthetic Value, Objectivity, and the Fabric of the World", in McDowell, *Mind, Value, and Reality* (Cambridge, Mass.: Harvard University Press, 1998).

———, "Gadamer and Davidson on Understanding and Relativism", in Jeff Malpas, Ulrich Arnswald, and Jens Kertscher, eds., *Gadamer's Century: Essays in Honor of Hans-Georg Gadamer* (Cambridge, Mass.: MIT Press, 2002).

———, "Hegel and the Myth of the Given", in Wolfgang Welsch and Klaus Vieweg, eds., *Das Interesse des Denkens: Hegel aus heutiger Sicht* (München: Wilhelm Fink Verlag, 2003).

———, "L'idealismo di Hegel come radicalizzazione di Kant", in Luigi Ruggiu and Italo Testa, eds., *Hegel Contemporaneo: La ricezione americana di Hegel a confronto con la traduzione europea* (Milan: Guerini, 2003).

———, *Mind and World* (Cambridge, Mass.: Harvard University Press, 1996 [second edition]).

———, "Reply to Commentators", *Philosophy and Phenomenological Research* 58 (1998).

———, "Responses", in Nicholas H. Smith, ed., *Reading McDowell: On* Mind and World (London: Routledge, 2002).

———, "Values and Secondary Qualities", in McDowell, *Mind, Value, and Reality* (Cambridge, Mass.: Harvard University Press, 1998).

Peacocke, Christopher, *Sense and Content* (Oxford: Clarendon Press, 1983).

Pippin, Robert B., *Hegel's Idealism: The Satisfactions of Self-Consciousness* (Cambridge: Cambridge University Press, 1989).

———, "Hegel's Practical Philosophy: The Realization of Freedom", in Karl Ameriks, ed., *The Cambridge Companion to German Idealism* (Cambridge: Cambridge University Press, 2000).

———, "Hegels praktischer Realismus: rationales Handeln als Sittlichkeit", in Christoph Halbig, Michael Quante, and Ludwig Siep, eds., *Hegels Erbe* (Frankfurt: Suhrkamp, 2004).

————, "Kant on the Spontaneity of Mind", in Pippin, *Idealism as Modernism: Hegelian Variations* (Cambridge: Cambridge University Press, 1997).

————, "Leaving Nature Behind, or Two Cheers for 'Subjectivism'", in Nicholas H. Smith, ed., *Reading McDowell: On* Mind and World (London: Routledge).

————, *The Persistence of Subjectivity: On the Kantian Aftermath* (Cambridge: Cambridge University Press, 2005).

————, "Recognition and Reconciliation: Actualized Agency in Hegel's Jena *Phenomenology*", in Katerina Deligiorgi, ed., *Hegel: New Directions* (Chesham, Bucks: Acumen, 2006).

————, "What is the Question for which Hegel's Theory of Recognition is the Answer?", *European Journal of Philosophy* 8 (2000).

Rorty, Richard, "McDowell, Davidson, and Spontaneity", *Philosophy and Phenomenological Research* 58 (1998).

————, *Philosophy and the Mirror of Nature* (Princeton: Princeton University Press, 1979).

————, "Pragmatism, Davidson, and Truth", in Rorty, *Objectivity, Relativism, and Truth* (Cambridge: Cambridge University Press, 1991).

————, "Solidarity or Objectivity?", in Rorty, *Objectivity, Relativism, and Truth* (Cambridge: Cambridge University Press, 1991)).

————, "The Very Idea of Human Answerability to the World: John McDowell's Version of Empiricism", in Rorty, *Truth and Progress: Philosophical Papers*, vol. 3 (Cambridge: Cambridge University Press, 1998).

Sellars, Wilfrid, "Being and Being Known", in Sellars, *Science, Perception, and Reality* (London: Routledge and Kegan Paul, 1963; reissued, Atascadero, Calif.: Ridgeview, 1991).

————, "Berkeley and Descartes: Reflections on the Theory of Ideas", in Sellars, *Kant's Transcendental Metaphysics: Sellars' Cassirer Lectures Notes and Other Essays*, Jeffrey F. Sicha, ed. (Atascadero, Calif.: Ridgeview, 2002).

————, "Empiricism and the Philosophy of Mind", in Herbert Feigl and Michael Scriven, eds., *Minnesota Studies in the Philosophy of Science*, vol. 1 (Minneapolis: University of Minnesota Press, 1956); reprinted (with some added footnotes) in Sellars's *Science, Perception, and Reality* (London: Routledge and Kegan Paul, 1963; reissued, Atascadero, Calif.: Ridgeview, 1991); reprinted as a monograph, with an Introduction by Richard Rorty and a Study Guide by Robert Brandom (Cambridge, Mass.: Harvard University Press, 1997).

————, "Foundations for a Metaphysics of Pure Process", *The Monist* 64 (1981).

————, "Imperatives, Intentions, and the Logic of 'Ought'", in Hector-Neri Castañeda and George Nakhnikian, eds., *Morality and the Language of Conduct* (Detroit: Wayne State University Press, 1963).

————, "The Language of Theories", in Sellars, *Science, Perception, and Reality* (London: Routledge and Kegan Paul, 1963; reissued, Atascadero, Calif.: Ridgeview, 1991).

————, *Naturalism and Ontology* (Reseda, Calif.: Ridgeview, 1979).

———, "Phenomenalism", in Sellars, *Science, Perception, and Reality* (London: Routledge and Kegan Paul, 1963; reissued, Atascadero, Calif.: Ridgeview, 1991).

———, "Philosophy and the Scientific Image of Man", in Sellars, *Science, Perception, and Reality* (London: Routledge and Kegan Paul, 1963; reissued, Atascadero, Calif.: Ridgeview, 1991).

———, "The Role of the Imagination in Kant's Theory of Experience", in Sellars, *Kant's Transcendental Metaphysics: Sellars' Cassirer Lectures Notes and Other Essays*, Jeffrey F. Sicha, ed. (Atascadero, Calif.: Ridgeview, 2002).

———, *Science and Metaphysics: Variations on Kantian Themes* (London: Routledge and Kegan Paul, 1967; reissued, Atascadero, Calif.: Ridgeview, 1992).

———, "Some Reflections on Perceptual Consciousness", in Sellars, *Kant's Transcendental Metaphysics: Sellars' Cassirer Lectures Notes and Other Essays*, Jeffrey F. Sicha, ed. (Atascadero, Calif.: Ridgeview, 2002).

———, "Some Remarks on Kant's Theory of Experience", in Sellars, *Kant's Transcendental Metaphysics: Sellars' Cassirer Lectures Notes and Other Essays*, edited and introduced by Jeffrey F. Sicha (Atascadero, Calif.: Ridgeview, 2002).

———, "The Structure of Knowledge", in Hector-Neri Castañeda, ed., *Action, Knowledge and Reality: Studies in Honor of Wilfrid Sellars* (New York: Bobbs-Merrill, 1975).

———, "Truth and 'Correspondence' ", in Sellars, *Science, Perception, and Reality* (London: Routledge and Kegan Paul, 1963; reissued, Atascadero, Calif.: Ridgeview, 1991).

Strawson, P. F., *The Bounds of Sense* (London: Methuen, 1966).

Stroud, Barry, "Sense-Experience and the Grounding of Thought", in Nicholas H. Smith, ed., *Reading McDowell: On* Mind and World (London: Routledge, 2002).

Thompson, Michael, "The Representation of Life", in Rosalind Hursthouse, Gavin Lawrence, and Warren Quinn, eds., *Virtues and Reasons: Philippa Foot and Moral Theory* (Oxford: Clarendon Press, 1995).

Travis, Charles, "The Silence of the Senses", *Mind* 113 (2004).

Wittgenstein, Ludwig, *Notebooks 1914–1916* (Oxford: Blackwell, 1961).

———, *On Certainty* (Oxford: Blackwell, 1969).

———, *Philosophical Investigations*, trans. G. E. M. Anscombe (Oxford: Blackwell, 1951).

———, *Tractatus Logico-Philosophicus* (London: Routledge and Kegan Paul, 1961).

Wright, Crispin, "Human Nature?", in Nicholas H. Smith, ed., *Reading McDowell: On* Mind and World (London: Routledge, 2002).

Credits

Essay 1: Originally published in *Journal of Philosophy* 95 (1998): 431–450.

Essay 2: Originally published in *Journal of Philosophy* 95 (1998): 451–470.

Essay 3: Originally published in *Journal of Philosophy* 95 (1998): 471–491.

Essay 4: Forthcoming in *International Yearbook of German Idealism* (Berlin: Walter de Gruyter).

Essay 5: Originally published in *International Yearbook of German Idealism* 3 (Berlin: Walter de Gruyter, 2005), 21–37.

Essay 6: Originally published in *Philosophical Topics* 33, no. 2 (Fayetteville: University of Arkansas Press, 2008).

Essay 7: Originally published in Günter Abel, ed., *Kreativität* (Hamburg: Felix Meiner Verlag, 2006), 1065–1079.

Essay 8: Originally published in *Bulletin of the Hegel Society of Great Britain* 47/48 (2003): 1–16.

Essay 9: Originally published in German translation in Wolfgang Welsch and Klaus Vieweg, eds., *Hegels Phänomenologie des Geistes—Ein kooperativer Kommentar zu einem Schlüsselwerk der Moderne* (Frankfurt a. M.: Suhrkamp Verlag, 2008).

Essay 10: Originally published in *European Journal of Philosophy* 15 (2007): 395–410. By permission of Wiley-Blackwell.

Essay 11: Originally published in *Crítica* 30 (1998): 29–48.

Essays 12 and 13: First published in this volume.

Essay 14: Originally published in Jakob Lindgaard, ed., *John McDowell: Experience, Norm, and Nature* (Oxford: Blackwell, 2008).

Index